The New Anti-Liberals

A. Alan Borovoy

Canadian Scholars' Press Inc.   Toronto   1999

The New Anti-Liberals
A. Alan Borovoy

First published in 1999 by
Canadian Scholars' Press Inc.
180 Bloor Street West, Ste. 1202
Toronto, Ontario
M5S 2V6

Copyright © 1999 A. Alan Borovoy and Canadian Scholars' Press. All rights reserved. No part of this publication may be reproduced in any form without written permission of the publisher, except for brief passages quoted for review purposes.

We acknowledge the financial support of the Government of Canada through the Book Publishing Industry Development Programme for our publishing activities.

Canadian Cataloguing in Publication Data

Borovoy, A. Alan
    The new anti-liberals

Includes bibliographical references.
ISBN 1-55130-137-7

1. Civil Rights—Canada. 2. Political correctness—Canada. I. Title.

JC599.C3B677 1999   323'.0971   C98-932474-5

Page layout and cover design by Brad Horning

Dedication

To Daniel G. Hill, life-long fighter against discrimination, for the way he has combined devotion to the particularity of his black heritage with commitment to the universality of liberal values.

Acknowledgments

Since I became general counsel of the Canadian Civil Liberties Association (CCLA) 30 years ago, the greatest number of my public utterances have expressed the views of the organization. While I have never said anything publicly I did not support privately, I have nonetheless declined to say a lot of things that did not accord with organizational policy. It would be very difficult, however, to write a book of this kind without revealing a number of my political opinions that, while not inconsistent with CCLA policies, are beyond the CCLA mandate.

Thus, I must acknowledge, with deep appreciation, the generosity of my colleagues on the CCLA Board for encouraging the ensuing exercise in individual self-expression. And I must simultaneously acknowledge that those CCLA directors and members who do not agree with the political views expressed here are in no way diminished as civil libertarians because of it. For CCLA purposes, there is no inconsistency in holding a wide range of opinions—from the democratic left to the democratic right—on both domestic and international matters. Indeed, as an organization, CCLA has taken on *all* of the major political parties and points of view in Canada. And I have every reason to believe it will continue doing so.

It would not have been possible for me to write this book without substantial support from a number of individuals. After all, I have continued to function as CCLA's full-time general counsel during the entire time that I was involved in writing.

Few attempts at authorship have had the benefit of the wise advice that I have received. In this regard, I particularly thank CCLA vice-presidents John McCamus and Sydney Goldenberg, my close friends Owen Shime and Dawn Cannon, and University of Saskatchewan law dean Kent Roach for reading and commenting so helpfully on the total manuscript. If that weren't enough, Sydney Goldenberg read and critiqued many of the book's subsequent revisions. And, as with a previous book, I owe a special debt of gratitude to John McCamus. He was involved in perusing so many additional drafts that he virtually became an on-going consultant. I received additionally helpful comments with respect to certain sections from Ken Swan, Susan Slater, Merilees Muir, Louis Greenspan, and Cyril Levitt. Moreover, a vote of thanks to Ontario Court of Appeal Justice Rosalie Abella, York University professor Irving Abella, and Bernie Farber of the Canadian Jewish Congress who, despite our many differences, graciously helped me to locate material that documented a number of my factual allegations.

I am also grateful for the research efforts of CCLA's staff lawyers Stephen McCammon and Shauna Weinberg, and for those of our law students Andy McDonald-Romano and Veronica Syrtash. Their contributions were effectively buttressed by volunteers Edmund Chan, Thom Mallinos, Clio Godkewitsch, Akiva Katz, Nicholas Kluge, and Alison Wilkie. Collectively, these very competent young people uncovered the documentation for many of the statements I make and they produced many of the notes that the book contains.

Other CCLA staff members made substantial contributions: our administrative assistant, Donna Gilmour, for her tireless work in typing the manuscript and its infinite revisions and our director of administration and education, Danielle McLaughlin, for her periodic editorial assistance and for the efficient and diplomatic way she managed the office of the organization while I was preoccupied with the book.

Despite the considerable help I have received, the final decisions were nevertheless my own. Thus, I do not request—and cannot expect—anyone else to share the flack that the book might evoke. That, especially, will belong to me alone.

A. Alan Borovoy
Toronto, Summer, 1998

Contents

Introduction
x

Among Feminists
1

Among Minorities
33

Among Professors and Students
79

Among Doves
111

Among Governments and Their Agencies
131

Among Theoreticians
153

A Perspective
187

Introduction

I

It's one thing to periodically disagree with your traditional allies. It's another thing entirely to write a whole book on the subject. Nevertheless, that's what I have decided to do.

I have long considered myself an egalitarian. All my life, I have opposed discrimination on the basis of factors such as race, creed, ethnicity, gender, and sexual orientation. It is no coincidence that my two major jobs—the Labour Committee for Human Rights and the Canadian Civil Liberties Association—have been deeply committed to the promotion of equality.

Yet, for more than a decade, I have been increasingly troubled by excesses among my fellow equality seekers. At the same time, I have been troubled by the prospect of voicing my criticisms publicly. I have not wanted to do anything that would strengthen those in society who are opposed to equality.

In the course of trying to resolve this dilemma, I was influenced by the early twentieth century plight of the democratic socialists in the Russian Social Democratic Party. They found themselves opposed to the totalitarian philosophy of their Bolshevik comrades in the party. They similarly did not want to do anything that would strengthen those in society who were opposed to socialism. They finally decided, however, to split from the Bolsheviks. For these social democrats, the commitment to democratic values outweighed such other considerations. If only many more had followed their lead much sooner, the world might have been spared the horrors of Bolshevik Communism.

This is not, of course, to compare the late-twentieth-century equality seekers with the early-twentieth-century Bolsheviks. It is, however, to recognize the need to ensure that no alliances be allowed to imperil our priority values. Today, the overriding issue concerns the response to liberal values. My quarrel with a growing number of my fellow equality seekers is that they have been attempting to promote their objectives in contravention of the liberal values that are the very essence of the democratic system.

At this point, I had better spell out where I am coming from, what I mean by liberal values, and why they should be the paramount considerations. (I use the word liberal here with a small "l" to distinguish the liberal philosophy from the Liberal party.)

II

I grew up on the streets and in the parks of downtown Toronto during the years of the Second World War. At that time, Toronto (or Hogtown as it was then appropriately called) was riddled with anti-semitism. And I experienced a good deal of it. We lived only one long block from the place where the infamous anti-semitic riot had occurred—the Christie Pits. And, even in my day, the Pits gang made periodic forays into our neighbourhood where they would severely beat up whatever Jews they found.

One of the most memorable experiences of my youth was the speech that my grandfather made at the dinner of the reception for my *bar mitzvah*. It was the late winter of 1945. Although the war was not yet over, the allies were well on the march through Europe. Around that time, a number of the concentration camps were being liberated. For the first time, the world was beginning to learn what the Nazis had done to the Jews. With tears streaming down his face, my grandfather talked about the catastrophe that had befallen European Jewry, and he admonished me never to forget—and always to protect—my people.

I think that my subsequent development was heavily influenced by the memory of my grandfather's tearful eloquence. As I made my way through high school, I became increasingly determined to be involved in issues that responded to his admonition. But I also became increasingly convinced that the best way to protect the Jewish people was to promote greater justice for *all* people. In this regard, the group in Jewish life with which I most identified—and of which I later became the director—was the Jewish Labour Committee. This was an organization of Jewish trade unionists and social democrats that, in partnership with the general labour movement, operated a program dedicated to fighting all kinds of racism in the community at large.

With the passing years, the labour committee spent relatively little of its efforts on strictly Jewish issues and much more of its efforts on the injustices facing other people. That was because the incidence of anti-semitism had receded substantially in the post-war period. In consequence, the labour committee program emphasized discrimination against blacks and later it became more involved with aboriginals. For years, I have drawn inspiration from recalling that older generation of Jews talking in Yiddish about fighting for the human rights of blacks and native people.

Another key influence on me was the phenomenon of Soviet Communism. As I began, in the early cold war years, to devour everything I could read on the subject, I became struck by the magnitude of the chasm between Communism's egalitarian pretensions and its dictatorial realities—the starvation of the Kulaks, the purge trials of the 1930s, the slave labour camps of Siberia, the notorious doctors' plot, the mysterious disappearance of the Soviet Yiddish writers, and the anti-semitic Slansky trials in Czechoslovakia, to name only a few.

Perhaps even more revealing was the behaviour of Communist party members. Invariably, they would deal with the litany of Soviet horror stories by denying that they ever happened. Party members denounced the reports of Soviet atrocities as "fabrications of the bourgeois press". I never adequately resolved the question: were these party members conscious liars or did they really believe what they said? Either way, I was chilled by my confrontations with them. These experiences impelled me to regard dictatorship, itself, as the overriding issue. No egalitarian rhetoric could redeem a system that so grotesquely warped human behaviour. Accordingly, I became increasingly convinced that the struggle for human rights required the existence of democratic freedoms. Indeed, I became convinced that liberal democratic values must be the centrepiece of all political life.

III

For purposes of this discussion, the essence of the liberal philosophy, a legacy of the Magna Carta and then the Enlightenment, is a commitment to three principles: freedom of expression, equality, and procedural fairness.

Freedom of expression and its corollaries, freedom of the press and freedom of association, are the vehicles that enable all of us to influence the conditions under which we live. If we don't like what is happening in our society, we are entitled to raise non-violent hell about it through our speeches, writings, picket lines, and demonstrations. The animating conviction is that these freedoms significantly improve our ability to correct—and even to deter—the injustices we might face. These freedoms also enable us to engage in a vigorous search for truth and even to fulfil ourselves aesthetically.

An important component of the expressive freedoms is the analytical methods of intelligence. This means that the test of truth is what accords with empirical evidence and what can be inferred rationally from such evidence. Thus, liberals do not permit Divine revelations, religious dogmas, or subjective intuitions to overcome the results of intelligent inquiry. For philosophical liberals, there are no first principles so absolute or immutable that they cannot be questioned by the methods of intelligence.

The second principle is equality. This means not necessarily equality of treatment, but equality of concern. No one is deemed to be more or less important than anyone else. Thus, while it is impossible to avoid laws that may benefit some and burden others, liberals believe in the principle of equal consideration. Even if people are often subject to differential treatment, they must receive equal consideration. The foundation for equality is the centrality of human dignity in the panoply of liberal values. Among other things, this means that everyone is entitled to be judged on the basis of individual merit rather than on happenstance affiliation.

In order to ensure greater equality, many liberals are prepared to use the financial and even the coercive power of the state. Thus, while liberals have sought the withdrawal of most state restrictions on permissible speech, numbers of them have promoted many state restrictions on permissible acts. Indeed, certain liberals (myself included) have campaigned for—or at least supported—human rights legislation, labour legislation, and a host of welfare state measures designed to reduce inequalities.

The third principle is procedural fairness. No one should be made to suffer a significant penalty without having an opportunity to influence the outcome. At the very least, this means the right to fair trials, including representation by competent counsel, the chance to present and challenge evidence, and resort to impartial adjudication. It also includes a requirement that hearings be held in public and judgments be published for all to inspect.

The importance of such liberal values is that they stand a better chance than any alternatives to command support that transcends our tribal loyalties. It's easy to understand, for example, why numbers of women would support women's liberation, but why should *men* do so? What's in it for them? Why should anyone but the beneficiary of a particular measure support it?

The most consistently coherent response to this question is liberal values. To whatever extent we want to avoid a society where might is right, it will be in our interests to strengthen the observance of some universal values. Such universality could emerge, of course, from religion, tradition, or perhaps even a lottery. But decision-making of this kind creates a significant risk of irrationality.

What is needed is a system of universality that appears equally fair to all. For such purposes, liberal values, with their reliance on the disinterested methods of intelligence, provide the best hope there is. Thus, a man whose approach to life has been shaped by such values will be more likely, than one who has not been so influenced, to support fairness for women. The same reasoning would apply, of course, to relations between Gentiles and Jews, blacks and whites, immigrants and aboriginals, and so on across the board. A society that promotes the observance of liberal values is one in which a greater number of people are more likely to support fairness for others.

Thus, these values are the prerequisites and the emanations of democracy itself. No approach to equality is acceptable, therefore, if it affronts or neglects the liberal essence of the democratic system.

IV

There is yet another reason why I am inclined to escalate the argument with my fellow equality seekers. I believe that their infringements of liberal values are also hurting the very principles of equality they are espousing. To whatever extent a particular approach to equality is publicly perceived as hostile to commonly shared notions of fairness, it stands to alienate widespread numbers of people.

I believe, therefore, that there is a causal relationship between the contemporary rise of anti-egalitarian conservatism in North America and the excesses committed by equality seekers during the preceding several years. Consider, for example, the fate of Ontario's law on employment equity. The illiberal preferential treatment authorized by the Ontario New Democratic Party (NDP) approach to employment equity gave rise to the complete annihilation of this law at the hands of the Ontario Tories. By the time the New Democrats had done their work, most of us who wanted to preserve employment equity, albeit in a modified form, were unable to hold back the Tory onslaught. The public had become overwhelmingly fed up with the whole idea of employment equity.

Similar situations have occurred time and again with respect to other issues. The approach adopted by many equality seekers has turned off a growing number of people. In the result, the conservative opponents of equality have become increasingly strong.

Indeed, as the twentieth century and the second millennium come to a close, such conservative forces may well be dominating the political agenda throughout much of North America—they are found among the Mike Harris Conservatives in Ontario, the Ralph Klein Conservatives in Alberta, the Reform Party in Western Canada, the right-wing Republicans and religious right in the United States. Even where some of these elements have somewhat declined in strength, much of their program has been appropriated by their adversaries.

This book advances the proposition that these conservative gains in North America have been helped considerably by the general weakening of liberal values, much of it perpetrated by the excesses of equality seekers.

V

Traditionally, those who have attacked liberal values have had little to do with the quest for equality. In North America, most of the attacks on free speech have been launched by right-wing, anti-communist witch-hunters. Consider, for example, the American Palmer raids of the 1920s, the attempts to outlaw the Canadian Communist Party in the 1930s, and the activities of the notorious U.S. Senator Joseph McCarthy in the 1950s. Some attacks on freedom of speech have come from the super patriots in both countries who tried to outlaw flag-burning. Business interests, together with certain conservative politicians and judges, evinced a recurring antagonism to picketing often in labour and other protest situations. For years, numbers of right-wing religious fundamentalists have campaigned for the censorship of what they have considered to be "filthy" films, pictures, and books.

The same is largely true about the various attacks on procedural fairness. Typically, such attacks have come from government bureaucrats and their political supporters who sought essentially to facilitate the administration and enforcement of the law. Not surprisingly, some of the strongest attacks on procedural fairness have come from police authorities, police unions, and national security agencies such as the Mounties, the Canadian Security Intelligence Service (CSIS), and the Federal Bureau of Investigation (FBI). Among other things, these elements have tried to widen the rules of evidence so that prosecutors could use material no matter how unlawfully obtained and, in other respects, they have attempted to narrow the rules of evidence so as to deny the defence whatever might raise problems for intelligence and law enforcement investigations.

With few exceptions, all of these attacks on liberal values have emanated from right-wing sources that were rarely distinguished for their championship of equality. Of course, the same has been true of the traditional attacks on the egalitarian aspect of liberal values. Such attacks usually emanated from business interests that wanted to be left alone and conservative activists who wanted business to be left alone.

VI

For more than a decade, however, a number of new constituencies have begun to attack liberal values. They have attacked freedom of speech, procedural fairness, and, in certain situations, even the accepted concepts of equality itself. In the case of free speech, these new attacks have taken the form, *inter alia*, of anti-hate laws, anti-pornography laws, and university speech codes. In the case of procedural fairness, these new attacks have included rape-shield measures that prevented accused people from probing even relevant evidence from a complainant's sexual history. In the case of equality, these new attacks have included the advocacy and adoption of measures to pressure employers into actually discriminating in favour of traditional discrimination victims.

With few exceptions, these new attacks are not from the right-wing. Indeed, many of them have been unmistakably *left*-wing. But the most common thread shared by these new opponents of liberal values is a commitment to equality-seeking. To a very great extent, these attacks have been perpetrated in the interests of promoting equality.

This is the factor that has inhibited the responses of the liberal community. Those committed to liberal values, of necessity, are themselves equality seekers. For liberals to criticize any of the equality seekers would have meant criticizing their allies. This, they have been understandably reluctant to do. In my view, however, these new "anti-liberals" have had such an impact that it is no longer acceptable for liberals to remain silent.

Another factor has kept liberals from speaking up about these things: many of the equality seekers stem from constituencies that have themselves suffered unjust discrimination. Thus, liberals are reluctant to criticize such people and thereby join the ranks of those who are hurting them. But, in the face of honest and important disagreements, to perpetually immunize such people is to effectively patronize them. Quite often, the best way to accord people genuine equality and respect is to express our differences with them. By refusing to do so, liberals put at risk one of the key ingredients in their professed liberalism.

What follows is an attempt to identify a number of these new anti-liberal developments. For such purposes, it is not necessary to paint a definitive, comprehensive, or even completely up-to-date picture. Indeed, change is constantly occurring. Thus, even between writing and publication, some situations could well have become modified. In any event, the focus here is less on narrative than on analysis. And, since the idea is to sensitize the reader to the nature of the new threats to liberal values, what is needed now is simply an indication of certain key trends. It will suffice, then, to discuss a number of typical and recurring issues.

I should point out that there is no attempt here to rank the threats to liberal values. The amount of attention that is paid to some subjects rather than to others is often more attributable to my readily available knowledge than it is to their relative importance. But, while I have not allocated space according to relative importance, I have nevertheless chosen subjects that I believe to be very important.

An entire chapter is devoted to trends within the feminist community. Of all the constituencies that are explored here, this one appears to have made the most remarkable progress in the shortest period of time. And it continues to wield a considerable amount of political and social influence.

The relative progress of certain minorities is also noteworthy. Here too, however, there are disquieting signs of illiberalism. An especially significant factor with the Jews, for example, is that, according to many surveys, they may rank as one of the most liberal of ethnic groups. This gives their drift from liberal values a special importance. In the case of the blacks, it was a mere generation ago that they spawned the most inspiring embodiment of liberal values this continent has probably ever experienced—the U.S. civil rights movement around Martin Luther King. Like the case with the Jews, this gives a special significance to antiliberal developments in the black community. The disabled are included because, in a recent highly publicized case, many of their organizations rejected the kind of liberal approach they generally support.

Similar developments are occurring on university campuses. As regards professors and students, we are talking about one of the most traditional bastions of liberal values. To whatever extent the universities lose their loyalty to liberal values, there would be much less hope for the rest of society. I also attempt to show how, in international affairs, some kinds of egalitarianism can undermine the power that is needed to safeguard liberal values. Hence, the chapter on the doves. Certain activities of governments are discussed because it is important to acquire a sense of what happens when some equality seekers acquire governmental power. All three issues that are explored, in the chapter on government, relate to objectives that are legitimate and even desirable: protecting French, securing abortion rights, and combatting discrimination. While the objectives are desirable, the methods identified are contentious. Finally, no discussion of such issues would be complete without some examination of their theoretical underpinnings—thus, the chapter dealing with theoreticians.

In summary: the old anti-liberals are defenders of inequality who cling to the status quo; the new anti-liberals are promoters of equality who have gone off the deep end. Some of the new anti-liberals continue to justify their attacks in the name of liberalism. Despite their growing alienation, these people continue to profess their loyalty to liberal values. Others, however, explicitly declare their hostility to liberalism. While a few of them are new conservatives, many of them portray themselves as authentically radical. For these radicals, liberalism is too wishy-washy. It's one thing, however, to claim that liberal values are inadequate; it's another thing entirely to claim that they are unacceptable. I believe it was Irving Howe, the American socialist, who argued that a healthy radicalism must fulfil, not reject, liberal values.

The ensuing discussion is dedicated to this proposition.

CHAPTER ONE

Among Feminists

At some point in the early 1980s, I received a sad telephone call from a former classmate, a woman I had not seen for more than twenty-five years. In many ways, her unhappiness symbolized the need for the modern movement known as "women's liberation". A top scholar throughout public and high school, she had been "talked out of" her burning ambition—to enter medical school and become a doctor. Parents, family, and friends had admonished her that medicine was not a suitable profession for a woman. And so, more than twenty-five years later, she was desperately unfulfilled, functioning at a level miles below her intellectual capacity.

By now, it is common knowledge that millions of women have suffered similar experiences. They have been pressured into occupations and roles that don't require even a particle of their talents. Since the inception of recorded history, the woman's "place" has been in the home or in some dreary occupation of the most menial kind. Only a handful aspired to more challenging roles, and so often their non-conformity required what was then considered a heavy price—single status or divorce.

Betty Friedan's 1963 book, *The Feminine Mystique*, widely identified as the spark for the current wave of North American feminism, contains a particularly moving description of life as a housewife.

> It is urgent to understand how the very condition of being a housewife can create a sense of emptiness, non-existence, nothingness, in women. There are aspects of the housewife role that make it almost impossible for a woman of adult intelligence to retain a sense of human identity . . . .[1]

Of course, child-rearing and home-making are crucial functions. For those who freely choose it, such a role can also be fulfilling and challenging. But, for those who are regimented by society into performing such jobs, the experience can be, as Betty Friedan suggests, soul-destroying. The issue here is that society has created conditions that have effectively deprived women of the freedom to choose.

Thanks to the advent of women's liberation, these oppressive conditions are undergoing a pervasive transformation. In rapidly growing numbers, women are penetrating all of the hitherto male sanctuaries—law, medicine, engineering, business, accountancy, banking, even truck driving, police, and the military. The situation is a veritable revolution; there are tremors everywhere. As women pour onto the job market, there is an escalation of demand for low-cost day-care facilities to look after their children. With the growth of financial independence, increasing numbers of women are opting for different lifestyles. No longer content in the role of homemakers, many women are choosing common-law relationships over marriage and many are choosing to live alone or with other women. And it is no longer rare or disreputable for single women to bear and raise children. The essence of what has happened is that this generation of women is determined to be autonomous.

It is inevitable that the transition from oppression to autonomy would trigger shock waves throughout the breadth of society. As more women compete for jobs, they insist on effective protections against discrimination. No longer satisfied simply to be hired in jobs that had been closed to them, they campaign for "equal pay for work of equal value". And how can they demand autonomy in their domestic and labour relations without asserting it also over their own bodies? Thus, key supporters of the women's movement have undertaken a relentless fight to liberalize the abortion laws. Nor will modern women any longer suffer in silence the unwelcome invasion of their bodies. Unlike their foremothers, they mount vigorous pressures to ensure that rapists will be brought to justice. Even pictorial and verbal abuses of women will no longer be tolerated. A growing segment of the women's movement has challenged the existence of so much of our society's pornography.

For such a relatively short period of time, the women's movement has achieved a number of considerable gains. These have included positions on the governing bodies of Air Canada, the Canadian National Railway, and the top position on the Canada Council. In some private sector jobs, women have made it right to the top: for example, Maureen Kempston-Darkes at General Motors of Canada and Diane McGarry at Xerox of Canada. Moreover, this country has had a female governor general (Jeanne Sauvé) and three women justices of the Supreme Court of Canada (Bertha Wilson, Claire L'Heureux-Dubé, and Beverley McLachlin). The New Democratic Party elected two women in succession to be its federal leader: Audrey McLaughlin and Alexa McDonough. A growing number of women have become cabinet ministers (they rose to 40% in Ontario's New Democratic Party government of 1990). And, for a brief time, one woman even became Prime Minister—Kim Campbell.

Perhaps more important are the pro-feminist changes in the law. A combination of action in both the courtroom and political arena has left Canada's criminal law free of restrictions against abortion. In virtually every jurisdiction, there are laws against gender discrimination and sexual harassment. Moreover, the women's movement has, by now, won an impressive number of court cases. Indeed, a recent study of feminist litigation experience since the advent of Canada's Charter of Rights and Freedoms[2] suggested "that the feminist success is indeed significant".[3] None of this is intended to describe the status quo as the feminist millennium. It is simply to acknowledge the magnitude and importance of the progress that has been made in so short a period of history.

I have often found myself wistfully wishing that women's liberation had been born at least a few decades earlier. Had that happened, my generation of women would have been spared so much of the misery it has suffered. And my generation of men would have enjoyed far more enriching and enlightened relationships with the women in their lives. This is not to suggest that every person would have been better off as a consequence of this revolution. To be sure, every benefit has its costs, and it is no different with this one. Nevertheless, I believe that women's liberation represents a substantial net gain: it has liberated a significant number of women *and* men.

To a great extent, the women's movement was based upon the liberal values of gender equality and human dignity. As it began to confront the institutions of our society, the movement was essentially calling upon those institutions to implement the professed values of our society. Not surprisingly, the women's movement attracted significant allies from the liberal community: labour unions, churches, academics, writers, and civil liberties organizations. The growing conglomeration of constituencies helped to overcome the resistance of various conservative establishments. The changes that society was undergoing were seen as victories for liberal values and liberal organizations.

Somewhere along the line, however, this informal coalition began to come apart. Numbers of feminists became increasingly hardline in their political demands. As this process developed, these feminists focused their attacks less on the traditional conservative bastions of male power and more on their liberal allies in the liberation struggle.

By the end of the 1980s and beginning of the 1990s, these growing antagonisms erupted in some surprising ways. York University president Harry Arthurs—probably the country's most liberal and pro-feminist university president—was accused by a large group of feminists of sexist discrimination in his choice of a male over a female candidate for dean of York's Osgoode Hall Law School.[4] June Callwood—long considered one of the most compassionate and egalitarian feminists in the country—was accused by certain black women of being a "racist".[5] The Canadian Civil Liberties Association (CCLA)—the largest human rights and civil liberties organization in Canada's voluntary sector—was attacked by a group of feminist leaders for being "a macho, male-focused organization with no sensitivity to women".[6]

In the case of Harry Arthurs, it seemed incredible that he, of all people, would be accused of employment discrimination. During the few years before these accusations were made, Arthurs had conceived some rather imaginative schemes to increase the hiring of women at his university. Moreover, close to 50% of the administrative positions that were filled during his tenure had gone to women.[7]

No less incredible—perhaps even more so—was the attack on June Callwood. Her profound compassion had propelled her over the years to create several social service agencies: for abused women, for children, and for those dying of AIDS, to name only a few. Never content simply to raise funds and sit on boards, Callwood had spent long hours—often nights on end—personally attending to the people her agencies had been established to serve. These involvements had included personal service to visible minority women and active efforts to bring such women into the governing councils of these organizations. In addition, Callwood had instigated and participated in numbers of demonstrations and delegations designed to promote a greater level of racial equality in the community. As one columnist wryly noted, if June Callwood is a racist, who isn't?[8]

There were some strange ironies in the feminist attack on the Canadian Civil Liberties Association. The issue that was probably most responsible for precipitating the attack was the CCLA's challenge of the rape-shield section of the Criminal Code.⁹ Yet, perhaps no other single issue better dramatized the growing power of women in the civil liberties organization. The board of directors meeting that almost unanimously approved the CCLA position was attended by a majority of women. The president of the organization was then—and at the time of the attack—a woman. The lawyer who initially argued the case in court for the CCLA, on a *pro-bono* basis, was also a woman.¹⁰

Moreover, it's not without significance that the Canadian Civil Liberties Association was probably the first voluntary group in the country to attack the old "spouse in the house" rule for welfare recipients. As long ago as 1970, the CCLA had identified this rule as a major breach of civil liberties.¹¹ The rule disqualified people for welfare if they were cohabiting with unrelated members of the opposite sex. This disqualification disproportionately affected unmarried women. At around the same time, the CCLA also challenged the practice that required women to take their deserting husbands to court in order to obtain welfare assistance.¹²

More than two decades before being attacked as a "male macho organization", the CCLA had launched both a legal and political attack on these special hardships that our welfare system was visiting upon women. It is important to point out that the CCLA's involvement in these issues was not confined to anything as routine as issuing press releases. On the contrary, the CCLA went to court, organized delegations to cabinet ministers, conducted nationwide surveys, published documents, and gave scores of interviews to the media.¹³ For years, this "male macho organization" was on the barricades on behalf of the poorest women in our society.

As long ago as 1973, the CCLA intervened in the Supreme Court of Canada appeal of convicted abortionist Dr. Henry Morgentaler.¹⁴ In that case, the civil liberties group argued that the procedures and policies of Canada's therapeutic abortion committees violated the guarantee of due process in the old Canadian Bill of Rights. In support of its position, the CCLA filed a nationwide survey it had conducted into the behaviour of various therapeutic abortion committees. When the government of Canada attempted to re-criminalize abortions after the old law had been struck down by the Supreme Court in 1988, the CCLA was the first to testify against it at the hearings of the parliamentary committee.¹⁵ It also participated in a press conference organized by the National Action Committee on the Status of Women (NAC).¹⁶ Despite this support on an issue of such importance to women, certain feminist leaders seemed unhesitant in describing the CCLA as a "male macho organization . . . insensitive to women".[17]

Significantly, the CCLA had not changed. It remained—and remains still—a pro-feminist and, in these respects, a liberal organization. It was these feminists who had changed. Those who surfaced in the attack on the CCLA were evincing distinctly anti-liberal proclivities. In my view, the issue is not determined by where one stands on feminism; the issue is where do you stand on liberalism.

THE CENSORSHIP OF PORNOGRAPHY— A CHALLENGE TO FREEDOM OF SPEECH

In the winter of 1992, a large number of Canadian feminists celebrated a development that they regarded as a major victory: the Supreme Court of Canada upheld the constitutionality of the Criminal Code section on obscenity.[18] Whatever merit there may be in regulating material that is available to children or imposed upon unwilling adults, it should be noted that the enactment at issue here extends to restrictions on material that *willing adults* may produce and consume.

The Supreme Court judgment was widely seen as having imbibed the ideology of the major feminist intervenor in the case, the Women's Legal Education and Action Fund (LEAF). To be sure, the Court made the essential distinctions that LEAF had urged. It agreed that the portrayal of sex coupled with violence "will almost always" be obscene and so will much of the material that is "degrading or dehumanizing".[19] By contrast, the judges held that the portrayal of explicit sex that "is not violent and neither degrading nor dehumanizing" will generally not be obscene.[20] LEAF couldn't have been more successful. It had won a unanimous judgment from the Supreme Court of Canada. Nine to nothing—seven male judges and two female judges had approved and entrenched in the Canadian Constitution the modern mainstream feminist ideology. The judges even accepted LEAF's rationale:

> . . . if true equality between male and female persons is to be achieved, we cannot ignore the threat to equality resulting from exposure to audiences of certain types of violent and degrading material.[21]

Only months earlier, the *Toronto Star's* feminist columnist Michele Landsberg had popularized the LEAF position. The similarities with the Supreme Court judgment are striking. According to Landsberg, "most pornography ... harms women as a group and hinders their quest for equality ... ".[22] Landsberg quoted LEAF as denying that pornography represents a dissenting or "repressed voice". Indeed, her column flatly declared that "pornography is hate propaganda against women".[23]

Within a mere few weeks of the Supreme Court decision, the obscenity provisions of the Criminal Code were invoked, not against material designed to arouse men, but against material designed to interest lesbians. Canada Customs also seized a comic magazine on the grounds that it was sexually degrading towards *men*[24] and, in one of the first charges that was laid under the obscenity section since the Supreme Court judgment, the accused were operators of a gay and lesbian bookstore and the material was a lesbian publication.[25] In short, the law that was supposed to protect women was being used against women and against the constituency of women that has long been a "repressed voice".

This targeting of the lesbian community is nothing new. The Glad Day Book Store reports that it has been experiencing regular customs' seizures for years. Every few weeks, according to the proprietors of the bookstore, they have been receiving notices indicating that Canada Customs has seized and detained material addressed to their store. One of the recurring grounds for this reported Canada Customs' action has been its finding that the material is "degrading". The manager of Glad Day points out that the store has lost thousands of dollars as a result of this practice. On the few occasions that the store has responded with court action, the legal costs have been prohibitive. On many of the other occasions, a finding is made that the material is contrary to the Criminal Code and, at that point, Canada Customs reportedly returns the material to the sender at Glad Day's expense. If Glad Day refuses to pay the shipping costs, it says that Canada Customs destroys the material. In that event, the store winds up having to reimburse the original sender.[26]

Inexplicably, LEAF managed to neglect one of the most "repressed" elements of its own constituency. What explains this remarkable ability to overlook Glad Day? Doesn't the championship of feminism include lesbians? It's not as though anyone should be surprised that women would be among the casualties of our obscenity laws. Feminist author Varda Burstyn had warned about this very development several years *before* the Supreme Court judgment.[27]

The pro-censorship feminists have also argued that legal restrictions on pornography are needed to protect the welfare of children. Yet, in some respects, children were also an early casualty of the obscenity law in the period following the Supreme Court judgment. In the spring of 1992, Canada Customs shredded the manuscript for a novel written by retired psychologist Robert Lally, even though children were among the novel's potential beneficiaries. The novel was designed to explore the mind of the pedophile. Significantly, this book was cleared as legally acceptable by the Alberta Ministry of the Attorney General.[28]

Small wonder that the authorities keep invoking this law against targets who don't bear the slightest resemblance to those the feminists are trying to nail. The Criminal Code definition of "obscenity" includes material characterized by an "undue exploitation of sex".[29] It would be hard to conceive of murkier terminology. What in the world is an "undue" or, perhaps even better, a "due" exploitation of sex?

At the urging of LEAF, the Supreme Court of Canada has told us that the portrayal of sex coupled with violence is "almost always" an undue exploitation.[30] In making such a statement, the Court appears to gloss over the fact that such depictions of evil behaviour are often important to legitimate art and literature. Consider, for example, the following: the rape of Leda by Zeus in the form of a swan from Greek mythology; the medieval paintings that depict the rape of the Sabine women; the famous rape scene from Ingmar Bergmann's classic film, *The Virgin Spring*; and even the sexual assault committed by the hero on the heroine in Ayn Rand's novel, *The Fountainhead*.

At least the notion of sex coupled with violence does not suffer from the defect of vagueness. Instead, it suffers from dangerous overbreadth. But what about the other standard that the Court read into the obscenity definition: "degrading or dehumanizing"? What are these words supposed to mean? Nor does it help for the Court to add the qualifier that Canadians generally must consider that exposure to such material would involve a substantial risk of harm. Consider the dilemma of convenience store owners who receive a batch of magazines with sexual content. How are they supposed to discern the limits of their fellow citizens' tolerance? Must they commission a nationwide Gallup poll?

The Court hastens to assure us that, in any event, material can be rescued if the portrayal of sex is essential to a "wider artistic, literary, or other similar purpose". It's hard to fathom why the Court would consider these defences to be adequate. How are those convenience store owners supposed to make a judgment of this kind? Incredibly, the Court insists that, read together, all of the foregoing represents an "intelligible" standard.[31]

But, "intelligible" to whom? Even if we trusted judges and juries to make such judgments, what about cops and customs officials? Nowhere does the Court acknowledge that the latter make many of the effective decisions concerning alleged smut. In so many cases, people will bow to their rulings because challenging them in court could be a financial and emotional ordeal. Yet, while judges and juries are required to hear both sides, cops and customs officials have no such obligation. Moreover, most enforcement officials would be the first to admit that literary and artistic expertise is not their forté. From reading the judgment of the Supreme Court and the adulatory comments of the Womens' Legal Education and Action Fund, you could never tell what actually happens in real life.

Significantly, there was a wealth of experience prior to this critical Supreme Court decision. Consider, for example, the following incidents affecting those who were involved in apparently legitimate activity:

> In the late 1980s, a police department in Alberta seized material belonging to an *anti*-pornography organization.[32]
>
> In the mid-1980s, Toronto police targeted a painting that depicted the rape of a Mayan woman by Guatemalan soldiers even though the painting was reportedly a political statement sympathetic to Guatemalan women.[33]
>
> In the mid-1980s, customs officials confiscated *Erotic Poems* from a Greek anthology of sixth century B.C. and a film on male masturbation that was headed for the University of Manitoba medical school.[34]
>
> In the mid-1970s, police laid charges over the widely acclaimed film, *Last Tango in Paris*, and the children's sex educational book, *Show Me*.[35]

Even if the authorities backed down or were overturned in most of these cases, the affected parties were unlikely to be consoled. In order to vindicate their right to engage in perfectly legitimate activity, they had to face the possible financial and emotional burden of going to court.

Moreover, the mere threat of a charge or confiscation is usually enough to intimidate people. In any event, it should be noted that all of these cases were handled under the very test for obscenity that the Supreme Court, with only marginal refinements, declared to be "intelligible".

One of the most disquieting features of the 1992 Court decision is that the impetus for it came from an organization dedicated to women's liberation. So determined were the leaders of LEAF to censor pornography that they were prepared to imperil not only freedom of speech but also fundamental principles of criminal law. In the interests of fairness, ordinary people should be able to know when they are committing a crime. Those who pick up guns to compel bank tellers to hand over money may not know whether their conduct will be labelled theft, fraud, or robbery—but they will surely know that they have broken the law. There is no such clarity for those who handle material with sexual content.

What justifies all these risks? The Court acknowledges that "a direct link between obscenity and harm to society may be . . . impossible to establish".[36] But it insists nevertheless on the reasonableness of assuming that exposure to pornography is causally related to harmful "changes in attitudes and beliefs".[37]

Apart from difficult matters of evidence, it is questionable for a democracy to criminalize, in this way, the influencing of people's attitudes and beliefs. If exposure to obscenity is seen as undermining attitudes towards women and children, what about exposure to materials like the Communist Manifesto? Couldn't such exposure just as validly be seen as disposing people to join in—or at least to accept—the atrocities perpetrated by the Communists? Similarly, might it not be argued that exposure to the Bible helped to create the attitudes and beliefs that paved the way for the mass suicide at Jonestown in 1978? The evening television news may generate comparably harmful attitudes.

Thus, it can be seen that key sectors of the feminist movement have contributed significantly to the erosion of the Charter protections for freedom of expression.[38] In large part because of their efforts, infringements on freedom of expression don't require actual evidence that the contested material will likely cause imminent harmful behaviour. All that may be needed is a reasonable belief that the material is related to the growth of harmful attitudes. But, unlike the situation with imminent behaviour, the influencing of attitudes is a long-term matter for which there is likely to be time within which counter-influences can make an impact. By adopting the approach it did, therefore, LEAF has evinced a willingness to risk a substantial and needless expansion of the government's censorship powers.

According to the liberal values that contributed so much to the growth of feminism, it was never necessary to choose between censorship and paralysis. Bad material can be counteracted with good material. To whatever extent pornography is seen as producing sexist attitudes, there is a range of activity that could help to produce anti-sexist attitudes—the counselling of rape victims to charge their assailants, the provision of shelter and assistance for battered women, stronger laws against gender discrimination, improved day-care facilities for working women, improved educational programs, and so on. The combined effect of such activities would be to impress the dignity of women on the psyche of society. All this could be done without any significant risk to freedom of expression. Moreover, these measures would very likely produce much greater benefits for the women of our society than could ever be achieved by these dangerous and dubious attempts to restrict pornography.

THE "RAPE-SHIELD" AND "PRIVACY-SHIELD" LAWS— A CHALLENGE TO PROCEDURAL FAIRNESS

In August of 1991, the Supreme Court of Canada struck down the rape-shield section of the Criminal Code.[39] Until then, the divisions between certain feminist organizations and the Canadian Civil Liberties Association had been simmering beneath the surface. The rape-shield decision, to use the words of the *Toronto Star*, "brought the rift out into the open".[40]

The decision was greeted by angry protests from numbers of feminist leaders. Doris Anderson, former president of the National Action Committee on the Status of Women, complained that "now any woman who makes a charge will once again run the risk of her sexual history being paraded through the courts".[41] In the *Toronto Star*, columnist Michele Landsberg bitterly attacked Justice Beverley McLachlin who wrote the decision for the Supreme Court of Canada and the Canadian Civil Liberties Association that had intervened at the court hearing against the rape-shield section. Landsberg then summarized her perception of the resulting situation: "no other criminals enjoy the special victim-bashing rules of evidence that have now been made available to the rapist".[42] And the then LEAF executive director, Christie Jefferson, joined in: "Where is the [Canadian Civil Liberties] Association's concern about a woman's right . . . not to be raped and her right to bring that rapist to justice if she is?"[43]

More than fifty people openly resigned their memberships in the Canadian Civil Liberties Association. Very likely, there were a number of others who left without declaring themselves.

All this controversy was focused on a section of the Criminal Code that had been enacted in 1983 in order to protect the privacy and dignity of those—overwhelmingly women—who made accusations of sexual assault. At one time, female complainants in rape cases could expect a demeaning and irrelevant inquisition into their past sexual practices. By impugning the woman's "chastity", defence counsel would attempt to impeach her credibility. The theory was that those who were sexually promiscuous were not worthy of being believed. Defence counsel would also argue that a woman who consented to sexual intercourse on previous occasions was more likely to have consented on the occasion in question.

The rape-shield section was designed to put an end to these inquisitions. To that extent, the section enjoyed a consensus of support in both the feminist and civil libertarian communities. There was simply no justification for allowing those humiliating probes into the complainant's sexual history. So often, those probes demeaned the victim without uncovering anything worthy for the accused. The defence theories to which I just referred amounted to nothing more than sexist assumptions. They were utterly devoid of redeeming merit. There is no legitimate equation between sexual and ethical looseness; nor can it legitimately be inferred that previous consent makes significantly more likely the consent in question. It was understandable that feminist organizations would seek a rape-shield protection in the law.

The consensus between many feminists and civil libertarians came apart over the scope, not the principle, of the rape-shield section. The section as finally enacted was so broad that it was capable of suppressing relevant evidence that might be needed for the defence of an innocent person wrongly accused of sexual assault. In this regard, it is important to ask some crucial questions of those who have criticized the 1991 Court decision. Are they saying, as a matter of logic, that elements of a rape complainant's sexual background could *never* be relevant to a fair trial? Or, are they saying, as a matter of policy, that such evidence should not be admitted, even if it is relevant?

University of Manitoba psychology professor David Koulack has a simple answer to this question. Writing in *The Globe and Mail* during the aftermath of the judgment, he made the following statement:

> Try as I may, I can't imagine a situation in which a woman's previous sexual experience would have a bearing on whether she is truly a victim of assault.[44]

Perhaps the most charitable way to respond is to note that Professor Koulack is remarkably unimaginative. I will set out a number of possible situations "in which a woman's previous sexual experience" would have all the bearing in the world on the believability of her current allegations. In this connection, it is helpful to point out that I will be dealing not with the totality of a complainant's sexual history but only with certain aspects of it. In short, we are not obliged to choose between admitting the complainant's entire sexual background or admitting none of it.

Suppose the accused's defence is that the woman voluntarily had sex with him but then tried to extort money from him under the threat of charging him with sexual assault? If she made good on her threat, suppose the accused learned of a number of other situations in which she had behaved in a similar manner? The rape-shield section, as enacted, could have deprived such an accused of the right to elicit evidence of the woman's apparent pattern in order to buttress the credibility of his defence. It must be obvious that, in such circumstances, to deny him the right to explore this evidence would incur a significant risk of an unfair trial.

Some people have responded to this example by suggesting that the woman's past sexual relations need not be exposed, only her past attempts at extortion. It is rarely possible, however, to package evidence for court in such an artificial way. In any event, an innocent accused in such circumstances could well find it necessary to invoke the complete *modus operandi* of the complainant. To whatever extent she had made it a practice to use sex as the basis for extortion, the accused might need to be able to demonstrate it.

How, then, shall we take Michele Landsberg's response to this example? "Women don't falsely report rape", Landsberg declared.[45] *Never?* Of course, a substantial majority of those who make criminal accusations of any kind are telling the truth. But there is a significant distinction between a substantial majority and complete unanimity.

After condemning this example as "male-invented" and "silly", Landsberg made the following statement: "Evidence of such extortion attempts *would have been considered admissible* under the now-destroyed rape shield law" [emphasis in the original].[46] To be fair, legal opinions can differ over what constitutes a proper interpretation of the rape-shield section. But, while there was some disagreement on the Court, seven of the nine justices believed that such evidence could have been suppressed under that section. On the narrow question of how the courts are likely to interpret a statutory enactment, so many Supreme Court justices are unlikely to be wrong.

Regardless of that argument, the questions remain: should such evidence be suppressed and is such an example beyond the range of reasonable expectation? While I would certainly agree that behaviour of this kind would be a relatively rare phenomenon, my reading of the human condition is that such regrettable things do happen. And, in the event they did, I think it would be monstrous to deny an accused person the opportunity to explore similar allegations from the complainant's background.

Consider another possible example. The complainant is a youngster who describes in vivid detail what the accused allegedly did to her. Because of her tender age, the jury might conclude that her story must be believed; without first-hand experience, no one that young could possibly know enough about sexual interactions to describe them in such detail. Suppose the position of the accused is that the complainant knows these things, not because of any experience with him, but because she had been abused by other men. The section could have denied him the right to raise those other experiences. But to deny him recourse to such evidence is to incur a significant risk of his being unable to address what would obviously be on the jury's mind.

For yet another example, the Supreme Court judgment mentioned a recent American case in which certain aspects of a complainant's sexual history related to her motive for charging the accused.[47] According to him, she made the allegations against him because he had put an end to her sexual affair with his son. Thus, he wished to cite this aspect of her sexual background in order to demonstrate to the court that anger was the reason she laid the charge in question. If an accused were prevented from invoking such situations, it might be impossible for him to effectively answer the allegations against him. Significantly, a similar scenario emerged in a subsequent Quebec case.[48]

If it is acknowledged that certain past sexual relations could sometimes be highly relevant, are the critics of the Supreme Court judgment prepared in such cases to squarely face the implications of their position—that in some circumstances, the accused will be denied a fair trial? In view of the likelihood that a conviction would result in a substantial jail term, such a prospect would be repugnant to anyone with the slightest respect for elementary justice.

Some of the critics of the judgment have challenged defenders to identify a situation in which the rape-shield section actually produced a wrongful conviction. But what would flow from an inability to provide such an example? The unwarranted imprisonment imposed by Nova Scotia on the disadvantaged aboriginal, Donald Marshall, did not come to light for more than ten years. And a demonstration of his innocence required an exhaustive re-investigation of the circumstances. Few people could hope to have that kind of information. In my view, it's enough to know that the section was logically capable of suppressing important evidence. Even if our society managed then to avoid a wrongful conviction for sexual assault, there was no need to await such a catastrophe before insisting that a demonstrably flawed enactment be corrected.

Some of the Court's critics have argued that a woman's sexual history is so rarely relevant that it was not worth risking the integrity of the section for such eventualities. Admittedly, such evidence would be relevant only in exceptional cases. But why is that a reason to jeopardize *anyone's* right to a fair trial? In any event, that argument is based upon the fallacious assumption that our society had to choose between the section enacted by Parliament or nothing whatsoever. That was never the case. Indeed, the Canadian Civil Liberties Association had long taken the position that, while the section was too tight, the old practice was too loose.[49]

Significantly, we asked the Supreme Court for guidelines to prevent the restoration of the old practice.[50] In doing so, we were the only party before the Court that even addressed the question of how to protect complainants in the event that the section was struck down. Inexplicably, neither the government nor the intervening feminist organization considered this question. In the result, the Court adopted the thrust of the CCLA's recommendations. While no one knows whether the Court might have done so anyway, the CCLA's involvement could be the reason that, in the aftermath of the case, there were measures in place to prevent a reversion to the old discredited practice.

The Supreme Court expressly forbade the admission at trial of the complainant's previous sexual experiences if such admission was sought on the basis of the old assumption that "unchaste" women are not worthy of belief.[51] It also expressly barred such evidence if its introduction was attempted solely to support the inference that a woman who said "yes" several times before was more likely to have said "yes" on the occasion in question.[52] For such purposes—those most often invoked in the past—no part of a woman's sexual history could be used. In my view, that constituted an effective rape-shield law.

Moreover, the Supreme Court included a procedural safeguard as well. Before evidence of any past sexual experience could be looked at, there would have to be a *voir dire*, i.e., a hearing within the trial but in the absence of the jury.[53] The trial judge would have to be satisfied that the particular evidence of past sexual practice the accused wished to explore would not run afoul of the Supreme Court's explicit prohibitions, would otherwise be relevant, and even if relevant, had a probative value that was not substantially outweighed by its prejudicial impact. Such restrictions represented substantial hurdles.

What, then, are we to make of Michele Landsberg's hyperbole: "No other criminals enjoy the special victim-bashing rules of evidence that have now been made available to the rapist"?[54] Similarly, we have David Koulack's argument that if a shopkeeper has been robbed before, does that mean he "was enticing criminals to attack his store?"[55]

These comments and rhetorical questions reveal remarkable knowledge gaps and logical flaws. A storekeeper's previous experience with allegations of robbery would not be admissible to suggest that he enticed his tormenters; but it could be included to show a pattern of false accusations. The Supreme Court made a similar distinction upon promulgating its guidelines to replace the rape-shield law.[56] Moreover, there is more "victim bashing" in our criminal law system than Michele Landsberg seems to realize. In many criminal cases, the question boils down to one of determining which of the contesting parties is telling the truth. In a *non*-sexual assault case, for example, there is a wide latitude granted to the accused in questioning the background of the complainant. In a very real sense, such a case represents a trial not only of the accused but also of the complainant. This results from society's reluctance to risk the jailing of an innocent person.

If anything, the Supreme Court guidelines granted *special* protections to the sexual assault complainant.[57] There are precious few other situations in which evidence favourable to an accused has to be vetted first in a *voir dire*. In this way, sexual assault complainants were to be afforded protections enjoyed by few other complainants in the criminal law of this country.

Some feminist representatives argued that the overwhelming number of male trial judges could not be trusted to make the distinctions that the guidelines required. This argument was often fuelled by invoking examples of sexist remarks that some judges had made during the course of certain trials. While it is true that some judges continue to harbour harmfully sexist attitudes, it would be unfair to characterize the bulk of our judiciary in this way. In any event, the Supreme Court judgment did not give trial judges an unfettered discretion. Their discretion was very much fettered by those guidelines. Indeed, the guidelines contained enough specificity to make it very unlikely that any evidence of sexual experience would be admitted on the basis of the old sexist assumptions.

Of course, the guidelines were not—and could not be—guarantees. They were reasonably sensible curbs on the judicial discretion. In any event, real-world measures have to be compared, not to imagined perfection, but to practical alternatives. Better to have the kind of guidelines promulgated by the Court that protected *both* complainant and accused, than to perpetuate the old section with its willingness to virtually neglect the accused altogether.

At the height of the controversy, the then federal justice minister Kim Campbell vowed to introduce new legislation in the area. She made good on the promise and, within a year, Parliament enacted a new section with rape-shield and sexual assault provisions.[58] It was reported that Ms Campbell consulted widely with feminist organizations before introducing her new bill. The section, as adopted, appears to have been influenced by the kind of anti-liberal sentiment that had greeted the Supreme Court decision.

Among other things, the new law bars the media from disclosing whether and why a judge excluded any part of a woman's sexual history from the evidence in a sexual assault trial.[59] There is one exception: the judge who made the ruling may grant permission for such a disclosure.[60] This is simply repugnant.

Without information as to what is going on, how is the public supposed to decide whether it approves of the new rape-shield enactment? Just as eternal vigilance is the price of liberty, so is relevant knowledge the prerequisite for vigilance. Any law that simultaneously muzzles what the media can say and restricts what the public can learn, necessarily begins life under a cloud of constitutional fragility.

Consider also what this section can do to a person who is wrongly accused of sexual assault (even though this may be rare, it can happen). Suppose the accused believed that his ability to defend himself could have benefited from the admission into court of certain evidence from the woman's past sexual practices that the trial judge saw fit to exclude? And suppose the accused could not persuade either the trial judge or the court of appeal that the evidence was relevant and worthy of admission? In such circumstances, the accused person's only recourse might be to go to the media with his story.

Freedom of the press is the ultimate safety valve against injustice in a democracy. After this country's ordeal with the case of Donald Marshall, there should be a deep reluctance to inflict such a disability on accused people. In the Marshall case, even the appeal court judges turned out to be wrong.[61] Redress was finally made possible because the press was free to complain and to protest. If that freedom had not existed, Donald Marshall could still be languishing in jail.

Those who believe that this provision was designed to protect the privacy of women in these situations may be surprised to learn that such privacy is already protected. Another section of the Criminal Code provides a mechanism for suppressing publication of material that can identify the alleged victim of a sexual assault.[62] And the courts have already upheld the constitutionality of that section.[63] Thus, what possible excuse can there be for this new publication ban, restricted as it must be to material that will *not* reveal the identity of the victim? Incredibly, this provision was enacted into law with hardly a peep of opposition. The new anti-liberals had apparently managed to intimidate the members of Parliament.

The rape-shield amendment was adopted when Kim Campbell was minister of justice and her Conservative party occupied the majority of seats in the House of Commons. Unfortunately, the situation did not much improve when Allan Rock became minister of justice with the Liberal party having a majority in the House of Commons. In the spring of 1997, Parliament enacted a "privacy-shield" law that was designed to protect the privacy of sexual assault complainants from having their therapeutic records made available to those they accuse.[64]

Of course, it *should* not be easy for anyone, including accused persons, to look at such records. Those seeking therapy reasonably expect that their disclosures will be held in confidence. Indeed, the very effectiveness of the therapy requires such confidentiality. Few people would readily unburden themselves to their therapists unless they could trust that their privacy would be respected.

But accused persons who face possible imprisonment for years must have a reasonable chance to defend themselves. This entails some right of access to any materials that could bear upon their guilt or innocence. A society that wrongly jailed not only Donald Marshall but also Guy Paul Morin and David Milgaard should feel a moral duty to ensure such minimal fairness to those accused of serious crimes.[65]

The 1997 "privacy-shield" law is a model of *unfairness*. Courtroom access to therapeutic records dealing with the complainant requires, among other things, that the judge be satisfied such records are "likely relevant" to an issue at the trial.[66] Fair enough. But the law also enumerates some ten grounds that, despite their potential relevance, will still not be sufficient to produce the desired access.[67] Incredibly, these grounds include material that discloses a prior inconsistent statement made by the complainant and material regarding the complainant's credibility.[68] Either of these matters could be highly relevant to a criminal trial. Yet, even if both were involved, that would not suffice.

But, as the saying goes, "that's only the half of it". The 1997 law does not only deny the accused person such access to the material, it even forbids the judges from looking at it on their own.[69] Thus, judges are required to assess the importance of the material *without even seeing it*. Remarkably, the 1997 law represented an attempt by the government to improve upon guidelines promulgated by a 1995 Supreme Court of Canada decision.[70]

In the first place, the court had made it less difficult for the trial judges to see the records. Pointing out that the test for requiring production of such records to a judge should not be onerous, the court talked about a "reasonable possibility" that the desired record contained relevant material.[71] This test made it obviously more than a mere routine matter to get the contentious material before the trial judge. But it was clearly a test that, unlike the one in the 1997 law, allowed a *reasonable level* of such access to occur. After all, the threat to the complainant's privacy is much reduced when only a judge is allowed to invade it.

But, before the Supreme Court would allow the accused person himself to see the material, a trial judge would have to be satisfied that the material's contributory value to a fair trial for the accused outweighed its deleterious impact on the privacy of the complainant.[72] To be sure, the Supreme Court did not make it easy for accused persons to peruse these confidential records. *But it was at least a practical possiblity*. That's why I believe that the Supreme Court struck a much fairer balance than did the government.

The critical influence was exerted by the anti-liberal feminists. They reacted angrily to the Supreme Court judgment and immediately began to pressure Justice Minister Rock for a new "privacy-shield" protection.[73] The minister and his minions responded favourably to these pressures. It is significant that, at the time of writing, two courts—one in Alberta and one in Ontario—have ruled the 1997 law unconstitutional.[74] These courts see the law as infringing the right to a fair trial. Regrettably, neither the mainstream feminist organizations nor the Liberal government evinced a comparable loyalty to liberal values.

EMPLOYMENT EQUITY—A CHALLENGE TO SOME CONCEPTS OF EQUALITY

On the issue of employment equity, Judy Rebick, then president of the National Action Committee on the Status of Women (NAC), was quoted in August of 1992 as follows:

> ... the Canadian Civil Liberties Association seems to be more concerned about reverse discrimination against white men than about the needs of women and minorities and justice for disadvantaged groups.[75]

Curiously, these comments were made less than eighteen months after the Canadian Civil Liberties Association had called upon the government of Ontario "to weather the criticism and stay the course" on employment equity.[76] And the very letter which took this position contained the results of a CCLA survey: of 1200 retail jobs that were examined in Sudbury and Sault Ste. Marie, only three were held by aboriginal people and, in a majority of the stores which cumulatively employed more than 850 people, there was not a single native job holder. (These cities have relatively large native populations.) All this was widely publicized across Ontario and much of Canada. Not bad for an organization that "seems to be more concerned about reverse discrimination against white men than about ...justice for disadvantaged groups".

It's also significant that less than a year before Ms. Rebick made this statement, a CCLA delegation had met with the Ontario citizenship minister and presented to her a brief setting out guidelines for acceptable forms of affirmative action. Among other things, the brief contended that "it will no longer suffice for human rights commissions to sit on their formal jurisdictions waiting for complaints to come along".[77] Rather, the CCLA argued that the commissions must be involved in "the self-initiated quest for and removal of obstacles to the participation of disadvantaged groups in various sectors of the economy".[78] In support of this thesis, the CCLA cited a 1991 survey that focused especially on the inequities suffered by women. Despite the fact that at least 70% of public elementary school teachers have long been women, the survey disclosed that fewer than 25% of principals were female and women occupied only 18% of supervisory positions. Not surprisingly in light of such statistics and proposals, the brief included the following statement: "The Canadian Civil Liberties Association, therefore, supports affirmative action."[79]

What, then, accounts for the fact that employment equity was identified as a source of difference between NAC and the CCLA? The likely explanation concerns the kind of programs favoured by each of the groups. While the CCLA urges special measures to increase the pace of job equity for women and other disadvantaged groups, it nevertheless insists that such programs observe liberal principles designed to achieve fairness for everyone. Admittedly, therefore, the CCLA is concerned to avoid reverse discrimination against white men—a concern that appears not to be shared by many of NAC's supporters.

This difference in approach surfaced most clearly in the controversy over "Equity 2000" at the Ontario College of Art. Despite an acknowledged plethora of available female talent, the overwhelming majority of teachers at the college have traditionally been male. Neither a generation of human rights legislation nor the expressed commitment of the administration to avoid discrimination had managed to alter the pattern. Understandably, there was a felt need to do something different. The college adopted a plan, to begin in 1990, whereby qualified women would be preferred over qualified men for all of the jobs vacated by retirement until the year 2000.[80]

It was estimated that approximately 50% of the available talent pool was female.[81] Accordingly, the objective of "Equity 2000" was to reach a 50% gender split in the faculty as soon as possible.[82] As noted in a

Saturday Night article on the subject, "Equity 2000 . . . is a misnomer. Equity *won't* exist by the year 2000; in that year . . . 38% of periods will be taught by women" [emphasis in original].[83] "But," observed the *Toronto Star's* Lynda Hurst, "it was a start".[84]

The plan ignited considerable controversy. It split the public as well as the faculty. The college administration was accused of reverse discrimination; the accusers, in turn, were accused of insensitivity to women. And the rhetoric kept escalating.

In such circumstances, it's hard for a genuine liberal to oppose the idea of a numerical target. As indicated, the preponderance of male over female faculty had endured for years without significant change. It appears, therefore, that the traditional enforcement methods of the Human Rights Code were inadequate to the task. This is, of course, understandable. Since there are so many factors—including subjective tastes—that normally account for who gets chosen, it is very difficult to prove the existence of discrimination in individual cases. In order to make many ordinary human rights complaints stick, the aggrieved parties must effectively demonstrate that they are *substantially* more qualified—an exceptional situation—than the successful applicants.

A key idea of employment equity is to reverse the onus. Employers who do not fulfil their numerical targets are required to demonstrate that the persons they chose were discernibly the best. They should also have to demonstrate the vigour of their recruitment efforts and the reasonableness of their selection standards. Considering everything—including the employers' obvious knowledge of the relevant facts—such a shifting of the onus had much to commend it in the case of the art college. Moreover, since the distinctions among the college's qualified candidates would often be marginal, this approach could also have minimized inequities.

The principles of liberalism are offended, not necessarily by the concept of a numerical target, but by the way this one was chosen. If it is believed that there are about as many qualified women as men, why wasn't the target for the period of the plan closer to 50% women rather than 100%? To the extent that employment equity was justified here in order to counteract discrimination, there was no reason for a numerical target of so much more than 50%.

The 100% target reveals a confused set of objectives. It could have meant that future hirings were designed to redress yesterday's discrimination. But why should an entire generation of men be shut out of certain jobs because of what happened to past generations of women?

How is this going to redress the injustice that was done to numbers of women who may now be retired or even dead? (Of course, preferential treatment could be appropriate for any of the *actual victims* of yesteryear's discrimination who remained able and willing to perform the jobs in question.) In short, innocent white males should not now be made to suffer for sins committed by guilty white males. The fact that—as one writer has noted—there may have been an unfair affirmative action program in effect for men heretofore cannot justify an unfair affirmative action program for women hereafter.[85] Discrimination based solely on gender is repugnant no matter which gender is being favoured. That remains a valid liberal principle.

The other possible objective for Equity 2000 was expressed by (now Madam Justice) Rosalie Abella whose 1984 report first coined the term "employment equity". In her view, success in reducing disadvantage can be measured by "the extent to which, over time, those who were inappropriately under-represented take their representative place throughout [our] systems and institutions."[86]

Indeed, this was the aim of the Ontario NDP government's 1993 approach to employment equity: places of business should contain, proportionately, the same racial and gender mix as exists in the general society. But why? I would have thought that the sensible objective of employment equity is to ensure that there will be no discrimination *from now on*. Numerical targets represent a practical device to demonstrate that those discriminatory barriers at long last are being removed. The racial and gender mix in the community at large is simply one barometer for helping to assess the effectiveness of our anti-discrimination efforts. But to say that institutions and places of business must reflect the exact mix in the general community is to confuse ends and means.

A more reasonable way to choose numerical goals is to make an assessment of how many from the targeted groups would likely be chosen if the recruitment were vigorous, the job eligibility requirements were fair, and the selections were non-discriminatory. On this basis, of course, it would be virtually inconceivable that any such category of jobs could become a male or female preserve. In order to predict the numbers who would be both able and willing, it would be useful to examine demographic and occupational profiles along with factors such as course enrolments and the experiences of employers in similar circumstances. For the purpose of such calculations, the most relevant racial and gender mix will be found, not in the community at large, but in the pool of qualified personnel.

And, in order to prevent numerical targets from spawning reverse discrimination, employment equity plans should ensure that, in general, the anti-discrimination provisions of the Human Rights Code would continue to apply. Even if employers such as the art college are required to justify any failure to select a prescribed percentage of women, that is no reason to discriminate against men. Apart possibly from certain special situations, *every* aggrieved person—male or female, black or white—should still have recourse to the normal protections of the Human Rights Code.

It's critical that we keep our eye on the ball. The legitimate purpose of employment equity is not compensation for the remote past or representativeness in the distant future; it's no discrimination in the present and hereafter.

Somewhere along the line, a number of feminist leaders lost sight of—or repudiated—the liberal principles which provide the most valid justification for employment equity measures. In any event, such liberal principles stand at the centre of the growing rifts between certain feminists and certain civil libertarians. Where you stand on those principles determines where you stand in these disputes.

A PERSPECTIVE ON DEVELOPMENTS AMONG THE FEMINISTS

In an attempt to summarize the essence of the growing conflicts between many feminists and civil libertarians, Judy Rebick made the following statement:

> There is a pattern to what they [the Canadian Civil Liberties Association] are doing, they are coming down for the rights of the individual against the rights of [an oppressed] group.[87]

A similar theme can be found in Rosalie Abella:

> Unless we come to terms with the sometimes dichotomous relationship between civil liberties and human rights, we will be in policy rigormortus over remedy . . . if choices sometimes have to be made, and they do, human rights argues that the choices be made on behalf of the arbitrarily

disadvantaged group not the temporarily inconvenienced individual.[88]

And, in the context of the rape-shield controversy, Michele Landsberg made the following comment:

> Once again, the individual rights of the accused criminal have been given far more weight than the rights of all women to equal justice.[89]

This analysis is beset with significant flaws. In the first place, it suffers from the packaging fallacy. Very often, a claim that is packaged as "individual" can be described as "group" and vice versa without any logical difficulty. Why, for example, describe the rape-shield dispute as a conflict between the individual accused and women as a group? It might be even more appropriate to describe the conflict as one between two groups: aggrieved women and accused men.

The same transposition will often work for Judy Rebick's description. She uses the term "oppressed" to describe those groups whose interests she would accord the priority. In sexual assault cases, it could well arise in some cases at least that the socio-economic circumstances of the accused would be more disadvantaged than those of the complainant. In such cases, then, shouldn't the accused have the benefit of the label "oppressed"?

The same with Judge Abella's statement. To the extent that the accused in sexual assault cases suffer a legal disability as a result of an unjustified rape-shield law, they could be described as an "arbitrarily disadvantaged group". Similarly, to the extent that we attempted to redress the unfair features of the rape-shield law, we could label the complainant facing an intrusive interrogation as the "temporarily inconvenienced individual". After all, the reverse situation would really strain Judge Abella's conceptualism. If the rape-shield law had been allowed to stand, we might be labelling an improperly jailed accused with the words "temporarily inconvenienced individual". Not a very felicitous description.

The second problem with the group versus individual characterization is that it contributes nothing to the consequent analysis. What difference does it make if a claim is designated as "individual" or "collective"? There are no absolutes that can be invoked to resolve the conflicts we face. Inevitably, claims have to be balanced against each other to determine their relative impact on the shared interests and values of the affected parties and the total society. This is an on-going process that must be applied to the resolution of all these problems. It simply doesn't matter whether the competing claims are characterized as "individual" or "collective". Despite the characterizations, they still must be evaluated comparatively.

Thirdly, words like "oppressed" and "disadvantaged" frequently contribute more confusion than clarity. A representative of LEAF, with whom I appeared in a law school class, rebuked me in the context of a debate on hate propaganda by alleging that the CCLA never looks at the balance of disadvantage in the parties that are coming before the courts. In her view, we should do so in order to redress such disadvantage. Since the issue had arisen during a discussion of hate propaganda, I replied by asking her a question: as between Nazis and Jews, which is the more disadvantaged group? I would have thought that, in some respects, Nazis were among the most disadvantaged groups in Canada, and I would hope that they remain so. Why would any sensible person want to redress that disadvantage?

Such comparing of relative disadvantage is not a principled way to resolve disputes. At base, this may be one of the most disquieting features that has affected much of the modern feminist movement. Many of these feminists are essentially saying that, in general, women have been more disadvantaged than men; therefore, their interests ought to prevail over those of men whenever they collide. The context doesn't matter and the other applicable values don't matter. To paraphrase Patrick Henry, it is a case of "my constituency right or wrong".

Apart from questions of morality, such a posture would constitute disastrous politics. The feminists are not going to win these battles by trying to overpower men. Indeed, with such a gender-centric posture they won't even be able to command the adequate support of women.

What they need is a position capable of transcending gender boundaries. That's why feminists would be wise to return to the liberal values that originally launched their movement. Those values address the needs of disadvantaged people and the requirements of fairness better than any nakedly self-interested posture could possibly do. The liberalism inherent in the essence of feminism has the capacity to create a mighty coalition. The best hope for the triumph of what is worthy in feminism is to embrace the principles of liberalism.

Notes

1. Betty Friedan, *The Feminine Mystique* (New York: Dell Publishing, 1962) p. 305.
2. The Charter of Rights and Freedoms was adopted in 1982 as part of the Canadian constitution.
3. F.L. Morton and Avril Allen, "Feminists and the Courts: Measuring Success in Interest Group Litigation," paper prepared for the 1997 Annual Meeting of the Canadian Political Science Association, p. 7.
4. *Canadian Press*, June 2, 1987.
5. "Racism charge the 'worst thing ever in my life'" *Toronto Star*, (15 June 1992).
6. "Women take aim at civil liberties group" *Toronto Star*, (30 August 1992) A1, A6.
7. "York University's response to the Fassel Human Rights Complaint #50-657B"
8. "If Callwood is a racist then so are we all" Pierre Berton in the *Toronto Star*, (23 May 1992) H3.
9. "Women take aim at civil liberties group" *Toronto Star*, (30 August 1992) A1, A6.
10. The CCLA's president, at the time, was Sybil Shack of Winnipeg, a retired high school principal. She served for more than ten years as head of the civil liberties organization. The lawyer who acted, *pro bono*, for the CCLA intervention in the rape-shield case was Osgoode Hall law professor and now judge Louise Arbour.
11. "Civil Liberties and the Administration of Public Welfare," CCLA brief to John Yaremko, Minister of Social and Family Services of Ontario, March 10, 1970, p. 7-10, 17 [hereinafter CCLA brief to Yaremko].
12. CCLA brief to Yaremko, p. 4-7,17.
13. See, for example, CCLA brief to Yaremko, Minister of Social and Family Services of Ontario, March 10, 1970; "Poverty and Civil Liberties," CCLA brief to the Special Senate Committee on Poverty, April 16, 1970; "Welfare Practices and Civil Liberties—a Canadian Survey," Canadian Civil Liberties Education Trust, 1973; "Social Assistance and the 'Man in the House' Rule," CCLA brief to John Sweeney, Minister of Community and Social Services of Ontario, March 25, 1986.
14. *Morgentaler v. The Queen*, [1976] 1 S.C.R. 616.
15. "Abortion bill called too vague" *Brantford Expositor*, (1 February 1990).
16. "Borovoy joins fight against law on abortion" *Globe and Mail*, (3 August 1989).

[17] "Women take aim at civil liberties group" *Toronto Star*, (30 August 1992) A1, A6.
[18] *R v. Butler* [1992] 89 D.L.R. (4th) 449 [hereinafter Butler].
[19] Butler at 471, per Sopinka J.
[20] Ibid.
[21] Butler at 479, per Sopinka J.
[22] "Porn mutilates women's fight for equality" Michele Landsberg in the *Toronto Star*, (11 June 1991) F1.
[23] Ibid.
[24] Bruce Walsh, "Canadian dissident" *Quill & Quire*, v. 59(3) (March 1993) 9.
[25] "Police raid gay bookstore" *Globe and Mail*, (1 May 1992) D1.
[26] Confirmed by Glad Day owner John Scythes in Feburary 5, 1998 interview with CCLA staff member; "Butler decision splits women's law conference," *XS*, (April 1993) 7.
[27] Varda Burstyn, "Censoring who?" *Our Times*, (November, 1984).
[28] "Pedophile novel in Customs' limbo" *Globe and Mail*, (22 June 1992) A1, A2.
[29] Canadian Criminal Code, Section 163(8).
[30] Butler at 471, per Sopinka J.
[31] Butler at 475, per Sopinka J.
[32] "Anti-porn group target of seizure" *Globe and Mail*, (17 October 1987) A6.
[33] Lynn King, "Censorship and Law Reform: Will Changing the Laws Mean a Change For the Better," in *Women against Censorship*, ed. Varda Burstyn (Vancouver: Douglas and McIntyre, 1985) p. 87.
[34] *Erotic Poems—Canadian Press*, (19 December 1986); *Canadian Press*, (26 January 1987).

Film on male masturbation—"Medical film ruled not porn" *Toronto Star*, (26 October 1983) C18. While the customs power talked about material "of an immoral or indecent character", it, like the Criminal Code, targeted material that "goes beyond what the contemporary Canadian community is prepared to tolerate."- *Re University of Manitoba and Deputy Minister, Revenue Canada* (1984), 4 D.L.R. (4th) 658 at 661. Following a later case, *Luscher v. Deputy Minister Revenue Canada [1985] 1 FC 85*, the customs power was changed to incorporate the *Criminal Code* definition of obscenity.
[35] "Last Tango in Paris" was at issue in *R v. Odeon Morton Theatres Ltd. and United Artists Corp.* (1974), 16 CCC (2d) 185 (Man. CA) and "Show Me" in *R v. Macmillan of Canada Ltd.* (1976), 31 CCC (2d) 286, 13 OR (2d) 630 (Ont. Co. Ct.).
[36] Butler at 483, per Sopinka J.
[37] Ibid.

³⁸ The Canadian Charter of Rights and Freedoms contains in s.2(b) a guarantee for "freedom of expression." This is the provision that was at issue in the Butler case.
³⁹ *R v. Seaboyer,* (1991) 2 S.C.R. 577 [hereinafter Seaboyer].
⁴⁰ "Women take aim at civil liberties group" *Toronto Star,* (30 August 1992) A1, A6.
⁴¹ "Supreme Court ruling ignores reality of rape" Doris Anderson in *Toronto Star,* (26 August 1991) A15.
⁴² "Rape shield law offered protection" Michele Landsberg in *Toronto Star,* (10 September 1991) D1.
⁴³ "Women take aim at civil liberties group" *Toronto Star,* (30 August 1992) A1, A6.
⁴⁴ "New rape shield is transparent curtain" David Koulack in *Globe and Mail,* (6 September 1991) A15.
⁴⁵ "Rape shield law offered protection" Michele Landsberg in *Toronto Star,* (10 September 1991) D1.
⁴⁶ Ibid.
⁴⁷ *State v. Jalo* 557 P.2d 1359 (Or. Ct. App. 1976).
⁴⁸ "Sex history questions barred, accused dad wins new trial from Quebec appeal court" *The Lawyers Weekly,* (3 April 1992) 2.
⁴⁹ CCLA letter to federal minister of justice, December 3, 1986.
⁵⁰ CCLA factum in Seaboyer, p. 21.
⁵¹ Seaboyer at 634-5, per MacLachlin J.
⁵² Ibid.
⁵³ Seaboyer at 633-4, per MacLachlin J.
⁵⁴ "Rape shield law offered protection" Michele Landsberg in *Toronto Star,* (10 September 1991) D1.
⁵⁵ "New rape shield is transparent curtain" David Koulack in the *Globe and Mail,* (6 September 1991) A15.
⁵⁶ Seaboyer at 615-6, per McLachlin J.
⁵⁷ Seaboyer at 611-2, per McLachlin J.
⁵⁸ *Bill C-49, An Act to Amend the Criminal Code (Sexual Assault)* [now s. 276 of the Criminal Code].
⁵⁹ Canadian Criminal Code, s.276.3.
⁶⁰ Canadian Criminal Code, s. 276.3(1)(d)(ii).
⁶¹ *Commissioners' Report, Findings and Recommendations of the Royal Commission on the Donald Marshall, Jr., Prosecution* , 1989, Volume 1, pp. 87-88.
⁶² Canadian Criminal Code, s. 486.
⁶³ *Canadian Newspaper Co. v. Canada (Attorney-General)* (1988) 2 S.C.R. 122.
⁶⁴ *Bill C-46, An Act to amend the Criminal Code (production of records in sexual offence proceedings)* [now s. 278 of the Criminal Code].

65 Donald Marshall, a native Canadian Micmac, spent eleven years in a Nova Scotia jail for a murder he did not commit. Despite an incompetent police investigation and perjured testimony, Marshall's conviction for murder in 1971 was initially upheld by the Nova Scotia Court of Appeal. Convicted at the age of seventeen, Marshall was later exonerated by the confession of another man. His conviction was quashed by the Nova Scotia Court of Appeal in 1982. A public inquiry into this miscarriage of justice found that racism against native Canadians played a part in Marshall's conviction. See—*Royal Commission of the Donald Marshall, Jr., Prosecution, Commissioners' Report, Findings and Recommendations* (Nova Scotia, 1989), volume 1, p. 148-193, 275.

David Milgaard was wrongfully convicted of the murder and rape of a Saskatoon nursing assistant in 1969. Imprisoned for twenty-three years, he was freed in 1992 when the Supreme Court of Canada, after reviewing the evidence, ordered a new trial. Since Saskatchewan authorities declined to convene a second trial, Milgaard was not cleared until DNA tests conclusively proved his innocence in July, 1997—twenty-eight years after the crime occurred. A week later, charges were laid against another suspect. See—"Victims behind bars" *The Halifax Daily News*, (18 December 1997) 16.

In Ontario, Guy Paul Morin was acquitted of murdering his next-door neighbour in 1986 but, at a second trial in 1992, the Crown obtained a conviction. Morin was exonerated by DNA evidence in 1995. A public inquiry into Morin's wrongful conviction criticized the handling of the case at every phase of the justice system. See—"Guy Paul Morin's vigil for truth" *Toronto Star*, (20 June 1997).

66 Canadian Criminal Code, Section 278.7.
67 Canadian Criminal Code, Section 278.3(4).
68 Canadian Criminal Code, Section 278.3(4)(d)(e).
69 Canadian Criminal Code, Section 278.5(1).
70 *R. v. O'Connor* [1995] 4 S.C.R. 411 [hereinafter O'Connor].
71 O'Connor, at 415.
72 O'Connor, at 441-442. In the *Mills* case (see infra note 74), the CCLA factum, applying for intervenor status, proposed a somewhat modified test.
73 "Women's lobby urges government to shield rape-centre records" *Canadian Press*, (9 June 1995).
74 "Medical records open in rapes" *Globe and Mail*, (3 October 1997) A1, A12. See the cases of *R. v Mills*, [1997] AJ No. 891, 12 CR (5th) 138 and *R. v Lee* (1997), 35 O.R. 594 and *R. v Lee* (1997), 35 O.R. 598. There are also some cases that uphold the constitutionality of the 1997 privacy shield law. See, for example, *R. v Hurrie*, [1997] B.C.J. 2634; *R. v Curti*, [1997] B.C.J. 2367; *R. v Hnyda*, [1997] B.C.J. No. 2600; *R. v E.M.F.*, [1997] O.J. No. 4828; *R. v Weeseekase*, [1997] S.J. No. 790.

[75] "Women take aim at civil liberties group" *Toronto Star*, (30 August 1992) A1, A6.

[76] CCLA letter to the provincial minister of citizenship, May 24, 1991.

[77] "Guidelines for Affirmative Action toward Employment Equity," CCLA brief to the provincial minister of citizenship, November 20, 1991, p. 6 [hereinafter CCLA brief on employment equity].

[78] Ibid.

[79] CCLA brief on employment equity, p. 7.

[80] "Equity 2000: a long range plan for employment equity, the Ontario College of Art, Phase I and II," Status of Women Committee, Ontario College of Art, March 28, 1989, p.10, 20 [hereinafter Equity 2000]; "Art college uproar: fairness or folly?" Lynda Hurst in *Toronto Star*, (21 January 1990) B1, B5.

[81] Equity 2000, p. 2.

[82] Equity 2000, p. 10.

[83] "Artful Dodgers" Morris Wolfe in *Saturday Night*, (December 1990) 77.

[84] "Art college uproar: fairness or folly?" Lynda Hurst in *Toronto Star*, (21 January 1990) B1, B5.

[85] "Old boys' art school painted a fake equity picture" Michele Landsberg in *Toronto Star*, (28 September 1991) G1.

[86] "Human rights in the twenty-first century; a global challenge," Rosalie-Silberman Abella in *The Law Society Gazette*, 25 (1991) 43-51, at 47.

[87] "Women take aim at civil liberties group" *Toronto Star* (30 August 1992) A1, A6.

[88] "Solidarity attacked by exclusion: respecting equality and diversity," Rosalie-Silberman Abella's keynote address to 'Human Rights in the 21st century: A Global Challenge', November 9-12, 1990, pp. 13-14

[89] "Rape shield law offered protection" Michele Landsberg in *Toronto Star* (10 September 1991).

CHAPTER TWO

Among Minorities

A few years ago, a friend of mine who was doing some research at Queen's University came upon a fascinating document: the minutes of a Queen's University Senate meeting for October 29, 1943.

Under the heading, Statistics on Jewish Registration, the document contained the following:

> At Toronto University, ... the percentage [of Jewish students] has been 6% but in medicine 25-30% on occasion. The University is much concerned about the situation in medicine ... at McGill University ... Jewish students in arts ... are admitted only on an academic standing of 75% or over; other students are admitted on standing of 60% or over. This regulation is publicly known and seems to operate without any friction.

Read these minutes aloud to an audience today and the response will be one of shock. It's the unembarrassed candour of the anti-semitism. By today's standards—incredible.

Even more incredible is the realization that these minutes are little more than fifty years old. In the sweep of history—a mere interlude. By today's standards it's also hard to believe that, not long before those Queen's University minutes were being written, the government of Canada denied entry to a ship full of Jewish refugees from Hitler's persecution.[1] And when we consider that, in the 1970s, the chief justice of Canada was the Jewish Bora Laskin, our credulity is strained by recalling what befell him some thirty-five years earlier. In the late 1930s, the same Bora Laskin—despite a brilliant academic record—was unable to obtain a job with a law firm in Toronto.[2]

Blacks in Canada have also suffered serious discrimination in virtually every walk of life. To begin with, Canadian immigration policies set quotas on the number of blacks who were even allowed to come here.[3] Then, when they were here, they could expect discrimination in jobs, public accommodations, and housing. For years, it was hard to find any blacks working at jobs other than the most menial ones. They seemed to have a monopoly, for example, as sleeping car porters on the railways. Yet, they did not obtain the more prestigious jobs as conductors.

Some of the more outrageous cases were nationally publicized. In the mid-1940s, a black woman in New Glasgow, Nova Scotia was jailed overnight because she refused to sit in the theatre balcony that had been allocated for blacks (whites sat downstairs).[4] In the mid-1950s, the prime minister of Barbados was denied a room in a Montreal hotel.[5] As late as 1968, a dead black child in Nova Scotia was denied burial in what was then an all-white cemetery.[6]

The foregoing are simply a few of the situations that have come to public attention. Inevitably, there have been scores of others that were never publicized. We can only speculate as to the many situations in which Jewish and black people suffered daily indignities. The magnitude of change is nothing short of astounding.

Although it was only a few years ago that Jews were not even allowed to study in certain university faculties, they currently occupy scores of faculty positions that include deanships and even presidencies. A recent special supplement of the *Toronto Star* outlined the growing role that Jews have been playing in all walks of Canadian life: the arts, the media, medicine, law, the academy, business, publishing, and so on.[7]

Since the 1960s, numbers of blacks and other visible minorities have been entering fields of activity where, just a few years earlier, they were virtually non-existent. These fields include jobs servicing the public (bank tellers, retail sales clerks, hotel receptionists), prominent positions in the Canadian media, and even some executive offices in the corporate sector. In the 1980s, Lincoln Alexander, a successful black lawyer and politician, became the lieutenant-governor of Ontario.

Perhaps nothing tells the story more effectively than a few comparisons. At the end of the 1930s, that boatload of Jews fleeing the horrors of Nazism was turned back at the Canadian border; the incident failed to provoke a significant controversy. In the 1970s, boatloads of Vietnamese fleeing the horrors of Communism were not only allowed entry to Canada but, in many cases, were also subsidized to do so. In the early 1940s, job discrimination, based on race, creed, and ethnicity, was not only legally permissible, it was socially acceptable. By the 1990s, such discrimination has become unlawful and is considered immoral. Every jurisdiction in this country—both federal and provincial—has legislation making racial, religious, and ethnic discrimination unlawful in employment, public services, and housing. Such legislation would not have been possible without deep changes in public norms.

None of this is to portray contemporary Canada as an inter-group Utopia. To be sure, racism and discrimination—particularly against blacks—remain a significant phenomenon in our society. Despite comparable education levels, a recent census, for example, showed blacks with 50% more unemployment than exists in the total population.[8] But even though we acknowledge—as we must—the survival in Canada of serious racial and ethnic injustices, we must also acknowledge the monumental progress that has been made in so short a period of time. In the early 1940s, racial and ethnic discrimination was practised overtly with public approval. By the 1990s, this discrimination is practised covertly over public objection.

How did it happen? What made it all possible? I have little doubt that, to a great extent, this dramatic progress is attributable to the spread of liberal values throughout the Western world. These are the values bequeathed to us by the Age of Enlightenment: freedom of religion; racial, religious, and ethnic equality; human dignity. For close to two centuries, our society professed to believe in these values. During the last part of this century, we have made phenomenal strides towards their achievement.

But this tells only part of the story. The process by which a society lives up to its professed values is not automatic. There had to be a catalyst. Something had to galvanize our social mores. To a great extent, I believe that other liberal values and instrumentalities have contributed substantially: freedom of speech, the integrated school system, and inter-group cooperation.

For these purposes, freedom of speech includes freedom of the press, freedom of association, and freedom of assembly. Jews, blacks, and other minorities began to protest publicly about racial and ethnic discrimination. They set up test cases, publicized incidents of discrimination, organized delegations to government, lobbied politicians, picketed, and demonstrated. These freedoms were exercised again and again to fight discriminatory practices.

I am in a position to testify personally about the impact of freedom of the press. As director of the Labour Committee for Human Rights, I invoked the press time and again to fight discriminatory practices. Even before some of our anti-discrimination laws were enacted, I was able, simply by threatening to go to the press, to obtain housing for blacks that had otherwise been denied them. Freedom of expression was critical, therefore, in the fight against discrimination.

All the while discrimination was being eroded in this way, another development was occurring. Within the public schools, youngsters of all religions, colours, and ethnicities were having the experience of daily collaboration under normal life circumstances. By eating together in the cafeteria, working together in the classroom, and playing together in the school yard, they were developing the habits of enduring respect. According to a review of the social science literature on the subject:

> Out of hundreds of tabulations, there emerges the major finding that *in all the surveys in all communities and for all groups, majority and minorities, the greater the frequency of interaction, the lower the prevalence of ethnic prejudice.* [emphasis in original][9]

The other factor that accelerated racial and ethnic progress was the state of collaboration that existed among various groups in the community. Those delegations that called upon cabinet ministers were composed of several groups, not just one. Blacks, Jews, unions, churches, and others forged coalitions to fight discrimination. No one group could have had the impact that the coalitions made possible. Moreover, many of the organizations that fought for equality were themselves composed of diverse groups.

One of the most remarkable of these organizations was the Labour Committee for Human Rights, a group officially sponsored by organized labour as a public service to fight racism in the community at large. The Labour Committee was a model of intergroup collaboration. It was administered by the Jewish Labour Committee, operated by union leaders drawn from the general labour movement, and buttressed by volunteers from the black community. This organization conducted the key campaigns that produced Canada's major human rights legislation and it set up test cases to ensure that the legislation functioned properly.

Its technique was to dig out and document discriminatory practices. Through the use of black testers recruited from groups such as the Brotherhood of Sleeping Car Porters and the National Unity Association along with white rank and file trade unionists, the Labour Committee systematically exposed racial barriers throughout the community—particularly against blacks. It did this in Dresden restaurants, Windsor golf courses, Muskoka resorts, and apartment buildings in Toronto, Hamilton, St. Catharines, and Windsor. Once the discriminatory practices were exposed, they became the focus of legislative campaigns and legal proceedings. The success of this organization depended largely upon the kind of cooperation that existed among blacks, Jews, and trade unionists.

In view of the extent to which both blacks and Jews have been the beneficiaries of liberal values, it is not surprising that the positions and policies of the major black and Jewish organizations were traditionally supportive of such values. While both black and Jewish organizations sought to protect their special interests, they did so in conformity with the broad principles of human rights applicable to everyone. Thus, the position of mainstream blacks and Jews was essentially universalist—liberal to the core.

Since the mid-1960s, however, this posture began to undergo some significant changes. The self-interest of nationalism began to replace the universal values of liberalism. Perhaps the ethno-centric nationalism of the era was contagious. New nations were forming throughout the Third World, and separatist movements, like those of the Québecois and the Basques, were appearing in more developed countries. Whatever the causes, the political positions of a growing number of black and Jewish organizations have become discernibly more parochial than their earlier counterparts had been. Unfortunately, the key instruments of yesteryear's liberalism—freedom of expression, the integrated school system, and inter-group collaboration—have become the casualties of this development. I will deal with each in turn.

THE CENSORSHIP OF HATE—A CHALLENGE TO FREEDOM OF SPEECH

Somewhere around the mid-1960s, a small group of neo-Nazis appeared on the Canadian scene. In ghoulish fashion, the group began to revive the symbols of the Holocaust—uniforms, swastikas, and blatant propaganda about international Jewish conspiracies. Understandably, these images proved too much for many Jews to bear. Despite the infinitesimal size and pathetic impotency of this neo-Nazi constituency, many sectors of the Jewish community became deeply upset. Those who had survived the Nazi death camps in Europe demanded action. If the Canadian Jewish Congress (CJC) would not provide the leadership, large numbers of survivors threatened to go it alone. One way or the other, they were not going to tolerate the existence of a Nazi organization here in Canada.

The Canadian Jewish Congress responded. But, in the process of doing so, it began a descent on a "slippery slope" of dubious policy positions. The major CJC response was to launch an action campaign for new legislation to outlaw hate propaganda. Admittedly, the CJC had long advocated some kind of legislation to deal with such hate utterances. In the early 1950s, for example, a CJC delegation had proposed some minor tinkering with the false news section of the Criminal Code and had also called for the expansion of sedition to include incitements to racial violence. But the campaign of the mid-1960s represented a difference in kind. No more minor tinkering with existing concepts. Once and for all, it must become a crime to promote hatred against racial, religious, and ethnic groups.

Of course, this change in policy was completely understandable. So few years after the Holocaust, it was simply outrageous for anyone to dress up in a Nazi uniform and taunt Jews once again. These outrages probably reached an epitome with the later inception of the propaganda that began to deny that there had ever been a Holocaust. It is hard to imagine a more malevolent obscenity to inflict on those who had suffered so much. As one writer so eloquently expressed it: it was not enough for yesterday's Nazis to extinguish six million Jewish lives, their modern sympathizers seek to extinguish six million Jewish *deaths*.

As understandable as the CJC position was, it exacted a significant price from one of society's most vital and liberal values—freedom of expression. Inevitably, the response to such concerns has been that free speech is not an absolute. This generality, of course, is true. But the mere fact that freedom of speech is legitimately susceptible to some infringements, does not mean that it should be susceptible to *this* one.

Even if it is not an absolute, free speech is, as we have seen, the life blood of the democratic system in general and an important weapon for the Jewish community in particular. It is the vehicle by which aggrieved people have the opportunity to recruit and mobilize public support in order to achieve redress. The assumption is that unjust policies and governments are less likely to endure—or even to emerge—in an atmosphere of free public debate. In this sense, freedom of expression is a strategic freedom—a freedom on which other freedoms depend. A wise old trade unionist once called it the "grievance procedure" of a democratic society.

When considering anti-hate legislation, it would be helpful to stop talking in the abstract about the desirability of suppressing hate and, instead, talk in the concrete about how to do it. Once that were done, we would confront the essence of the problem: the hopelessness of formulating a legal prohibition precise enough to nail these unredeemed expressions of hatred without, at the same time, catching other speech—including valuable speech—in the same net.

Canadian law now makes it an offence to engage in the wilful promotion of "hatred" against people distinguished by race, religion, or ethnicity.[10] There could be no reasonable objection to a law that prohibited the incitement of racial *violence* in situations of imminent peril. But what are the boundaries of "hatred"? We know that free speech is often most important when it expresses strong disapproval. The battles to which I earlier referred were not waged and won by adhering to the admonitions of Emily Post. The speech that was used often had to be tough and biting. But where does strong disapproval leave off and hatred begin? And, in any event, how does a blunt instrument like the criminal law formulate the relevant distinction? I don't think it can be done without undue risk, and I believe that, at this stage of Canadian history, it's unwise even to try.

For the most telling examples to make my point, we need look no further than the actual experience of the last twenty-five years or so since the hate propaganda law has been on the books. Although it has managed on a couple of occasions to convict genuine hate mongers,[11] this law has been used against a wide variety of others.

In the mid-1970s, some young people were arrested for distributing literature at the Shriners' parade in Toronto. Their literature bore the words "Yankee go home". The charge was distributing hate propaganda. And, while the crown attorney had the good sense subsequently to withdraw the charge, we should not be overly consoled. In the meantime, those young people suffered the suppression of their perfectly legitimate political protest and they spent a couple of days in jail.[12]

In the late 1970s, there was a dispute in Ontario's Essex County over public support for French education. Two French-Canadian nationalists, feeling frustrated over the apathy of the French community, composed and distributed anti-French material. Their goal was to arouse pro-French sympathy. Even if their conduct might appear somewhat bizarre, it is clear that these two activists were not involved in the kind of behaviour for which our anti-hate law had been designed. Nevertheless they were charged with, and even convicted of, distributing hate propaganda. It was not until the court of appeal reviewed the case that the conviction was quashed and a new trial was ordered. Fortunately, the prosecution declined to resume the matter.[13]

In the mid 1980s, a mainstream publisher was under the gun for having published the pro-Zionist novel, *The Haj*, by best-selling author Leon Uris because, in the opinion of an Arab organization, the book seriously maligns the Arab people.[14] Not long after that, a film sympathetic to South Africa's Nelson Mandela was held up at the border for longer than a month because of allegations that it promotes "hatred".[15] Consider the ironies. Legislation designed to protect minorities like Jews and blacks winds up being used against them.

In 1989, there were two incidents. A Jewish leader, Edgar Bronfman, became the target of a hate propaganda complaint because he used harsh language against the Austrians for their failure to renounce Kurt Waldheim as their president despite the reports of Waldhein's pro-Nazi activities during the Second World War.[16] And Salman Rushdie's book, *Satanic Verses*, was ordered detained at the Canadian border because of allegations that it is offensive to the Muslim religion.[17]

Our democratic consciences should not be appeased by the fact that none of these cases produced a lasting conviction. Freedom of speech is undermined not only by the convictions that are ultimately registered but also by the prosecutions that are initially threatened. If we cannot speak our minds publicly without the fear of facing a criminal charge, we are not enjoying a meaningful freedom of speech. This is the phenomenon that certain American courts have so sensitively labelled "the chilling effect".[18] The risk of having our speech chilled increases with the vagueness of the laws that might apply. In order to avoid the possibility of prosecution, many people would be impelled to ensure that their speech steered as far as possible from the prohibited zone. The casualty of such self-censorship could well be perfectly legitimate speech.

The fact that those French-Canadian nationalists ultimately avoided conviction does not tell us what an ordeal it was to go through a criminal trial. The fact that charges were withdrawn against those anti-American activists does not tell us what it was like to be arrested and to spend a couple of days in jail. The fact that the Jewish leader and the publisher were never charged does not tell us how potentially intimidating it would be for many people to be the subject of governmental scrutiny. Nor does it guarantee that, in a very different political climate, charges would not be laid over the speech in question.

Even if material is temporarily detained rather than permanently seized at the border, our democratic consciences should not be appeased. In the case of the Mandela film, we do not know the extent to which the one month delay might have undermined the anti-apartheid activities that had been planned. In the case of the Rushdie book, we can imagine how a different political climate might have produced a more serious consequence than a forty-eight-hour detention order.

In retrospect, I shudder to think of what would have happened to the Jehovah's Witnesses in the early 1950s if the anti-hate law had been enacted then. Believing as they did that the Roman Catholic church was behind the persecutions they were suffering at the hands of Quebec's Duplessis regime, the Jehovah's Witnesses published some bitter attacks on the Catholic church. Duplessis responded by charging their leaders with seditious libel. The Supreme Court of Canada ultimately acquitted the Jehovah's Witnesses on the grounds that seditious libel had to be confined to the incitement of violence or disorder against constituted authority; it could not be stretched to prohibit the promotion of inter-group ill will.[19] The decision was widely applauded in Canadian liberal circles, including those of the Jews. But where seditious libel had failed, the anti-hate prohibition might have succeeded. The intriguing question emerges: to what extent would the Jewish leaders who applauded the acquittal of the Jehovah's Witnesses now be prepared to risk their conviction?

Some defenders of the anti-hate law have argued that there is a certain amount of vagueness in *all* legislation. According to them, arguments such as mine make the case not against the hate law in particular, but against all law in general. There is, of course, an element of truth to this contention. It fails, however, to adequately address two critical issues:

(1) Most of our criminal law is nowhere nearly as vague as the anti-hate provision. Murder, kidnapping, arson, robbery, and theft, for example, are defined with much more precision.
(2) Where there is comparable vagueness, the values put at risk involve matters such as driving a car (it requires "reasonable care") not values like freedom of speech, which engage the very grievance procedure of the democratic system. Those who seek to control dangerous instruments such as automobiles *should* be chilled into being exceptionally careful. Those who seek to speak their minds in order to redress grievances should not be commensurately chilled.

Significantly, if the Canadian Jewish Congress had had its way, the anti-hate law would have been even wider. In the early 1980s, the CJC had called for removing the requirement that the provincial attorney general must consent to certain anti-hate prosecutions.[20] Ironically, therefore, that mainstream publisher could well have faced criminal charges for putting out the pro-Zionist book and the Jewish leader could have suffered a similar fate for his anti-Nazi criticism of the Austrians. As anyone who has ever faced a criminal trial can readily testify, it's a harrowing ordeal. Eventual acquittal can never adequately obliterate the experience.

Within the next few years, there is a not insignificant risk that Jews will become more serious targets of the anti-hate law. The risk could be triggered by the ways in which Jews decide to deal with the disquieting signs of resurgent anti-semitism in Europe and elsewhere. One way to counteract these trends is to pressure governments in North America to take retaliatory action against those foreign governments that either unduly encourage or inadequately address anti-semitic activities within their borders. This will require mobilizing public opinion here at home.

Such mobilization could, in turn, require some tough talk. Canadian Jews might well have occasion to condemn, in general terms, the behaviour of certain foreign governments and their peoples. To whatever extent Canadian Jews believe that large numbers of people in other countries are behaving in an unacceptable manner, there will be a felt need to excoriate them in the harshest terms. The stronger such language becomes, the greater the risk of crossing the boundaries of the anti-hate law.[21]

Moreover, there is good reason to question how well the cause of racial and ethnic dignity is otherwise served by the anti-hate law. In significant ways, the requirements of a criminal prosecution are at variance with the canons of common sense. From the standpoint of common sense, the one thing you should not do is debate the merits of a malevolent obscenity. As Toronto Rabbi W. Gunther Plaut once observed, if someone calls your mother a whore, that is not a fit subject for a debate.[22]

But, when you prosecute, you are often forced to debate the merits of the accused's position. Small wonder, therefore, that in the Zundel false news case, there was a discussion in court over the monstrous proposition that Auschwitz was not a Nazi death camp but a Jewish holiday resort.[23] And the prosecutor, not the defence, called a non-Jewish banker to the stand and asked him if he was being paid by an international Zionist/Communist/banker/Jewish/Freemason conspiracy.[24] The *question* was an obscenity. I am not necessarily blaming the prosecutor for this; he may well have felt that he had to cover all of the elements in the accused's defence. I am simply suggesting that the risk of farce is endemic to the very nature of such proceedings and that it materialized in the Zundel case.

It's no secret that the publicity surrounding the first Zundel prosecution was very upsetting to many members of the Jewish community. A number of those Jews found consolation by persuading themselves that it was all a new experience for the media that was bound to be significantly improved in the event of any further such prosecutions. Unfortunately, however, much of the publicity surrounding the second Zundel prosecution achieved only marginal improvements over what happened the first time. Note, for example, the following extract from a *Toronto Star* report of the second trial:

> Christopher Browning, Professor of History at Pacific Lutheran University in Tacoma, Washington, said [Zundel's]

pamphlet *Did Six Million Really Die?* underestimated the number of Jews in Europe before the war and overestimated the number of Jews who emigrated from Europe.[25]

Here, we have the report of a professor calmly and politely treating Zundel's pamphlet as though it had engaged in a mere miscalculation of statistics. The Zundel pamphlet, of course, contained malevolent obscenities. But the very process of prosecution forced the authorities to treat it with a respect that it did not deserve. In the Keegstra anti-hate prosecution, the accused lectured the judge and jury as though they were his high school students. (In that case, James Keegstra, a high school teacher, was prosecuted for propagating, in the classroom, his anti-semitic interpretation of world events).[26] The courtroom became a forum for further ventilating his fatuities about an international Jewish conspiracy. I do not complain of this publicity because of a fear that these trials created a significant following for the hate mongers. I simply regard such trials as a gratuitous affront to the community's dignity and common sense.

There is yet another consideration. Not only is this law dangerous to Jews and other victims of discrimination, not only is this law potentially offensive to the dignity of the very groups who seek to enforce it in the courts, but it is also unnecessary in order to contain the influence of the hate mongers themselves. In this regard, we should consider the actual developments in the James Keegstra hate case. When the public became informed about his anti-semitic activities as a teacher, he was removed from the classroom by the school board, decertified as a teacher by the professional association, and ousted as mayor by the voters of Eckville, Alberta. In short, he was denuded of his clout and standing in the community. All this happened to him *before* any charges were laid against him.[27]

At the time of the charge, he was working as a garage mechanic. I don't want to disparage the importance of fixing cars, but an auto garage is hardly a centre of political influence in our society. At that point, Keegstra should have been allowed to wallow in the obscurity he so richly deserved.

This basic approach has demonstrated its utility on numbers of occasions. Certain persons in respected positions make racist or prejudiced statements in public and their fellow citizens pressure them to retract or resign. We all know of people in high places to whom this has happened—judges, politicians, and journalists, among others.[28]

In general, therefore, democracies should seek not to muzzle racists, but to marginalize them. It's too dangerous for the law to censor; it's appropriate for citizens to censure. Instead of trying to stop racists from speaking, it's usually better to focus on reducing their impact. In this regard, it would also help to improve the administration and enforcement of our anti-discrimination laws that deal with the serious racial and ethnic problems—in areas such as jobs and housing. A stronger program against racist *deeds* will weaken the impact of racist *words*.

In any event, there is no need for a choice between prosecution and doing nothing. There are other weapons that can be used to contain the influence of society's hate mongers. Such other weapons are significantly less dangerous than are curbs on freedom of expression. At least at this stage of history and in the foreseeable future, Canadians have more to fear from the censorship powers of their governments than from the racist invective of these extremists.

Unfortunately, the Canadian Jewish Congress's drift into pro-censorship positions has not stopped at the anti-hate law. The CJC wound up supporting the false news prosecution of Holocaust-denier Ernst Zundel. This section of the Criminal Code was particularly dangerous. It prohibited the conscious dissemination of false material that was "likely to cause injury . . . to a public interest".[29] Nowhere, however, did this section define its terms.

While it might appear acceptable in the abstract to ban the deliberate telling of lies, in the concrete such a ban could endanger much political and even historical discussion. As reprehensible as Holocaust denial is, we must remember that the law at issue had the capacity to muzzle *other* speech. If denying the Holocaust could provoke a criminal prosecution, what about denying the enormity of Stalin's crimes or denying the magnitude of the Inquisition?

Indeed, people in political situations frequently accuse each other of falsehood, and frequently there is at least an arguable basis for the charge. At the time of Canada's 1988 election campaign on free trade, for example, virtually all parties accused each other of lying. What is often at issue, of course, are not matters of fact at all but matters of opinion. In any event, the parties to the 1988 campaign might well have tended to exaggerate their own claims and minimize those of their adversaries. But imagine the impact on the debate if such exaggerations and minimizations had produced serious threats of criminal prosecution.

Even if the defendants would ultimately have been cleared because of inadequate proof that they had *knowingly* lied, the campaign would have suffered. A critical danger to freedom of speech is the very existence of a law that could threaten us for engaging in normal democratic debate. Moreover, the people most likely to be intimidated are those with unpopular ideas. Unless they were particularly imprudent or exceptionally courageous, they could well decide that it is better to be quiet than to risk the ordeal of a prosecution. That's why public opinion, rather than legal coercion, should decide the truth and falsity of most public policy claims.

The Supreme Court of Canada recognized all this even if the Canadian Jewish Congress did not. In the context of the Zundel case, the Court struck down the false news section as an unconstitutional infringement of free speech.[30] This doesn't mean that any kind of false news law would have suffered such a fate. There could be no reasonable objection, for example, to a law which prohibited the spreading of false news in situations where there was an imminent peril to life or limb. It would be acceptable, therefore, to punish a television station for falsely broadcasting that enemy missiles were on their way to strike Canadian cities. But such a law would have to define its terms in the kind of precise language that was nowhere to be found in the section that the Court invalidated and the CJC sought to uphold.

In the late fall of 1992, the Canadian Jewish Congress went a step further: it petitioned the Canadian government to keep the Holocaust-denying, U.K. historian David Irving out of this country.[31] Of course, Canada owes nothing to such an alien who wishes to come here. But this country does have an obligation to its citizens and permanent residents who seek access to him. Their free speech is the central issue.

But there is a section in the Immigration Act that potentially excludes foreigners on the basis of their having been convicted in another country of an offence that, if committed here, could be prosecuted "by way of indictment".[32] (The CJC argued that Irving's conviction in Germany for Holocaust-denying statements was analogous to a Canadian conviction under the anti-hate law).[33] The problem with this provision is that it is so wide that it could have denied Martin Luther King admission to Canada. During his battles against racial segregation in the American south, King was convicted and jailed for conducting demonstrations in violation of court orders.[34] That was an offence that, if committed here, could have been prosecuted "by way of indictment".[35]

It would have been more appropriate for the Canadian Jewish Congress to campaign against any law that could deny access to foreign speakers on such dubious grounds. Instead, it wound up encouraging public support for this unduly restrictive law. This is not to say that all aliens should be admitted here simply because there are some citizens who wish to engage with them. There is nothing wrong with devising criteria that would keep out foreigners who actually endanger the social peace of this country. All I am saying is that the criteria at issue here exceeded such legitimate considerations. The methods matter. For the CJC, the long-term implications were subordinated to the short-term objective.

In the fall of 1996, the Canadian Jewish Congress took yet a further step in this pro-censorship direction. It invoked another section of the Immigration Act in an attempt to stop American black leader Louis Farrakhan from keeping a speaking engagement in Toronto.[36] As head of the Nation of Islam, Farrakhan had compiled a dismal record of anti-semitic pronouncements. But, unlike David Irving, he had not been criminally convicted for these pronouncements. In the United States, where Farrakhan spends most of his time, there is no legislation akin to our anti-hate law. Such legislation would offend American notions of free speech.

Since there was no indication that Farrakhan had already been convicted of an offence unacceptable in this country, the CJC invoked a section that would keep out aliens if there were reasonable grounds to believe they *would* violate a Canadian law. In this case, the CJC argued that Farrakhan was likely to breach our anti-hate law.[37]

There was a special problem with using the anti-hate law in this way. With such a precedent in place, Canadian citizens might be denied access to many foreign speakers on a wide range of important subjects including the conflicts between Serbs and Muslims in Bosnia, Protestants and Catholics in Ireland, and Hindus and Sikhs in India. In at least some of those situations there is, to use the CJC's words, a "reasonable likelihood" that speakers expressing their indignation would attract action under the anti-hate law.[38]

Nor was there any reason to believe that such an appeal to the immigration authorities was the only way for Jews to lodge an effective protest against Farrakhan's visit to Canada. The CJC could have picketed the site of the speech and it could have publicly rebuked those Canadians who were prepared to make alliances with such a divisive demagogue. There could also have been appeals to various human rights organizations to join in a vigorous repudiation of Farrakhan and any Canadian allies he might have. Even if such organizations declined to participate, the exercise of making the request would have succeeded in raising many people's consciousnesses about the issue. In any event, it is likely that at least some of these organizations would have accepted such a CJC invitation.

In an earlier period, I believe the Canadian Jewish Congress would have objected to the very existence of immigration criteria as dubious as those it invoked in this case. But a combination of its short-term objectives (to keep out an undesirable) and the record of the positions it had already taken constituted an imposing barrier to the resurrection of the CJC's earlier liberalism. Sometimes, apparently, there really *is* a slippery slope.

In 1997, the Canadian Jewish Congress took an even steeper step. The CJC's Pacific region filed an anti-hate complaint under the British Columbia Human Rights Code. The target of the complaint was Doug Collins, a columnist for a neighbourhood newspaper whose writings had disparaged the Jews and expressed certain doubts about the reality of the Holocaust.[39] And, in Ontario, the Canadian Jewish Congress appeared before a tribunal in support of a complaint that had been filed under the telephone hate messages section of the Canadian Human Rights Act. The target of this complaint was Ernst Zundel, and the basis for the complaint was the Holocaust-denying messages he was disseminating through his website on the Internet.[40]

The factor that makes these cases so significant is the sheer breadth of the prohibition against speech in both of the human rights statutes.

They address statements that are "likely to expose" people to "hatred or contempt" on grounds that include race, creed, and ethnicity.[41] Unlike even the anti-hate section of the Criminal Code, these provisions do not require a guilty intent and there is no defence of truth or reasonable belief in the truth of the statements at issue.

On this basis, truthful discussions of racial, religious, and ethnic warfare in Bosnia, Rwanda, or Northern Ireland could very well run afoul of these human rights statutes. Couldn't such discussions be seen as "likely to expose" Serbs, Croats, Muslims, Hutus, Tutsis, Catholics, or Protestants to hatred or contempt? Or suppose a complaint were filed regarding Daniel Goldhagen's recent book, *Hitler's Willing Executioners*? Since the book argues that German people by the thousands participated eagerly in the Holocaust, might it not be said that the book is "likely to expose" a whole generation of Germans to hatred or contempt? Indeed, considering how much anti-semitism existed in Nazi-occupied Europe during the war, these human rights statutes might render it unlawful simply *to tell the truth* about the Holocaust. After all, truthful accounts of the anti-Jewish collaboration the Nazis received from some of the indigenous populations in the countries they occupied could well be seen as "likely to expose" the people of those countries to "hatred or contempt".

If such complaints were ever filed, what position would the Canadian Jewish Congress take? In view of its support for the complaints against Collins and Zundel, what position *could* it take? The CJC might find itself handicapped in its attempt to defend constructive, truthful discussions of these historical episodes. Such sad ironies not infrequently accompany the infringement of liberal values.

For the Canadian Jewish Congress, irony was further compounded in the spring of 1998. A New Brunswick judge held that newspaper cartoonist Josh Beutel had defamed former New Brunswick school teacher Malcolm Ross in a cartoon presentation to a 1993 teachers' seminar. Ross, who had been removed from his teaching position because of his anti-semitic writings, sued Beutel for depicting him as a Nazi. While acknowledging the racist and anti-semitic nature of Ross's beliefs, the judge held that calling the former teacher a Nazi "goes too far". Beutel was ordered to pay Ross $7500.00 in damages.⁴²

The Canadian Jewish Congress reacted with understandable anger. According to *The Globe and Mail*, a CJC representative charged that the judgment would "put a chill" on commentators wishing to criticize public figures. In the reported words of CJC lawyer Hal Joffe, "How are commentators to determine how something like this will impact them? As a result people who have appropriate comments to make may just shy away from making them."⁴³

Exactly. Hyperbole is the stuff of political commentary and, even more so, of political cartooning. As Mr. Joffe rightly notes, the attempt here to target what is illegitimate creates a significant risk of inhibiting what is legitimate. The murkier the legal criteria, the greater this risk will be. Not the least of the difficulties is the recurring problem of distinguishing declarations of fact from expressions of opinion. Is it a statement of opinion or purported fact, for example, to accuse certain logging companies of "genocide" for conducting their activities on land claimed by aboriginal people? What about the charge we often heard that the Americans were committing "genocide" during the Vietnam war?

The Canadian Jewish Congress sees the problem clearly when the speech of *its* supporters attracts legal sanctions. But its perceptions become clouded when the shoe is on the other foot. The CJC's criticism of this court decision is almost a replica of the criticism that has been made of the anti-hate law that the CJC supports. Murky criteria wind up imperilling legitimate expression.

Incredibly, according to *The Globe*, Mr. Joffe went on to advocate a still wider law of defamation. He reportedly proposed changing the law in this area to give groups such as the Canadian Jewish Congress a right of legal action against individuals who attack Jews.⁴⁴ Having so correctly analyzed the problem, the CJC recommends making the situation even worse. A not unexpected consequence of straying so far from liberal values.

THE PUBLIC FUNDING OF RELIGIOUS SCHOOLS—A CHALLENGE TO INTER-GROUP INTEGRATION

As I indicated earlier, the public schools have been one of the most integrative forces in our community. They have contributed immeasurably to the increased mobility and equality of the Jewish community and indeed other minority groups.

Jewish organizational involvement over the schools has usually concerned the place of religion in them. Historically, the position of the Jewish community has coincided completely with liberal values and the requirements of human rights.

In 1944, the Ontario government enacted a regulation requiring two one-half-hour periods per week of formalized religious instruction for its public schools.[45] The content of the instruction would represent the doctrines shared by the major Protestant creeds in the community. By virtue of a pre-Confederation agreement, Roman Catholic separate schools would continue to be financed out of state taxes at least from kindergarten to Grade 10 inclusive.[46] The question for the Canadian Jewish Congress was whether the Catholic situation should be treated as a precedent or an exception. For more than three decades, the CJC treated it as an exception. Taking the position, therefore, that public funds and public schools should not promote anyone's personal faith, the CJC mounted a vigorous and forthright campaign against the 1944 public school regulations.

Throughout the years, the CJC's campaign enjoyed increasing success. Major school boards such as those of Toronto and North York sought and received formal exemption.[47] The original guide books, long a source of bitter controversy, simply went out of print and were never republished. By the early 1970s, a major government committee headed by J. Keiller Mackay, former lieutenant-governor of Ontario, recommended the total removal of this program from the public school system.[48] A growing number of mainstream Protestant leaders also spoke out against the government regulation.[49] As the years went on, the regulations were increasingly ignored. It became harder to find school boards and classrooms where the program was being taught according to the curriculum requirements. In the mid-1980s, however, we discovered a few areas where religious instruction, of a particularly sectarian character, was still being given. This discovery triggered new action.

By the end of the 1980s, the Canadian Jewish Congress intervened in support of a constitutional court challenge launched by the Canadian Civil Liberties Association.[50] That case finally won the day: the 1944 regulation was invalidated under the Canadian Charter.[51]

At some point during the 1970s, however, another form of Jewish self-interest intruded in this issue. I refer to the growing Jewish day school movement. For a number of years, some of the larger urban centres in Canada began to experience a substantial increase in the Jewish day school population. Many of the major ideologies in Jewish life established their own day school facilities—Orthodox, Conservative, Reform, and even secular. Increasingly, the Jewish day school movement was being relied upon to stem the tide of assimilation.

The problem was that it is extremely expensive to maintain such a separate school system. And these expenses are compounded to the extent that Jewish day school supporters must also pay taxes in support of the public school system. As the expenses mounted, a growing number of Jews began to argue that they should receive some relief from the public purse. After all, they were being forced to pay for facilities that they were not using. Moreover, why shouldn't the Jews be entitled to at least some of the benefits that the Catholics receive? Doesn't such differential treatment amount to unwarranted religious discrimination?

Those who disagreed with these arguments pointed out that citizens without children are nevertheless required to support the public school system. Indeed, the argument was made that, since the public schools enrich the whole society, *everyone* should be required to pay for them. Denominational schools serve only the adherents of such demoninations. Hence, there was no inequity in requiring the beneficiaries of such schools to support them and the public schools. As for religious discrimination, the argument was made that the favourable treatment of the Catholic schools was inherited, not initiated, by contemporary society. Indeed, the public funding of Ontario's Catholic schools was entrenched in the Canadian constitution. And, in any event, the need to prevent the erosion of the public schools was seen as good reason to hold the line at the Catholic schools.

For present purposes, however, I shall not address the general question of whether any such aid to Jewish day schools could be considered desirable. Rather, I wish to look at the concrete methods by which the Jewish community has been prepared to obtain such support. From the standpoint of liberal values, there are three developments in particular that I find disquieting.

The first one occurred in the mid-1970s. The Associated Hebrew Schools, a Jewish religious day school system, devised a plan with the North York Board of Education whereby this Jewish school system would be transformed into a public school so that it could obtain North York board funding for the secular portion of its curriculum.[52] As ingenious as this plan was, it contained a fatal flaw. Despite their proposed receipt of public funds, the Associated Hebrew Schools insisted upon retaining their mandatory classes in the Jewish religion.[53]

Mandatory Jewish instruction, of course, is perfectly acceptable in a Jewish day school. But how could it be justified in a common public school? It was bad enough for the Associated Hebrew Schools to propose this plan; the situation became exacerbated over the methods by which they were prepared to fight for it. When the Ontario government refused to accept the arrangement, the North York Board of Education, with the support of the Associated Hebrew Schools, took the government to court.[54]

Consider the implications: if the North York board had won that case, mandatory Jewish instruction would have become acceptable in some public schools. At that point, why wouldn't mandatory Christian instruction be acceptable in other public schools? Thanks, in part, to the Associated Hebrew Schools, the Jewish and liberal community would have lost a major weapon in their fight against Christian indoctrination in the public schools. Fortunately, the court ruled against their claim.[55]

The second development occurred in the mid-1980s. I refer to the policy of the Canadian Jewish Congress regarding the Ontario government plan—Bill 30—to extend the full public funding of the Catholic separate schools from Grade 10 to Grade 13. (As indicated, those schools were being fully supported by public funds up to Grade 10.) The issue was referred to the Ontario Court of Appeal and it then went to the Supreme Court of Canada. Many organizations participated.

Faced with the prospect of such additional aid for the Catholic schools, it was understandable that the Canadian Jewish Congress would argue that Jewish and other denominational schools were entitled to comparable benefits. But while the CJC did make this argument, it also took the position that it "supports the extension of the public funding of Roman Catholic denominational schools through the completion of secondary school...."[56]

Unfortunately, Bill 30 contained some problematic features. It recognized that, because of funding arrangements, a number of non-Catholics in certain areas would be effectively forced, by reason of distance and the need for special programs, to attend the Catholic schools. It was especially anticipated that such arrangements would be made for non-Catholic students whose public schools were slated to become Catholic schools because of the large Catholic populations in those areas. Accordingly, Bill 30 provided that non-Catholics in this position could be exempted from the religious classes in those Catholic schools.[57]

The problem with this provision is that the Catholics have traditionally said that, in their schools, religion is not confined to any one class. It permeates the atmosphere. It is not possible, of course, to obtain exemption from the atmosphere. In the result, therefore, Canadians were treated to an unfortunate spectacle: the Canadian Jewish Congress went to court to support a program that contemplated the foisting of Roman Catholicism on non-Catholics. This represented a remarkable departure from the traditional Jewish commitment to the liberal principles of religious freedom.

Again, it seems likely that such parochialism will wind up damaging a number of Jewish self-interests as well. Among the non-Catholics forced into the Catholic school system, there could well be a number of Jewish youngsters. Thus, in its eagerness to obtain public funds for the Jewish day schools, the Canadian Jewish Congress took a position potentially harmful to some of its own constituents. After all, only the Jews in some of the larger centres would ever be in a position to benefit directly from the public funding that the Jewish Congress was seeking for the Jewish day schools. No matter what level of funding might be forthcoming, there is little likelihood that Jewish day schools would ever be established throughout the province. Thus, the CJC seemed prepared to trade off the well-being of its most vulnerable members who would never have a practical option but to attend schools in which they would be a minority.

The third development arose in the early 1990s. It came in the wake of the victory won by the Catholic schools and the Ontario government in the above case.[58] Now that the Catholic separate schools were entitled to full funding from kindergarten to Grade 13, the Canadian Jewish Congress made its next move. It went to court seeking an order that the Jewish day schools are constitutionally entitled to parity with the Catholic schools.[59] A group of private Christian schools joined the case as co-applicants.

In fairness, I must acknowledge once again some merit in the CJC's argument. In all equity, if the Catholics are entitled to a certain amount of public support for their schools, the Jews also have a persuasive claim.

On the other hand, the obligation to fund the Catholic schools was inherited from an arrangement made in 1867.[60] (Indeed, the Supreme Court of Canada held, in the Bill 30 case, that Ontario was constitutionally *compelled*—not simply allowed—to finance the Catholic schools up to the end of Grade 13).[61] Thus, the special treatment for the Catholics did not result from a contemporary decision; it was foisted on us by history.

In any event, when you go to court and ask for a ruling as a matter of constitutional law, the risk you run is that the result could be rigidified in the Constitution. It follows that, if the CJC had won this case, virtually all religious day schools—not just the Jewish ones—would have acquired a constitutional right to the level of funding the Catholic schools get.

What, then, would have become of the public schools? Full funding would be likely to entice a wide variety of religious groups to open their own schools, including at some point those mainstream Protestants who are smarting from the defeats they have suffered over having their prayers and instruction removed from the public schools.[62] Attendance in the public schools could severely decline.

To its credit, the CJC did not contest the importance of the public schools. Instead, it pointed to the experience in the Western provinces and argued that public funding of religious day schools would not, in fact, erode the public schools. But public assistance to independent schools in the West is a relatively recent development.[63] The brevity of the experience does not warrant the breadth of the conclusions the CJC has drawn from it. Even at that, there has been a dramatic increase in private school attendance since the funding began.[64] In any event, however, the level of funding at issue in this case—parity with the Catholic schools—would substantially exceed the amounts provided in the West. Not surprisingly, many religious schools in the Western provinces continue to charge onerous fees.[65]

A more analogous situation is that of the Netherlands—the only place in the world that provides full public funding for private schools in coexistence with public schools. Following the change in funding arrangements in the early part of the century, public school attendance in that country went from more than 65% in 1901 to less than 30% today.[66] Even if, as some suggest, Holland today embodies "social integration, not social division",[67] we should not expect Ontario to fare as well if its public schools could no longer perform their integrative function. After all, inter-group tolerance appears to have deeper roots in Dutch history than it does in the history of many other nations.[68] And, as indicated earlier, intolerance and discrimination were quite respectable in Ontario as recently as the 1940s.

Thus, if the schools of Ontario were to become religiously Balkanized, the province could well become a much less tolerant place than it is today. In view of what this century has revealed about the potential fragility of religious and ethnic coexistence, the Jewish community should be especially wary about the changes that would occur in the event that the public schools became significantly weakened. A wise policy would aim to do everything possible to create and sustain a strong, viable public school system in which youngsters of all religions and ethnicities would have the experience of cooperative interaction. In serving liberal values, such a course would also serve the best interests of the Jews themselves.

A PERSPECTIVE ON DEVELOPMENTS AMONG THE JEWS

On both of these issues—freedom of expression and the viability of the public schools—the Jewish community has been moving away from its traditional support of liberal values. And I think it's fair to say that this trend is compromising the long-term interests of the Jews as well.

One factor that gives me hope is the continuing state of internal democracy within the Jewish community. Despite everything I have written here, it remains very much a Jewish characteristic to encourage debates on these very subjects. The Jewish community is a highly pluralistic one including in its leadership and ranks those who are Orthodox, Conservative, Reform, secular, right-wing Zionist, left-wing Zionist, peacenik, and even non-Zionist. A climate as rich in diversity as this creates the opportunity and even the requirement that its policies and practices will be under constant scrutiny and review.

In this regard, I am reminded of the old story concerning a Jewish Robinson Crusoe who had been marooned on an island by himself for many years. When his rescuers came, they wanted to see how he had been living during that time. He took them on a tour of his island. At one point they came upon a beautifully constructed lean-to. "What is that?", they asked him. "It is my synagogue", he proudly replied. But later that day, the rescuing party came upon another well constructed lean-to at the other side of the island. "What is that?", they asked. "It is a synagogue", he answered. "Why does one Jew need two synagogues?", they asked. *"In dos shul gay ich nisht"*, he retorted. (In that synagogue, I don't go.) Jews always need a synagogue they refuse to attend.

So long as such pluralism remains a key component of Jewish life, there is a chance that the Jews will reclaim their traditional liberalism. In my view, it is more important than ever that they do so. It was liberal values that set the Jews free; it is liberal values that can *keep* them free.

THE TOLERANCE OF ETHNIC ANIMOSITY—A CHALLENGE TO INTER-GROUP COOPERATION AND RAPPORT

While cooperation among groups such as blacks and Jews continues to exist, the last several years have seen the development of some disquieting tensions. These tensions are putting a strain on the levels of cooperation that are needed for further progress in race and ethnic relations.

I

In October of 1995, several hundred thousand blacks—primarily men—peacefully assembled in the "Million Man March" on Washington. The central figure in the march and the principal speaker for the day was Louis Farrakhan, leader of the Nation of Islam, a black nationalist organization based on the Muslim religion. Despite reports linking Farrakhan to racism, anti-semitism, anti-Catholicism, sexism, and homophobia, mainstream black leaders—including former presidential candidate Jesse Jackson and a number of members of the Congressional Black Caucus—participated as platform speakers.[69]

Two years earlier, according to *Commentary* magazine, Farrakhan had told an audience in Harlem that Jews "are the most organized, rich, and powerful people, not only in America, but in the world" and that they were "plotting against us even as we speak".[70] And, in an interview with a Chicago newspaper during that same year, Farrakhan reportedly made the following statement: "When I talk to the Jews, I am talking to a segment of that quorum that holds my people in their grip. And I can't get to you [the media] unless I get to them first because they got a grip on you whether you want to admit it or not . . .".[71]

In addition to its well-known reference to the Jews as "bloodsuckers", Farrakhan's organization, the Nation of Islam, distributes the notorious anti-semitic tract, *Protocols of the Elders of Zion*, and publishes material purporting to prove that the slave trade was dominated by Jews.[72] Another representative of the Nation of Islam reportedly declared that Jews work "to keep blacks ignorant and repressed" and that Jews have used blacks "as cannon fodder".[73]

Notwithstanding all of this evidence, Reverend Benjamin Chavis of the National Association for the Advancement of Colored People (NAACP) declared that Farrakhan was "neither anti-semitic nor racist",[74] and the chairman of the Congressional Black Caucus was prepared to enter into a "sacred covenant" with the Nation of Islam to pursue a shared civil rights agenda.[75] And, together with the Reverend Jesse Jackson, a number of these mainstream black leaders participated in the Million Man March.

In view of all this mainstream collaboration, it is no surprise that a survey conducted under the auspices of the University of Chicago found 67% of black respondents considered Farrakhan a positive force in the black community and only 28% viewed him negatively.[76] Similarly, a *Time*/CNN poll found 70% of black respondents agreeing that Farrakhan "says things the country should hear", 63% agreeing that he "speaks the truth" and only 34% saw him as "a bigot and a racist".[77] Moreover, a 1992 survey, conducted for the Anti-Defamation League of B'nai Brith (ADL), showed a higher level of anti-semitism among blacks than among other groups. In this survey, only 14% of black respondents registered no anti-semitism while 37% were in the category of most anti-semitic, more than double the level found among non-Jewish whites.[78]

Such disquieting attitudes are to be expected when the likes of a Louis Farrakhan can engage in such anti-semitic demagoguery with so little opposition—indeed, with apparent cooperation in a number of cases—from mainstream leaders of the black community. It would be unfair, of course, to characterize all the current mainstream black leadership in this way. To be sure, there are important black leaders who have been openly critical of Farrakhan and his organization: Congressman Major Owens of New York, Mel Reynolds of Chicago, John R. Lewis of Atlanta, and General Colin Powell, as well as former Georgia state legislator and newly elected NAACP chairman Julian Bond, to name a few.[79]

The significant fact is that the American black community has changed dramatically in the last thirty years. By contrast with what is happening today, the mainstream black leadership of the 1960s embraced liberal values. In so doing, they set an inspiring moral example for all of America. Martin Luther King, of course, was described—and appropriately so—as the "moral leader of America". So many of his colleagues were also distinguished by their commitment to liberal principles: Roy Wilkins and Thurgood Marshall of the NAACP, Whitney Young of the Urban League, A. Philip Randolf and Bayard Rustin of the labour movement. For these leaders, the priority was racial integration and equality. Yet a larger number of the current black leaders appear more focused on nationalist and ethnocentric concerns.

It is simply inconceivable that the mainstream black leaders of the 1960s would have responded with anything but denunciation in the face of anti-semitic invective. This is not to say that they never had differences with the Jewish community. But it is to say that those differences were addressed in tones of mutual respect. Moreover, King, Wilkins, and the others were attempting to build a liberal, labour, civil-rights coalition as the vehicle to right the wrongs of America. Thus, they were committed to working hard for a united front with constituencies such as the Jews.

At some point in the late 1960s, schisms developed within the black community. When Stokely Carmichael (as he then was known) uttered the words "black power", he sparked the launching of an ethno-centric nationalism within the black community. To a great extent, a similar orientation evolved around Elijah Mohammed, Malcolm X, and the Black Muslims. These people challenged the liberal philosophy of the integrationists around King. Aided and abetted by the growth of nationalism throughout the world, additional sectors of the American black community became increasingly sectarian and, of course, less liberal.

By the time of the Million Man March, a new generation of black leaders had emerged. Unlike those who were at the helm in the sixties, this group felt the need to accommodate the anti-liberal nationalism that was gaining such momentum. When asked about making common cause with the likes of Farrakhan, the current mainstream leaders pointed to the legitimate objectives of the march—the need, in black communities, to increase the cohesion of families and to decrease the commission of crimes. Whether or not we agree that such objectives could justify the collaboration of mainstream black leaders and the consequent political empowerment of a hate monger like Farrakhan, it is important to recognize how the relative decline of liberal values in the black community helped to create such a dilemma for mainstream black leaders.

Perhaps the growth of black nationalism in the United States was causally related to the perceived failures of liberal integrationism. The dismantling of racial segregation that occurred in the 1960s did not appear to be accompanied by a significant improvement in the daily lives of many black Americans. Millions of them continued to languish in the terrible, teeming ghettos of the big cities.

Nevertheless, discernible progress *had* occurred. In education, transportation, and public accommodations, the walls of segregation were crumbling. Moreover, comprehensive anti-discrimination laws had been enacted for many sectors of community life. And, with voting rights being enforced more than ever before, blacks were being elected to key positions of power—even in the old south. Since these changes were largely attributable to the tactical brilliance and moral courage of the integrationist leadership around Martin Luther King, there was reason to believe that the civil rights movement was on something of a roll. After all, King had only begun to address the problems of economic inequality. He was assassinated before this next phase of the movement was able to get underway.

In any event, the fight against the economic injustices was going to require disciplined hard work. Civil rights leaders like Bayard Rustin continued to urge their fellow blacks to resist the temptations of nationalism in favour of building coalitions with other groups in order to increase their victories at the political level.[80] Rustin criticized the "black power" nationalists because, in his view, their approach was a recipe for defeat. He acknowledged the psychological satisfactions that nationalism could bring, but he warned that this was no substitute for political success.[81] Despite King's legacy and Rustin's efforts, the nationalists continued to gain ground at the expense of the integrationists.

As ethno-centric nationalism became a more influential philosophy in the black community, there was a drop in the number of black leaders who were committed to liberal values. Thus, Farrakhan and the Nation of Islam have been inadequately challenged by their fellow blacks for a considerable period of time. Such circumstances enabled the Farrakhan entourage to increase their standing and prestige so that they could command a substantial following. As a result, a number of the mainstream leaders believed that the achievement of the march's legitimate objectives required them to compromise with Farrakhan and his people.

As is so often the case, developments in Canada are behind those in the United States. Fortunately, this applies as well to the advance of nationalism and the decline of liberalism in the black community. It would be wise, however, to learn from the American experience in order to avoid the potential strengthening of extremists here. Certain recent incidents in this country are worth noting as potential barometers of an unhealthy development.

II

An incident that warrants concern is the 1993 controversy over the use of the musical *Showboat* to open the North York Centre for the Performing Arts in Toronto. Soon after the planned production was announced, a political storm emanated from key parts of the black community. Numbers of black activists complained that this American musical would perpetuate false stereotypes about blacks and thus strengthen community prejudices against them.[82]

What creates the concern is not the protest over the musical. People can have legitimate differences of opinion about such matters. No doubt, a decision to open the centre with Shakespeare's *The Merchant of Venice* might well have evoked some Jewish protests over the stereotypes involved in the Shylock character. It's not without significance, however, that the appearance of *Showboat* in a number of American communities created no comparable controversy there.[83] In any event, not having seen the show, I have no comment on the propriety of the production or of the protest. (Fortunately, the protest did not include any demands for government censorship.) My concern is focused on the extremist language with which the Toronto controversy was conducted in some quarters. I refer primarily to the recurring resort to expressions of an anti-Jewish nature.

Some of the most disturbing examples of anti-Jewish sentiment were contained in the pages of the black newspaper *Share*. This newspaper has a circulation of several thousand; it reaches many people in the black and general community. Its editor, Arnold A. Auguste, wrote not one, but several editorials in which he made Jewishness an issue in his protest over *Showboat*. To him, it was significant that the musical was written by a Jew, it was being produced in Toronto by a Jew, and the North York mayor who was slated to preside over the inaugural ceremonies at the theatre was also a Jew.[84] So what, it might well be asked. Indeed, this is exactly what was asked by the Canadian Jewish Congress in a letter to Mr. Auguste.[85]

In his reply, the editor of *Share* exacerbated the conflict. In addition to repeating the number of Jews that were involved, he made the following comment:

> You complained that I labelled 140,000 Jews in Toronto . . . . You are more concerned that some Jewish people's feelings may be hurt by my expression of my pain, than for the hurt that I feel for your people's refusal to accept my pain.[86]

Here we have a major black newspaper expressing a notion of collective guilt. The Canadian Jewish Congress is faulted because a number of Jews have allegedly refused to accept Mr. Auguste's pain. If the editorials had simply appealed to the conscience of the Canadian Jewish Congress as an organization of fellow discrimination victims with a mandate to promote equality, the issue would have been much less contentious. But these editorials went much further. According to them, the Jewish ethnicity of the writer, producer, and mayor requires special action from the CJC.

Indeed, in yet a subsequent editorial, Mr. Auguste actually said that he "had hoped supportive voices— . . . in the wider Jewish community—would have publicly dissociated themselves from such an affront to us . . . ."[87] If Jews commit an impropriety, other Jews, according to this view, bear a special responsibility for it unless and until they "dissociate themselves".

Such a doctrine has the ability to eradicate years of progress in racial and ethnic relations. I would have thought that the principle for which both the black and Jewish communities had fought was the idea that people should be judged on the basis of their individual worthiness and not as members of groups. On this basis, for example, many human rights and civil liberties organizations challenged certain newspapers for playing up the fact that a number of crimes had been committed by black people. If anyone had suggested that blacks in general had a special responsibility for the crimes committed by certain blacks, there would have been hell to pay. For some reason, Arnold Auguste did not seem to appreciate the connection between this example and his condemnation of the Canadian Jewish Congress when it refused to take special responsibility for the Jews connected with *Showboat*.

Indeed, every time Auguste commented on the issue, such difficulties were compounded. Perhaps they reached their zenith in the following remarks he made:

> All this talk coming from some people in the Jewish community about my identifying those connected with *Showboat* as Jews, thus negatively labelling all Jews, is just a smoke screen—absolute nonsense. The people involved in this denigration of black people *are* Jews. They are not Chinese. They are not East Indian. If they were, I would have said so. [emphasis in original][88]

After fighting for so many years to promote the principle that ethnicity is presumptively irrelevant in assessing the propriety of people's behaviour, we are now told by a leading black publication that we must have been wrong. In this quote, Mr. Auguste answered the Canadian Jewish Congress, not by addressing the question of whether ethnicity is relevant in these circumstances, but rather by insisting that he got his irrelevant facts straight.

The most troubling aspect of this controversy is the paucity of responses it elicited from those not directly associated with the Canadian Jewish Congress. While Arnold Auguste's remarks may have been the most frequent and widely circulated, certain other comments from the black community also expressed disturbing anti-Jewish sentiments.[89] Apart from a few notable exceptions such as columnist Robert Fulford, former Ontario Ombudsman Daniel G. Hill, and the Canadian Civil Liberties Association, hardly anyone else challenged the anti-Jewishness in the *Showboat* protests.[90]

At this point, I had better anticipate a possible problem. Lest I be thought of as inconsistent, I should point out that I am not faulting blacks, in particular, for failing to challenge the anti-Jewish expressions of their fellow blacks. In my view, blacks no more than Jews should be responsible for each other in this way. What I am concerned about is the failure of agencies and organizations, normally concerned with race relations, to apply their principles in this case. The blacks and whites connected with operations such as the Ontario Human Rights Commission, the Urban Alliance on Race Relations, and the various human rights committees of churches and labour unions would have jumped if any major white organization had said some of the things about blacks that this black publication said about Jews. Yet, almost without exception, these organizations maintained a public silence about the way Jewishness was intruded into the *Showboat* debate.

III

Another incident worthy of mention here occurred in September of 1996. I refer to the visit of Louis Farrakhan to Toronto. (The Canadian Jewish Congress failed in its attempt to have him barred from Canada.) Despite the fact that there was less than one week's notice of his visit, more than 2500 people, mostly blacks, overflowed the convention room at the Harbour Westin Hotel on a Sunday night to hear his speech.[91]

I have already mentioned the allegations of Farrakhan's sexism, anti-Catholicism, and homophobia. I have also cited reports of his anti-semitism. Indeed, outside the convention room where he was speaking, his organization was selling booklets entitled *The Jewish Onslaught* and *The Jews and Their Lies*.[92]

As indicated earlier, I am opposed to the kind of efforts made by the Canadian Jewish Congress to keep Farrakhan out of Canada. In my view, the CJC's arguments represented an undue threat to the free speech rights of Canadian citizens who seek encounters with foreign speakers on Canadian soil. It's one thing, however, to defend such rights; it's another thing entirely to endorse the propriety of making common cause with a man like Farrakhan. Even though there was no suggestion of any anti-semitic invective on this occasion, his record was accessible to anyone who wished to scrutinize it.

The disquieting feature about Farrakhan's visit was the torrent of adulation it set off in Toronto's black community. *Toronto Star* columnist Cecil Foster, for example, swooned about how Farrakhan had "spread his charm, using his charisma to strongly connect with blacks living in this country".[93] Dudley Laws, Executive Director of the Black Action Defence Committee, described Farrakhan as a "great man".[94] June Veacock of the Ontario Federation of Labour said she was "particularly impressed"; black educator Oscar Braithwaite said that "Farrakhan has a positive message to give black people";[95] and an editorial in *Share* said that "Farrakhan, the intelligent individual that he is, made certain that his message was relevant, not only to his Muslim brothers and sisters, but also to those blacks who are Canadian-born or may have come here from Asian countries, the Caribbean and other parts of the Diaspora".[96]

Even more disappointing is the fact that, despite Farrakhan's record, there was a dearth of commentary in the black press that expressed any misgivings about him or the value of alliances with him.[97] To be fair, Farrakhan does address genuine problems in the black community. There is no question of the bleak circumstances that millions of blacks are suffering in America today. A combination of drug abuse, violent crime, and oppressive poverty has made life a nightmare in the U.S. black ghettos. It was understandable—indeed desirable—for black leaders to do something in order to turn these conditions around. The question, however, is whether this laudable objective justifies the political empowerment of a hate monger. Is there no other way to champion the legitimate interests that Farrakhan addresses?

Consider, for example, how Nazism grew. Many non-Nazis initially supported or declined to oppose Hitler because his movement gave disheartened Germans a sense of purpose and his program promised an end to unemployment. This is not to compare Farrakhan with Hitler. It is simply to illuminate the nature of the ethical choices involved. To serve otherwise legitimate objectives, many black leaders have been prepared to legitimize a dangerous demagogue.

It might be helpful to consider certain other situations closer to home. Despite the well-known benevolence of the Lions' organization, many Canadians (myself included) picketed a convention it held in Toronto because that convention welcomed then segregationist governor of Alabama, George Wallace. Admittedly, an angry demonstration of responsible citizens might have hurt some of the worthy charities supported by the Lions' organization. But, during that very period, George Wallace was turning dogs and hoses on innocent civil rights demonstrators, including children. For us, the importance then of de-legitimizing a racist tyrant trumped such other considerations.

In all these situations, the fight against racism and hate has collided with other worthy objectives. Such is the nature of the human condition. Everything we humans want usually requires some sacrifice of something else we want. But, while there are no absolutes, the suffering caused by hate mongering in the twentieth century should make people especially wary about this particular evil.

A PERSPECTIVE ON DEVELOPMENTS AMONG THE BLACKS

Of course, a few incidents do not warrant large generalizations. The black community in Canada remains—like most racial and ethnic groups—highly heterogeneous. Yet such incidents do indicate the growth of certain trends—unfortunately, of an anti-liberal character. It would be fruitful if these incidents served as stimulants to action.

To learn the lesson of the American experience is to realize that a tolerant reception of anti-Jewish or any bigoted pronouncements will very likely strengthen the anti-liberal elements in our community. Had Farrakhan, for example, been more vigorously opposed earlier, he might never have acquired the clout he ultimately did. The key lesson is that when expressions of hostility against certain groups emanate from any otherwise respectable sources, it is important that they be challenged strongly and quickly. In this way, other members of the public are helped to see the unacceptability of racist and bigoted pronouncements. Blacks as well as whites should be censured for daring to promote such unfair notions.

A most encouraging development during the *Showboat* controversy was the public apology tendered by a black politician. Having made some anti-Jewish statements about the issue, she recanted, acknowledging the impropriety of her remarks. The significance of her reversal is that it was urged upon her by a number of black leaders.[98] The forthrightness of these black leaders stands in the best traditions of the black community's historic liberalism. No less encouraging in this respect is the kind of cooperative spirit that characterizes many of the relations among blacks, other visible minorities, and whites in organizations such as the Urban Alliance, the labour movement, and the Canadian Civil Liberties Association.

Again, the best hope there is for preventing the kind of developments in Canada that have occurred in the United States is to avoid judging such issues on the basis of blackness, Jewishness, or any other tribal affiliation. The central issue should be the universal liberal values that would judge all of us by a common standard. That is what must be reclaimed and extracted from these controversies.

A WORD ABOUT DEVELOPMENTS AMONG THE DISABLED

Where the discrimination against blacks and Jews has often been based on animosity, the discrimination suffered by people with disabilities has been more attributable to condescension. Unlike the situation with racial and ethnic minorities, the disabled have been more patronized than criticized.

Yet, while people with disabilities have traditionally evoked compassion, more recently they are also commanding respect. This development is largely attributable to the fact that the disabled, like many other constituencies, have organized themselves to exert political pressures on the powers that be. These pressures have won increasing public and governmental support for the equality-seeking demands of the disabled community. Of course, the aspirations of these people have been enhanced by the conspicuous competence of certain disabled people who have entered public life—Charles Krauthammer, the American newspaper columnist; Catherine Frazee, former chair of the Ontario Human Rights Commission; and David Lepofsky, legal counsel for the Ministry of the Ontario Attorney General, to name a few. Not surprisingly, much of our human rights legislation has been amended in recent years in order to prohibit various forms of job discrimination based on disability.

Unfortunately, certain segments of this constituency have started to show some of the anti-liberal proclivities that have affected so many of the other equality seekers. This became particularly evident in the mid-1990s case of Robert Latimer, the Saskatchewan farmer who killed his severely disabled thirteen-year-old daughter Tracy. Since Latimer admitted that he planned the killing, he was convicted of murder—in his case, second-degree murder.[99] In Canadian law, such a conviction carries an automatic life prison sentence with no chance of parole for at least ten years.[100] Initially, this was the sentence that the trial court imposed upon Latimer and it was upheld by the court of appeal.[101] Due to certain technicalities, the Supreme Court of Canada ordered a new trial.[102] At the second trial, Latimer's lawyer persuaded the judge to grant his client a constitutional exemption from the statutory sentence on the grounds that, in the circumstances of this case, such an outcome would amount to "cruel and unusual punishment". In the result, the judge sentenced Latimer to one year in jail and one year under house arrest.[103]

This diluted punishment triggered a wave of protests across the country. One disabled representative after another denounced the judge's decision. Hugh Scher of the Council of Canadians with Disabilities probably expressed the views of many of his constituents when he warned that the sentence "sends a message that what Robert Latimer did was okay".[104] Indeed, many others did echo Scher's rhetorical question: "Would the sentence even be an issue if Tracy Latimer wasn't disabled?"[105]

The two-year sentence imposed upon Latimer hardly suggests that what he did "was okay". Yes, it does suggest that what he did was not as bad as what other second-degree murderers have done. But that's a far cry from total exoneration.

According to the Canadian Association for Community Living, "had Tracy not been disabled, Robert Latimer would be serving a minimum ten year prison term. There can be no double standard".[106] Catherine Frazee, former chair of the Ontario Human Rights Commission, charged that Canadians are feeling compassion for the wrong person, "No one speaks for Tracy. No one knows what she thought, or wanted".[107]

It's true that we don't know what Tracy wanted. Indeed, this turned out to be one of the mitigating factors in the case. According to the evidence—most of which was uncontradicted—the girl was so severely disabled, physically and mentally, that she was effectively unable to communicate.[108] On the basis of all the evidence, the judge found that Robert Latimer honestly—and apparently with good reason—believed that his daughter was suffering unremitting agony that only her death could relieve.[109] It may be, of course, that some people disagree with these findings of fact. Since I was not there and did not read the transcripts, I am unable to second guess the judge on his assessment of the evidence. I suspect that many of the other commentators are similarly unqualified. Unless they have examined the evidence with some thoroughness, they have no basis to prefer any findings of fact over the ones made by the judge.

If the judge's understanding of the facts is to be accepted, it becomes very hard to quarrel with his exercise of compassion. When Catherine Frazee argues that the compassion of Canadians is misdirected, she is assuming, with no way of knowing, that Tracy preferred her painful life to an early death. In view of the fact that we have all known of cases where people experiencing certain kinds of pain *chose* death over life, how can we make such assumptions about Tracy Latimer? Moreover, our compassion need not be an either/or proposition. Why can't we show compassion to Tracy *and* her father?

When Hugh Scher and others claim that Tracy might still be alive if she hadn't been disabled, they are omitting a crucial ingredient. It wasn't simply her disability that brought about her death; it was her father's reasonable belief that she was suffering unbearable, unrelievable agony.

In some ways, one of the most disappointing responses was made by the Association for Community Living when it argued that "Tracy's death should be treated like any other murder . . . there is no room . . . for . . . compassion . . . as justification for a lenient sentence".[110] On the basis of this argument, Robert Latimer should serve at least ten years in jail. The exceptional circumstances of this case would, therefore, count for nothing. If this organization had its way, Latimer would be punished as though his deed were the outgrowth of hate rather than of love. What could be more illiberal than this refusal to make distinctions? Again, this is to argue for mitigation not exoneration. In any event, automatic justice is for automatons, not for humans.

What these representatives of the disabled community seem to fear most is how this lenient sentence will affect subsequent situations. In the words of Diane Ritcher of the Association for Community Living, "if you have a disability, you're not going to sleep very well".[111] Such comments reveal a lack of perspective. The leniency shown to Robert Latimer is a function of the rather exceptional circumstances of this case. Anyone else seeking to use this case as a precedent would be effectively required to satisfy a court that all of these factors were present. This would be no easy burden. Even at that, this case could not be invoked to completely liberate an accused person in such circumstances. A not insignificant amount of jail time would still be forthcoming. Moreover, anyone contemplating such a deed would also have to reckon with the intimidating processes of arrest, prosecution, and then the anxious uncertainty over what penalty would be imposed. At best, these are unpleasant prospects. Thus, there is simply no basis to believe that the leniency shown here will open the floodgates.

In supporting mandatory minimum jail sentences, these organizations for the disabled are rejecting vital prerequisites of a liberal penal policy. In this regard, it would be helpful to consider research conducted in the 1980s by the Canadian Sentencing Commission. In a survey of judges, 91% said minimum penalties restricted their ability, at least sometimes, to give a just sentence.[112] Ninety-five percent said the existence of such sentences contributes, at least sometimes, to inappropriate plea bargains.[113] Commission surveys among both prison inmates and members of the public revealed widespread unfamiliarity with the provisions for minimum sentences. When asked to name an offence carrying such a penalty, very few were able to do so.[114] How in the world is a minimum sentence supposed to deter if its very existence is unknown? Small wonder that, according to the Law Reform Commission of Canada, the reported research does not show that such harsh sanctions are more effective than less harsh ones in preventing crime.[115]

And how necessary are minimum punishments for keeping dangerous criminals off the streets? A perusal of the published sentencing decisions for the 1990s conveys the impression that heavy penalties are not infrequently imposed upon violent offenders. For aggravated assault, there have been sentences of eight years and nine years, and as high as ten years and twelve years for aggravated sexual assault.[116] Even without minimum sentences, the Criminal Code permits substantial penalties, and experience suggests that the Canadian judiciary is hardly a sanctuary for bleeding hearts.

In view of all this, why insist on such rigidity? In many ways, a mandatory minimum sentence is an arbitrary penalty. It imposes jail terms according to an abstract formula rather than on the basis of concrete circumstances. Not surprisingly, the above report of the Canadian Sentencing Commission contained the following statement: "In the past 35 years, all Canadian commissions that have addressed the role of minimum mandatory penalties have recommended that they be abolished".[117]

It is disappointing indeed to see organizations for the disabled—that otherwise promote liberal and progressive policies—become advocates of such regression.

Notes

1. Irving Abella and Harold Troper, *None Is Too Many* (Toronto: Lester & Orpen Dennys Limited, 1982), 64.
2. "Laskin Obituary" *Canadian Press*, (26 March 1984).
3. James W. St.G. Walker, *A History of Blacks in Canada* (Ottawa: Minister of State Multiculturalism, 1980), 93-4.
4. Walker, p. 125.
5. Daniel G. Hill and Marvin Schiff, *Human Rights in Canada: A Focus on Racism* (Ottawa: Canadian Labour Congress and the Human Rights Research and Education Centre, University of Ottawa, 1985) 15.
6. Walker, p. 89-90.
7. "Shalom: Making A Difference" *Toronto Star* Supplement, (3 Dec 1992).
8. See the various statistical studies of the Employment Equity Data Program, part of the Housing, Family and Social Statistics Division, Statistics Canada in 1991. This particular conclusion is derived by collating the education levels measurements (177-199) and the labour force activity measurements (223-232) of the black subgroup and the total population.
9. Robin Williams Jr., *Strangers Next Door: Ethnic Relations in American Communities* (Englewood Cliffs: Prentice-Hall, 1964), 167-8.
10. *Criminal Code*, R.S.C. 1985, c. C-46, section 319(2).
11. *R.* v. *Keegstra*, [1990] 3 S.C.R. 697; *R.* v. *Andrews and Smith*, [1990] 3 S.C.R. 870.
12. "Hate literature charges against 3 to be dropped" *Globe and Mail*, (4 July 1975) 1.
13. *R.* v. *Buzzanga and Durocher* (1979), 101 D.L.R. (3d) 488 (Ont. C.A.).
14. "Libraries won't ban Uris book" *Globe and Mail*, (11 October 1984) 20.
15. "Customs pledges procedure review after film seizure" *Toronto Star*, (26 Dec 1986) A3.
16. "Bronfman is target of complaint" *Globe and Mail*, (26 May 1989) A11.
17. "Ottawa halts Satanic Verses imports" *Canadian Press*, (18 Feb 1989).
18. See, for example, *Dombrowski* v. *Pfister*, 380 U.S. 479 at 487 (1965).
19. *Boucher* v. *The King*, [1951] S.C.R. 265.
20. "Measures proposed to discourage spread of hate propaganda" *Globe and Mail*, (2 June 1984).
21. Admittedly, it is a defence under the anti-hate law, section 319 of the Criminal Code, to make statements that are intended to reduce "feelings of hatred" toward racial, religious, and ethnic groups. Such a defence, however, requires that such groups be "in Canada". Moreover, the defence also requires "good faith". In the wrong political climate, this latter requirement

might be difficult to establish. In any event, in such a climate, charges might be laid, or at least threatened, in response to certain impassioned Jewish criticisms of anti-semitism in other countries. That, in itself, would imperil the free speech at issue.

22 "Prosecution in Zundel trial faced long odds" *Globe and Mail*, (1 March 1985) 15.

23 "Rosy views of death camp challenged by prosecutor" *Toronto Star*, (5 March 1988) A3.

24 "Banker bemused at examination in Zundel trial" *Globe and Mail*, (30 Jan 1985) M1.

25 "Zundel's statistics on Jews wrong, historian tells trial" *Vancouver Sun*, (16 Feb 1988) A7.

26 "Keegstra lectures courtroom on Jewish conspiracy theory" *Globe and Mail*, (30 May 1985).

27 D. J. Bercuson and D. Wertheimer, *A Trust Betrayed: The Keegstra Affair* (Toronto: Doubleday Canada, 1985), 108, 122-3, 168-9.

28 For example, Toronto radio broadcasters Dick Smyth and Brian Henderson aired comments on their shows in September, 1995, claiming that a disproportionate number of lawyers, doctors, and dentists are Jewish. Consequently, they said, those professions were too crowded. The remarks were condemned by members of the Jewish community and by radio station management. Demands were made for the hosts to apologize and retract their statements. Both broadcasters did apologize publicly for their comments (*Canadian Press*, 21 Sept 1995). Similarly, in March, 1998, newly appointed Supreme Court Justice Ian Binnie used the phrase "faggoty dressup party" during a keynote speech at an international legal fraternity dinner. The comment created an uproar in the legal community, and had gay activists calling for the judge's removal from a high-profile gay rights case. Binnie quickly apologized in a letter to the dean of Osgoode Hall Law School (*Canadian Press*, 13 March 1998).

29 *Criminal Code*, R.S.C. 1985, c. C-46, section 181.

30 *R. v. Zundel*, [1992] 2 S.C.R. 731.

31 Verified on April 27, 1998 by Bernie Farber, an official of the Canadian Jewish Congress.

32 *Immigration Act*, R.S.C. 1985, c.I-2, s.19(2)(a.1).

33 Verified on April 27, 1998 by Bernie Farber, an official of the Canadian Jewish Congress.

34 In April, 1963, Reverends King, Abernathy, and Shuttlesworth led a march in Birmingham in defiance of a court injunction against such demonstrations. The United States Supreme Court upheld the conviction of King and others for disobeying the court order. *Walker v. City of Birmingham*, 87 S.Ct. 1824 (1967).

35 Section 127 of the *Criminal Code*, R.S.C. 1985, c. C-46, makes it an offence to disobey an order of court. The offence is punishable by way of indictment, and an offender is liable to imprisonment for a term not exceeding two years.
36 "Farrakhan here to tell 'the truth'" *Toronto Star*, (16 Sept 1996) A1, A4.
37 Verified on April 27, 1998 by Bernie Farber, an official of the Canadian Jewish Congress.
38 "Thousands attend Farrakhan speech: Jewish groups object to black leader's visit" *Globe and Mail*, (16 Sept 1996).
39 "Freedom's just another word . . ." *Saturday Night*, (Nov 1997) 59 at 60.
40 "Genocide viewed as fable: Witness" *Canadian Press*, (16 Oct 1997).
41 *Canadian Human Rights Act*, R.S.C. 1985, c.H-6, s. 13(1); *British Columbia Human Rights Code*, R.S.B.C. 1996, c.210, s. 7(1). Although the board of inquiry in the *Collins* case found that the material in question would not likely expose Jews to hatred or contempt, this does not assuage my general apprehension concerning the enactment at issue. The result in the case cannot be seen as a precedent; it may represent nothing more than the response of a particular tribunal to a particular piece of writing.
42 *Malcolm Ross v. New Brunswick Teachers' Association and Josh Beutel* (17 April 1998) Trial Division, Judicial District of Moncton.
43 "Jewish group opposes ruling on cartoonist" *Globe and Mail*, (12 April 1998) A6.
44 Ibid.
45 "Appeal Court asked to curb religion classes in Ontario" *Globe and Mail*, (12 Sept 1989).
46 "Hearing opens on school funding" *Globe and Mail*, (26 May 1992).
47 Ministry of Education Internal Memorandum from R.A.L. Thomas (Executive Director of Curriculum Development) to G.R. Podrebarac (Assistant Deputy Minister), October 22, 1979.
48 J. Keiller Mackay, Chair, "Religious Information & Moral Development: The Report of the Committee on Religious Education in the Public Schools of the Province of Ontario" (Toronto: Ontario Department of Education, 1969).
49 Signatories to the CCLA's Statement on Religious Education in Ontario's Public Schools, sent to the Minister of Education, included the following Protestant leaders: Rev. Donald Gillies, Rev. Carl Moore, Rev. Victor Dell, Rev. J.A. Davidson, Bruce McLeod.
50 *Canadian Civil Liberties Association v. Ontario (Minister of Education)* (1990), 71 O.R. (2d) 341 (C.A.).
51 Ibid.
52 Minutes of the Board of Education for the Borough of North York (Sept. 22, 1975).

53 Ibid.
54 *Re Board of Education for the Borough of North York and Ministry of Education* (1978), 19 O.R. (2d) 547.
55 Ibid.
56 Factum of the Canadian Jewish Congress in the matter of *Reference re an Act to Amend the Education Act (Ontario)*, paragraph 26, submitted to the Supreme Court of Canada.
57 *Act to Amend the Education Act*, S.O. 1986, c-21, s. 136o(5).
58 *Reference re an Act to Amend the Education Act (Ontario)*, [1987] 1 S.C.R. 1148.
59 "Hearing opens on school funding" *Globe and Mail*, (26 May 1992).
60 *Constitution Act, 1867*, s.93.
61 *Reference re an Act to Amend the Education Act (Ontario)*, [1987] 1 S.C.R. 1148.
62 *Canadian Civil Liberties Association* v. *Ontario (Minister of Education)* (1990), 65 D.L.R. (4th) 1 (C.A.); *Zylberberg* v. *Sudbury Board of Education (Director)* (1988), 65 O.R. (2d) 641 (C.A.).
63 Funding began in Saskatchewan and Alberta in the mid-1960s, in British Columbia in 1978, and in Manitoba in 1980: J.D. Wilson, ed., *Canadian Education in the 1980s* (Calgary: Detselig Enterprises Limited, 1981); R. Everhart, ed., *The Public School Monopoly* (Cambridge: Ballinger Publishing Company).
64 Private school attendance in Alberta was 5509 in 1978-79 and rose to 13,630 in 1989-90 (Alberta Department of Education, "Education in Alberta: Facts & Figures, 1989"); in British Columbia the number of students enrolled in private schools rose from 4.3% of the student population in 1977 to 8.2% in 1994 (Sweet, L. *God in the Classroom* (Toronto: McClelland & Stewart Inc., 1997), 117); and, in Manitoba, 0.2% of students in private schools in 1986 rose to 6.6% in 1995-96 (Manitoba Education and Training, 1995 Statistics); CEA Information Note (Canadian Education Association, Feb. 1992).
65 For example, Vancouver Christian School charges $345 per month per student (approximately $3450 per year, grades 8-10); North Edmonton Christian School charges $3850 per year per student (above kindergarten level); Calgary Jewish Academy charges $3420 per year per student (Grade 9). Information given by the schools' secretaries, April, 1998.
66 S. Lawton, "Public Support for Catholic and Denominational Schools: An International Perspective" (Paper prepared for the Annual Conference of the Ontario Association of Education Administrative Officials, Toronto, Ontario, Oct. 31-Nov.2, 1984).
67 Sweet, p. 136.
68 For more on the roots of tolerance in Dutch history, see Kennedy, R. *The Ageless Indies*, (New York: John Day, 1942) 143-4, quoted in Bagley, C. *The*

Dutch Plural Society: A Comparative Study in Race Relations (London: Oxford University Press, 1973):
"Nowhere in Europe is Christianity, whether Protestant or Catholic, taken more seriously than in the Netherlands .... But the people of Holland have displayed *throughout their three centuries of independence* a strong regard for religious liberty . . . Holland has rightly been honoured as a sanctuary of religious tolerance . . . " [emphasis added]
See also, Shetter, W. *The Pillars of Society: Six Centuries of Civilization in the Netherlands*, (The Hague: Martinus Nijhoff, 1971); Price, J.L. *Holland and the Dutch Republic in the Seventeenth Century: The Politics of Particularism*, (Oxford: Clarendon Press, 1994).

69 "Thousands of U.S. blacks join rally" *Globe and Mail*, (17 Oct 1995) A1.
70 Arch Puddington, "Black Anti-Semitism and How it Grows," *Commentary*, (April, 1994), 19-24.
71 Puddington, p.21.
72 "Blacks rally in U.S. in midst of controversy" *Globe and Mail*, (16 Oct 1995) A1; Puddington, p. 20.
73 Puddington, p. 22.
74 Puddington, p. 20.
75 Ibid. There is some indication that other members of the Congressional Black Caucus have denied the existence of this covenant, saying it was never put to a vote. See "Farrakhan gets muted response from black causus," *Associated Press* (4 February 1994).
76 Puddington, p. 21.
77 Ibid.
78 Ibid.
79 Puddington, p. 20; Julian Bond, "NAACP Head: Better Jewish Relations," *Canadian Press*, (7 April 1998); "A Year after Chavis's Ouster, Search for NAACP Head Continues," *Canadian Press*, (18 October 1995).
80 Bayard Rustin, " 'Black Power' and Coalition Politics," in *Down the Line: The Collected Writings of Bayard Rustin* (Chicago: Quadrangle Books, 1971) 154-165.
81 Ibid.
82 R. Breon, "Show Boat: The Revival, the Racism" (1995) Summer, *The Drama Review*, 86.
83 Breon, p. 102-3.
84 Arnold Auguste, "Tired of being your niggers" *Share*, (1 April 1993).
85 Gerda Frieberg, letter: "Jewish Congress Responds" *Share*, (8 April 1993).
86 Arnold Auguste, "Jewish community must take stand" *Share*, (8 April 1993).
87 Arnold Auguste, "More than just 'Show Boat'" *Share*, (22 April 1993).
88 Ibid.

[89] See, for example, "B.C. man responds to Thorsell" *Share*, (29 April 1993); "Israel and South Africa are allies" *Share*, (6 May 1993); "An uncivilized, racist act against us" *Share*, (20 May 1993); "Get off the fence United Way" *Share*, (1 April 1993); "Showboat and racism" *Canadian Press*, (9 March 1993).

[90] Robert Fulford, "When indignation obscures truth" *Globe and Mail*, (2 June 1993); A. Alan Borovoy & Daniel G. Hill, "Ethnicity of 'Show Boat' producers is wrong issue" *Toronto Star*, (19 April 1993), A15.

[91] "Thousands attend Farrakhan speech" *Globe and Mail*, (16 September 1996), A12.

[92] Ibid.

[93] Cecil Foster, "Farrakhan's charm has West Indian flavor" *Toronto Star*, (23 September 1996), A13.

[94] "Nothing wrong with Farrakhan" *Share*, (19 Sept 1996) 18.

[95] "Farrakhan 'relevant'" *Share*, (19 Sept 1996) 1.

[96] "A man of influence" *Share*, (19 Sept 1996), 7; "It's time to heed Farrakhan's words" *Share*, (19 Sept 1996) 8.

[97] My authority for the absence of criticism regarding Louis Farrakhan in the Canadian black press is Bernie Farber, a staff official of the Canadian Jewish Congress. In the wake of the Farrakhan visit, he scoured the black press in search of relevant commentary. He also reports that, in the aftermath of Farrakhan's subsequent visit to Toronto in 1998, the black press did little more than report on his speech, an event apparently not as well attended or as widely discussed as its predecessor.

[98] "Rocking the boat (Controversy over Show Boat has heightened racial tensions in Toronto)" (Nov 1993) 27/16 *Toronto Life*, 49-56.

[99] *R. v. Latimer* 126 D.L.R. (4th) 203 (Sask. C.A.).

[100] *Canadian Criminal Code*, section 745(c).

[101] *R. v. Latimer* 126 D.L.R. (4th) 203 (Sask. C.A.).

[102] *R. v. Latimer* 142 D.L.R. (4th) 577 (S.C.C.).

[103] *R. v. Latimer* (Oral judgment: December 1, 1997), S.J. No. 701 (Saskatchewan Court of Queen's Bench); "Latimer to spend a year in jail for killing daughter" *Canadian Press*, (1 Dec 1997).

[104] "Latimer sentence may go to top court" *Globe and Mail*, (1 Dec 1997), A10.

[105] Ibid.

[106] "Canadian Justice System Fails Tracy Latimer," Press release issued by the Canadian Association for Community Living, December 2, 1997.

[107] "Judge's decision 'terrifying', advocate for disabled says" *Toronto Star*, (2 Dec 1997).

[108] *R. v. Latimer* 126 D.L.R. (4th) 203 (Sask. C.A.) at 209.

[109] *R. v. Latimer* (December 1, 1997), S.J. No. 701 (Saskatchewan Court of Queen's Bench).

[110] "CACL to seek Intervener Status in the Robert Latimer Appeal," Press release issued by the Canadian Association for Community Living, December 18, 1997.

[111] "Judge's decision 'terrifying', advocate for disabled says" *Toronto Star*, (2 Dec 1997).

[112] *Sentencing Reform: A Canadian Approach, Report of The Canadian Sentencing Commission* (Ottawa: Minister of Supply and Social Services, 1986), p. 180.

[113] Ibid.

[114] *Sentencing Reform*, p. 181.

[115] *Sentencing Reform*, p. 179.

[116] For aggravated assault see, for example, *R. v. Lavoie* (12 janvier 1994), No. C.A. Montreal 500-10-000341-931 (C.A. Que) or *R. v. Robertson* (March 23, 1994), Doc. Barrie 3392 (Ont. Gen. Div.). For aggravated sexual assault, see, for example, *R. v. Jack* (June 25, 1992), Doc. V01578 (B.C.C.A.) or *R. v. Patey* (September 23, 1992), Doc. S.C.C. 02593 (N.S.C.A.).

[117] *Sentencing Reform*, p. 178.

CHAPTER THREE

Among Professors and Students

I

In the mid-1970s, a debate raged at the University of Toronto over the action of a radical student group in physically preventing an American urbanologist from addressing a planned campus meeting. (The students had actually used strong-arm tactics to keep him from the platform.)[1] Because of his conservative views on issues of urban social policy, Professor Edward Banfield (the proposed speaker) was considered by many to be a "racist".[2] In the aftermath of the incident at which he was stopped from speaking, the issue for members of the university community was whether free speech or racism should enjoy priority concern.[3] Those who took the free speech side denounced the radical students. Those who took the racism side defended—or at least excused—the student action.

But, by the end of the next decade and a half, much campus opinion had changed. The University of Toronto was debating a proposed policy that would impose certain restrictions on various forms of speech—not only on speech considered racist but also on that which was considered sexist or homophobic, among others.[4]

Similar speech codes were being adopted at universities across the country. In Ontario, the government was actively promoting the idea.[5] Profound changes were occurring in the universities. Once considered the very centre of university life, freedom of expression was losing its preferred position. Indeed, it was often seen as an actual impediment to the realization of the value that had begun to dominate campus thinking—equality. Thus, traditional equality seekers were lining up to promote campus speech codes—they included many women, blacks, Jews, gays, and lesbians backed by numbers of traditional liberals in the mainstream churches and social democratic organizations. The speech codes were seen as measures to protect vulnerable students from the consequences of a hostile learning environment. Women, visible minorities, and homosexuals should not have to endure the kind of demeaning invective that could jeopardize their ability to function. The speech codes—usually referred to as policies on "discriminatory harassment"—were designed to promote dignity and equality in the university experience of vulnerable people.

Unquestionably, this was a laudable objective. To be sure, women and minorities had encountered their share of discrimination and harassment. In days gone by, there were open quotas on the number of Jews admissible to certain faculties.[6] Until recently, women professors were an extremely rare phenomenon. Indeed, there are still relatively few. On more than one campus, engineering newspapers periodically produced deeply sexist publications.[7] Much of the adolescent humour contained in those publications could be described as devoid of redeeming merit. It was understandable that female faculty and students would be resentful.

But, while it had long been considered legitimate to outlaw discriminatory conduct, it was now becoming acceptable to prohibit discriminatory *statements*. Remarkably, the main impetus for these restrictions on speech was coming not from the right but from the left. This represented a virtually diametric reversal of roles. In the 1950s, it was the left—liberals, social democrats, and other equality seekers—that bore the brunt of the battle against McCarthyite threats to free speech. In the 1980s and 90s, many members of those constituencies were seeking to limit free speech. This irony is further compounded by the extent to which the current advocates of censorship are the beneficiaries of the very freedom they would curb. As I have indicated earlier, the progress made by women and ethnic minorities is nothing short of remarkable. While they are a long distance from an acceptable state of equality, they have come a long distance in a relatively short period of time.

Essentially, freedom of expression made it possible. At the universities, scholars such as Ashley Montague, Gordon Allport, and Ruth Benedict used their academic freedom to challenge the conventional beliefs in racial superiority.[8] They and those they influenced said and wrote many things that offended the sensibilities of many people. Religious fundamentalists, southern Bourbons, and assorted bigots reacted with hurt and anger to the egalitarian findings of these scholars and their disciples.

Protected by employment tenure that guaranteed them academic freedom, the scholars continued to challenge the orthodoxies of their era. Increasingly, those scholars sought to shield their students from the consequences of asking embarrassing questions and making critical comments. In that atmosphere, students were encouraged to question and challenge everything, including the most cherished values with which they had been raised. Small wonder that students played such a critical role in the American civil rights movement that finally dismantled racial segregation in the American south. And small wonder that freedom of expression was one of the chief weapons employed by the civil rights movement in that struggle.

Of course, the current proponents of campus speech codes would not suppress speech that is friendly to equality; they would curb only expression that is hostile to equality. A workable free speech, however, cannot be so selective. Unless a speech code said explicitly that you may not insult women, racial minorities, or homosexuals, it would very likely be used, at some point, against some of the very groups it was designed to protect. That is because, as indicated in the chapter on minorities, no prohibition would likely be precise enough to nail the expressions of unredeemed racism, sexism, and homophobia without catching a great deal of legitimate speech as well.

In that earlier chapter, I enumerated the variety of constituencies that have been targeted under Canada's anti-hate law. (Such casualties have included anti-American demonstrators, French-Canadian nationalists, an anti-apartheid film, a pro-Zionist book, a Jewish community leader, and Salman Rushdie's *Satanic Verses*.) The significance of this experience derives from the fact that the anti-hate law is much narrower in its scope than are any of the campus speech codes. Very likely, therefore, those codes will also wind up attacking an even wider variety of legitimate speech.

It is nevertheless argued that there can be no meaningful free speech without equality; in a setting of unequal relations, free speech serves the interests of the more powerful against the less powerful. Even if this were so, what should be done about it? How is greater equality to be secured in an atmosphere that imposes significant restrictions on free speech? As noted above, such restrictions are very likely to be applied, at some point, against the very groups they were designed to protect. This means that the road to equality will have to increasingly rely on what the existing power structure is prepared to deliver. If equality seekers don't have the faith in the power structure when there is a more vigorous free speech, why should they have faith in it when there is a less vigorous free speech? Indeed, such faith is akin to a belief in the tooth fairy.

The whole point of a university is that, while it must treat its constituents with equal fairness and dignity, it cannot insist on a belief in equality or any other ideology as an institutional truth. Thus, for example, even if the university is obliged to obey our human rights laws, the members of the university must remain free to advocate the repeal of such laws. For such purposes, the institutional commitment is to the process by which individual professors and students will reach their own conclusions about the truths to which they will subscribe.

The validity of this position is enhanced by fleshing out the implications of possible alternatives to it. If equality—between the genders and sexual orientations and among the races and ethnicities—is to be accepted as mandatory truth for members of the university, on what basis should this happen? Is it because a belief in such equality accords with scientifically verifiable inquiry? Many believers in equality—myself included—believe, indeed, that the weight of scientific evidence supports this concept of equality. Suppose, however, additional scientific evidence emerges that challenges this hypothesis? Do we dismiss such conflicting evidence without subjecting it to the process of intelligent inquiry? If we do, we will no longer be able to claim that our support for equality is scientifically based. Alternatively, if we subject the conflicting evidence to scientific inquiry, we will no longer be accepting equality as a mandatory institutional truth.

On what other basis, then, would the university declare equality to be an institutional truth? Religion? Ideology? Dogma? Any of these replies would contradict the university's role as truth seeker. How could the university promote the methods of intelligent inquiry as the basis for discovering truth and simultaneously exempt certain positions from those methods?

There are additional risks as well. If equality is eligible for such exceptional treatment, why not other values and ideologies? Some may well argue, for example, that capitalism deserves such institutional reverence. With the collapse of Communism and the various failures of socialism, the proponents of capitalism have a seductive argument that only their system can provide both the freedom and the equality for which humans yearn. On that basis, they would contend—in the way that many equality proponents now do—that expressions of support for systems other than capitalism are antithetical to the best interests of the university. Still others would declare that religion in general or even Christianity in particular is no less entitled to institutional reverence. For these people, such theology provides the only adequate justification for beliefs in human dignity. If that position were to prevail, the advocacy of atheism, secular humanism, or even Judaism might become unacceptable in a campus context.

Indeed, the moment we depart from the principle of institutional neutrality on such questions, we incur a considerable risk that raw political power will determine the scope of permissible campus speech. Such an outcome, of course, represents the very antithesis of intellectual and academic freedom. The right to speak, write, question, and challenge would become dependent upon the vagaries of what ideology or point of view enjoyed political ascendency in the university at any given time. Thus, the best hope there is for a meaningful state of intellectual freedom is to promote as wide a consensus as possible that the university itself must eschew ideological positions of this kind. Those left-wingers who may be enjoying campus power today are being awfully short-sighted. They are paving the way for right-wingers to behave similarly on behalf of their favourite ideologies as soon as power alignments begin to change.

For such reasons, one of the central tenets of a university education has become the adventurous search for truth. This means that faculty and students must be free to ask challenging questions and to express provocative opinions. There are no institutional truths to which members of the campus community must submit. They should not be required to subscribe to capitalism, socialism, Marxism, Catholicism, Protestantism, Judaism, Islam, humanism, feminism, elitism, egalitarianism, or any comparable doctrine. As an institution, the university's commitment should not be to any particular ideology, but to the methods of intelligent inquiry itself. This entails a regime of vigorous free speech.

It follows that university members must be at liberty to challenge even free speech itself. There is no contradiction. As institutions, universities should practise free speech and equality. But the *members* of the universities should be free to question or disapprove of either or both.

II

So what happens, in actual fact, when universities adopt explicit measures to curtail free speech? Since such measures have been in effect for a number of years, it would be useful, at this point, to examine some of the real-life situations that have occurred on a number of Canadian campuses.

A case of some importance is the one involving Richard Devlin, who taught legal writing at the Osgoode Hall Law School in the mid-1980s. In a law journal article, Devlin tells of how, as a pro-feminist male, he tried to sensitize his students to feminist legal theory.[9] One way he did it was to ask his students to prepare legal briefs on the constitutionality of a hypothetical anti-pornography law. Half of the class would argue for it and the other half would be against it. Despite the professed nobility of his intentions, he ran into trouble. Since he had randomly divided the class for the assignment, a number of female students wound up arguing against their personal convictions. At some point afterward, Devlin learned that the sexual harassment centre at the university was making inquiries about him. This led to a meeting involving him and two of the centre's counsellors.

Although he was assured that he was not then the target of a sexual harassment complaint, Devlin reports the counsellors as saying that "one of the major criticisms" of him was the way he had divided the class for the assignment: it could create serious distress for those who had to argue against their own personal opinions. Indeed, the counsellors reportedly said that some of the women were undergoing identity crises as a result of the assignment. According to Devlin, the counsellors warned him that "if a similar situation were to occur again, there would be a possibility of an investigation to determine whether sexual harassment was actually taking place".[10]

For these purposes, sexual harassment was defined as "sexually oriented remarks and behaviour which may be reasonably perceived to create a negative psychological and emotional environment for work and study".[11] It is not necessary now to dwell on the applicability of this definition to Mr. Devlin's behaviour. Suffice it, at this point, to note both the breadth of the definition and the fact that those in authority, in fact, threatened to use it in response to this situation.

In his article, Devlin confesses that he was frightened, "indeed sick" because of what this incident could mean for his reputation "and career".[12] If this situation were not so dangerous, it would be laughable. Here we have the official policy of a university threatening a law teacher for employing laudable pedagogy. After all, a good lawyer must be able to advance and appreciate the arguments on all sides of a question. The complainants in this case stood to benefit from having to prepare arguments against their own point of view. We can only imagine how the publication of the Devlin story may have served to deter other teachers from adopting similarly helpful pedagogical techniques.

According to the student newspaper at Toronto's then Ryerson Polytechnic Institute, the first complaint under the policy adopted there was filed in December of 1990 against two engineering students for the way they had reportedly criticized the awareness day planned by the campus gay and lesbian club. One of the students allegedly called the event "totally unacceptable and immoral". In his view, "society has allowed that nonsense to build up" over time. The other student is quoted as saying, "I think homosexuality is a social or genetic problem and society is way too tolerant". According to this report in the *Ryersonian*, this student said of the gays and lesbians, "they used to be a quiet group on campus, but now they advertise their existence like they're totally normal".[13]

Fortunately, in mid-February of 1991, this complaint was dismissed. Unfortunately, however, the grounds for the dismissal reveal an unsatisfactory situation. The adjudicator held that the impugned comments were not "unsolicited" as required by Ryerson's anti-harassment policy.[14] Apparently, the students' statements were made in response to questions that had been asked by a *Ryersonian* reporter. Does this result mean that if those students had initiated the remarks in question without having been contacted by the campus press, they might well have been disciplined? Suppose, for example, they had written letters to the *Ryersonian* or they had requested an opportunity to appear before the ruling bodies at Ryerson in order to advance their case against gay and lesbian awareness day?

There is something deeply wrong about a campus policy that could leave these questions in such doubt. Even if the accused students had clearly initiated the remarks at issue, there should be no question of disciplining them. Neanderthal as I believe their statements were, they should not be allowed to trigger discipline in an institution of higher learning. To punish students for such remarks is to infringe a vital component of intellectual freedom.

As free as the members of the gay and lesbian club must be to promote a positive awareness of their sexual orientation, other members of the campus community must be no less free to criticize them. Campus activities should not be enjoyed only by those who agree with the policies of the gay and lesbian club. They should also be enjoyed by those who disagree with such groups. The proper response to students who express reactionary views is not coercive discipline, it's open debate.

Another troubling aspect of this case is the time it took: two months. This is not necessarily to say that there was undue delay. Rather, it is to acknowledge the inevitability of such delay if cases are to be handled properly. What is troubling is the fact that these two students were obliged to live under a cloud of uncertainty for as long as they did, despite the fact that their behaviour had not violated the policy. The lesson is clear: if you want to avoid having to worry about possible discipline, avoid controversy on such topics. That's quite an outcome for an institution of higher learning to create.

Some months after the furore over this complaint had subsided, I participated in a panel discussion on the Ryerson campus. At one point, I suggested the possibility that those students could have been subject to discipline if their remarks had, in fact, been unsolicited. I then asked whether such an outcome would be appropriate. Significantly, no one in attendance even attempted to answer my question. What a commentary on the contemporary commitment to intellectual freedom!

On January 9, 1992, Professor Marjorie Ratcliffe of the Spanish Department at the University of Western Ontario (UWO), was notified of a racial harassment complaint against her. On June 10, 1992, the university received the adjudicator's decision dismissing the complaint. For legal bills alone, Professor Ratcliffe had incurred, during this five-month period, expenditures of more than six thousand dollars.[15]

Professor Ratcliffe was accused of violating the racial harassment policy which was defined as:

> . . . unwelcome attention of a racially oriented nature, including remarks, jokes, gestures, slurs, innuendoes, or other behaviour, verbal or physical, which is directed at an individual or group by another person or group who knows or ought reasonably to know that this attention is unwanted.[16]

The alleged violation of this policy occurred in the professor's Spanish class on December 6, 1991. In attempting to assist the complainant—a young man from Iran—to understand the correct use of the word "condemn", Professor Ratcliffe reportedly referred to the experiences of condemnation suffered by the people of Iran. While this incident appears to be the one that triggered the complaint, there was apparently a previous occasion in which Professor Ratcliffe had remarked that "immigrants" whose mother tongue is neither English nor Spanish have particular difficulty in mastering certain Spanish expressions.

The adjudicator took the position that "a discussion about religious or ethnic persecution does not seem inappropriate".[17] The decision did add that a different view of the incident might have been taken "if there was any reason to believe that Prof. Ratcliffe knew that the discussions about Iran were painful" to the complainant. In the circumstances, however, it's unthinkable that her comments warranted the remotest threat of disciplinary action. The situation was aggravated by the fact that she was left out of pocket to the tune of more than six thousand dollars.

On July 31, 1992, less than two months after receiving the decision, Professor Ratcliffe wrote to the president of the university requesting an apology and compensation for various expenses including her legal bills.[18] On November 20, 1992, the president's reply refused outright to grant what Professor Ratcliffe had requested. The following are extracts from his letter:

> ... I would stress that the Policy specifically states that costs will be borne by the parties, should they seek representation by external counsel . . . Therefore, in accordance with this Standing Policy, I will not accede to your request that the University provide compensation for your legal expenses.... As for the matter of an apology, I believe that the confidence and good faith of the University community have been severely and inappropriately imposed upon, but I do not believe that this imposition has come from the institution or from those officers of the University who have striven to discharge their roles . . . to the best of their ability. It is they, in my judgment, who are deserving of an apology.[19]

At that point Professor Ratcliffe sought and received the help of the faculty association at UWO. For the next several months, her grievance became the focus of a heated controversy in the university newspaper and even in the daily press.[20] Finally, on March 5, 1993, the president of the university offered something more. He said, "I wish to express both personally and on behalf of the University deep regret for the pain and suffering that you have endured, however inadvertently caused, as a result of the application of the University's race relations policy in its present form".[21] In addition, he offered to reimburse her for her legal costs and for the airfare cost of bringing a witness to the hearing. He noted that he was making these gestures "unilaterally" because he wished to resolve the issue and go on to other things.

It is not my function here to assess the negotiating posture of either the university or Professor Ratcliffe. Perhaps, as some have suggested, she could have been more flexible earlier on and thus have avoided the ensuing loss of time, productivity, and money. Perhaps the university could have issued earlier a more forthright and gracious apology than it did, acknowledging her request that it describe her behaviour as "innocent". Perhaps the university should have promptly provided the compensation she requested for the loss of research time she sustained. My present concern is not with the merits of the various offers and counter offers—although I can't help wondering why the president would use the word "unilaterally" to describe an offer that had resulted from months of correspondence, meetings, and controversy. My primary concern, at this point, is with the merits of the *policy* that produced this regrettable situation. When "unwelcome verbal behaviour of a racially oriented nature" can trigger disciplinary action against a professor or student, unwarranted complaints become virtually inevitable. The policy reeks of subjectivity and overbreadth. At the same time, it's entirely understandable that those who believe themselves improperly accused of racial harassment will go to great lengths to seek complete vindication.

Of course, we must also realize that not all members of the university community have the kind of fortitude that Professor Ratcliffe has. The most likely consequence of such a policy is that many members of the university community will muzzle *themselves* rather than risk the ordeal that Professor Ratcliffe suffered. Thus, we can expect an avoidance of candid discussion about racial questions, at a time when society so badly needs a forthright exploration of such issues. While the policy at

UWO has undergone some amendment, it remains vulnerable to contentious interpretations. The key factor, of course, is whether enough people in that community are prepared to accord freedom of expression the kind of priority it warrants.

It appears likely that a strong impetus for the racial harassment policy at the University of Western Ontario came from the case of Phillippe Rushton.[22] In the late 1980s, Rushton, a UWO psychology professor, made international headlines with his research into the brain sizes and certain other physiological characteristics of three racial groups. In correlating these matters with intelligence, Rushton declared that Orientals had the highest intelligence, the white race was next, and, in third place, were the blacks. Not surprisingly, his findings ignited a major controversy. His conclusions, at variance with numbers of preceding scientific studies, were seen as an intellectual justification for anti-black racism.

It seemed incredible that an apparently reputable scholar was using the methods of science to resurrect the discredited notion of racial superiority. A significant risk emerged that, as a consequence of Rushton's theories, racial discrimination would become clothed in a mantle of academic respectability. Moreover, I couldn't help wondering *why* such research had been done. The imputation of inferiority to a group would hardly justify discrimination in individual cases. For these reasons, I hoped that competent scientists and intellectuals would take him on. While some scholars did indeed accept this challenge, the responses of many other people created a separate set of problems for liberal values. A growing number of Rushton's critics evinced a willingness to violate the principles of academic freedom. More and more of these people began to demand that Rushton be fired.

It's one thing to challenge a professor's work, but it's another thing entirely to punish him for reaching conclusions you don't like. Regrettably, one of these critics calling for Rushton's dismissal was the then premier of the province—David Peterson.[23] His comments legitimated the idea that professors could be disciplined for ideological reasons. In principle, this was no different from the demand in the 1950s to discipline professors for their communist ideas. Even more contentious was the order from the then attorney general that the Ontario Provincial Police conduct an investigation with a view to prosecuting Rushton under the hate propaganda section of the Criminal Code.[24] The implication of this action was that it wasn't enough to fire a professor for such research, it might be more suitable to *jail* him for it.

In the result, Rushton was not fired, jailed, or even charged. He was, however, subjected to a number of official pressures. While the university said that it must protect his academic freedom, it initially accorded him an unsatisfactory rating.[25] Potentially, this could have triggered a subsequent review of his tenure. However, he was able to successfully appeal the low rating he had received. In addition to the many demands for his dismissal and the recurring demonstrations against him, Rushton was also the target of an official investigation under the Human Rights Code. A formal complaint alleged that he violated the code by "poisoning the academic learning environment".[26] Although the complaint was filed in the spring of 1991, the commission did not dispose of it until 1995—that meant four years of uncertainty about the legality of his scholarship. Even then, it appears that the complaint was dropped—not because of a finding on the merits—but because the complainants had become unavailable.[27]

Professors are, of course, fair game for scientific and intellectual controversy. By all means, their research should be subjected to the severest scrutiny. That's what a university, as a community of scholars, should be all about. Nor do I suggest, for a moment, that professors with tenure should be completely immune to discipline. But, for such purposes, their performance should be judged, not on the philosophical acceptability of their findings, but on the scientific integrity of their methods. And so their fate should be determined, not by the society outside, but by the faculty inside. Even at that, there would have to be a substantial onus on anyone calling for their dismissal. Once professors are granted tenure, the faculty has already determined that they have the requisite competence and integrity. Academic freedom would be very fragile if dismissals could be facilitated with ease. Essentially, therefore, those skeptical of Professor Rushton's work should be seeking, not political influence to dismiss him, but intellectual arguments to rebut him.

As one of these skeptics myself—indeed, as a life-long enemy of racism—I regretted, even from a tactical point of view, the misconceived focus of the energy against Rushton. When so much effort is directed to punishment rather than to argument, the impression could well be created that the critics are bereft of argument. This could give society's racists an unwarranted advantage in their conflicts with egalitarians. Unlike Zundel, Rushton was not an impotent crank whose views could be summarily dismissed. He was a widely published academic with apparent standing in his field. It was important, therefore, that his analyses be debated and challenged.

Despite what I would have thought were the clear requirements of academic freedom, the Rushton case helped to precipitate the adoption of the university's dangerous policy on racial harassment. Muddled thinking and "political correctness" conspired to put in place an ongoing threat to the fundamental role of academic freedom.

Toward the end of 1993, mathematics professor Matin Yaqzan was suspended from his position at the University of New Brunswick for writing an article in the campus press in which he said that, if a woman visited a man's quarters after hours, she was implicitly consenting to sexual intercourse. He also described date rape of "promiscuous" women as an "inconvenience" rather than a "moral outrage".[28]

Tom Traves, the university's academic vice-president, reportedly said that Professor Yaqzan's article might violate the university's policy on sexual harassment.[29] Mr. Traves apparently pointed out that the policy contains a prohibition against behaviour that creates an intimidating, hostile, or offensive environment. According to a statement attributed to Mr. Traves, "we have to see whether these statements create such a situation for students who would be enrolled in this professor's class".[30] While the suspension was lifted a few weeks later, Professor Yaqzan never returned to the classroom. Shortly thereafter, he took early retirement under conditions that were not publicly disclosed.[31]

I have little difficulty describing Professor Yaqzan's impugned article as an exemplary piece of foolishness. Moreover, I can claim the distinction of having been personally attacked by Professor Yaqzan on previous occasions. As regrettable as I find that particular article and his judgment on some other issues, I nevertheless deplore the suspension he sustained. In a community of scholars whose role is to search for truth, the opinions of a Professor Yaqzan must receive, not disciplinary coercion, but critical discussion. That is the essential role of a university.

In 1992, a bizarre incident occurred at Toronto's Seneca College. Four students, members of a business club, put up a poster advertising a seminar on business protocol that was to be held the following week. The poster contained a portrait of the Queen (taken from a two-dollar bill and enlarged) with a "talk bubble" coming out of her mouth.[32] The bubble contained a series of questions and answers relating to business protocol in other countries and the eyes on the Queen's portrait were turned so as to make it appear that she was looking at the bubble.

This triggered allegations that the poster violated the Seneca policy on discrimination/harassment. According to these allegations, the picture of the Queen was a mockery of Canada's sovereign and an insult to the British heritage.[33] The policy includes the following:

> ... all visual displays (e.g. posters, advertisements, graphics) appearing on College property shall be free of discriminatory biases and stereotypes.

and "discrimination" is declared to be:

> any action, behaviour, or attitude which negatively affects or could negatively affect the ... academic status of a student that has been based on race, ancestry, creed, sex, age, marital status, family status, criminal charges or criminal record, mental or physical disability, sexual orientation, political affiliation, or union membership of the individual.[34]

In the circumstances, it appears that formal complaints were not filed. But there is reason to believe that members of the Seneca administration took the allegations seriously. Indeed, one of the teachers claims that he was berated by a superior for not having stopped the students from putting up the impugned poster in the first place. In the controversy that ensued, the complicit students took the path of least resistance—or most discretion. They simply removed the poster.[35] Thus, a policy that was designed to protect vulnerable minorities from serious indignities wound up censoring a mild caricature of the Queen. The incident could hardly be considered an advance on the road to equality.

In 1995, the University of British Columbia ordered a halt to all graduate student admissions to its political science department. This decision was based upon a report from an outside lawyer who had been retained by the university to investigate whether there was any "basis" for the allegations of a number of graduate students that the department had a problem with "pervasive racism and sexism".[36] At no point, did the outside lawyer make any findings of discrimination against any of the faculty members. Indeed, the lawyer conceded she had no basis to conclude that any of the professors were prejudiced or that they intended to discriminate.[37] The culprit, according to the report, was the "culture" of the department that "may well have an adverse impact on those students who do not share its prevailing characteristics".[38]

As examples of this culture, the report contains pages and pages of alleged incidents. The problem is that, in a good many cases, it is not at all clear that the example represents any kind of inappropriate discrimination—whether "direct" or "systemic".

Consider the following:
- In one class, a white male professor reportedly said, "Let's get on with it" when one non-white female student challenged the "colonialist and ethno-centric" comments of another student.[39] It is conceivable that the professor was being unwarrantedly abrupt and perhaps even discriminatorily condescending in the way he chose to deal with this situation. But, in the absence of further detail, the professor's behaviour here could also be seen as stemming from a legitimate wish to keep the class discussion focused on what he then regarded as issues of greater priority.
- In view of the poor grades obtained by a female student of colour, a white male professor suggested that she withdraw from the program until her children were older.[40] Perhaps this advice was an unjustified "put-down" of a vulnerable person. Without more detail, however, it is also possible to regard such advice as sound and helpful. Perhaps the professor knew that the woman's obligations to care for her young children were undermining her ability to function in the course.
- A white male professor omitted the name of a female student from a conference program even though she was supposed to be a presenter.[41] Admittedly, such evidence could reflect an insufficiently respectful attitude towards women. But, in the absence of further evidence about the matter, it is also possible to perceive the professor's error as genuinely inadvertent and essentially devoid of negative prejudice.

Another set of the author's examples requires separate treatment. The report cites the case of a white male professor who defended the use of "gender exclusive" language in the classroom.[42] Again, it is possible to interpret this case as an example of sexism. But, without more detail, it is also possible to view this professor's behaviour as a legitimate expression of opinion on a subject of interest. Why are professors obliged to agree with gender neutral language? Why are they not entitled to argue against it? The report is laced with further examples of this phenomenon. There are allegations that professors were teaching from the perspective of white scholars, that a course on aboriginal people was taught from "a very Euro-centric attitude",[43] and that feminism was dealt with as "a point of view" and not as a "theoretical approach".[44] The faculty was criticized for its failure to broaden the curriculum beyond a "very male and very white" base.[45]

It is not within the purview of this book to take sides on the continuing controversies in campus circles about the propriety of focusing on Western scholarship. Suffice it here simply to acknowledge the legitimacy of such differences of opinion. What is *illegitimate*—without more specifics in individual cases—is the condemnation of one side as racist or sexist.

To be fair, the report contains a large number of other allegations that, if true, could well be described as racist, sexist, or at least seriously unfair conduct on the part of certain faculty and administration members.[46] But the inclusion of the previous examples I have cited raises questions about the validity of the ultimate conclusions. This problem is compounded by the author's acknowledgement that the allegations have not been "proven to be 'true'".[47] The report simply reproduces a pile of allegations and, without attempting to determine their truth or to assess their relative importance, reaches the conclusion that they constitute a "basis" for the student accusations of pervasive racism and sexism in the department.[48]

Without the kind of rigorous analysis that was not even attempted here, the report is vulnerable to the perception that it was influenced more by ideology than by evidence. At one point, admittedly, the report seems to require objective evidence: "Just because a student says that she has experienced racism or sexism does not mean that discrimination has been proven, as a matter of fact, to have occurred."[49] But then the report hastens to add a subjective qualification: "However, the fact that the behaviours are being *experienced as racism and sexism* . . . is, at the very least, some evidence" of a chilly climate for women and people of colour [emphasis added].[50]

In summary, consider what the report contains: allegations that, if proved, would be serious, but they are not proved; allegations that, even if proved, could well be more exculpatory than incriminating; and the subjective impressions of the people affected. What is troubling is that, on the basis of this questionable conglomeration of material, the report recommended the extraordinary action of halting all admissions to the political science department until the authorities were satisfied that the department was "discrimination-and-harassment-free".[51] What is even more troubling is that the university immediately adopted the recommendation.

This is not necessarily to absolve the implicated department. It is simply to contend that the material cited does not warrant the action taken. After all, the suspension of admissions throws a cloud over the entire faculty—not only over those whose conduct was impugned. Moreover, how was the determination to be made as to when discrimination and harassment were adequately purged? Lie detector tests? Sensitivity groups? Scouts' honour? All of which is a manifestation of academic justice according to the canons of political correctness.

On February 10, 1998, at the University of Waterloo, a student complaint was dismissed against sociology professor Ken Westhues.[52] The original complaint was governed by a university policy against any "communication . . . which lacks any redeeming artistic, intellectual or literary merit and which promotes disrespect or intolerance for any person(s) based [*inter alia*] on . . . race, ancestry, place of origin, colour, [and] ethnic origin . . . ".[53] The complaint charged that, in class, the professor had made statements that were "racist" and "unbalanced" so as to cause the complainant "undue stress, humiliation, and embarrassment".[54] These allegations emerged from a classroom lecture in which, according to the complainant, the professor had failed to adequately define such terms as "employment equity" and "affirmative action".

Although the complaint was originally filed in March of 1996, the significant events, for my purposes here, began with a letter that the Canadian Civil Liberties Association (CCLA) sent to the provost of the university on September 3, 1996. That letter included a document setting out the reasons why, in the opinion of the civil liberties organization, the complaint should be dismissed.[55] At that time, the CCLA did not know that the ethics hearing committee (the first rung of the procedural ladder) had already written a report to the provost in which it concluded that there was substance to the complaint and, accordingly, it recommended that Professor Westhues be required to undergo counselling, to write letters of apology, and to attend a workshop on "smart strategies for a safe, open classroom".[56]

The provost, not being satisfied that the complaint disclosed an offence on Professor Westhues's part, rejected the recommendations of the ethics committee.[57] But the provost proceeded nevertheless to conclude that there were other matters on the basis of which Professor Westhues should be disciplined. In the result, he declared that Professor Westhues should be suspended for one month without pay.[58] From there, Professor Westhues appealed to the university president. On April 2, 1997, the CCLA wrote to the president indicating why, in its view, the record could not justify the penalty that the provost sought to impose.[59]

Somewhere around that time, Professor Westhues expressed concern about the ability of the president to adjudicate the appeal "without bias or the apprehension of bias".[60] Although the president rejected this point, on June 11, 1997 he requested that Dr. Peter Mercer of the University of Western Ontario resolve the complaint in his stead.[61] It is not without significance that, in part at least, the president's referral of the matter to Dr. Mercer was designed to produce a resolution "as expeditiously as possible".[62] As already indicated, the final decision was not reached until February 10, 1998. This is not necessarily to blame Dr. Mercer for the delay. In fairness, it takes time—especially for strangers to a dispute—to process such cases.

My purpose in setting out the chronology of these events is to provide some indication of the extent to which the anti-liberal forces of "political correctness" appear to have influenced some university faculties and administrations. I say this because I believe that the case was a rather simple one: there was no excuse in principle for (1) the recommendations of the ethics committee, (2) the decision of the provost to impose discipline, and (3) the decision of the president to refer the matter to Dr. Mercer.

As far as point (3) is concerned, I make this comment notwithstanding the fact that Professor Westhues himself questioned the president's impartiality. But, since the CCLA had sent copies of all its earlier correspondence to the president, he should have realized that, by June 11, 1997, when he referred the case to Dr. Mercer, there was no justification for doing anything but dismissing the complaint. Obviously, if the president had done that, Professor Westhues could hardly have complained of bias against him. The only thing that the referral to Dr. Mercer did accomplish, apart possibly from protecting the president's political position, was to prolong the anxiety of the accused faculty member.

I shall now try to demonstrate just why, at every stage along the way, the only reasonable outcome was the dismissal of the complaint. For these purposes, it will help to compare the arguments made by the CCLA with the reasons ultimately produced by Dr. Mercer. It should be borne in mind that, even in those cases where the CCLA was writing to someone else, it sent a copy to the president. As will readily be noted, there was a substantial concurrence between the CCLA submissions and the Mercer decision. The significance of this concurrence is that, as soon as an independent adjudicator dealt with the issues, it became clear that the CCLA position was right all along.

This is not to congratulate the CCLA. On the contrary, my point is that it never required special originality or insight to resolve this case. From the beginning, the resolution should have been obvious. Nor is this to minimize the important contribution made by Dr. Mercer. It is simply to observe that even obvious right was not likely to be done without the involvement of an outside adjudicator who was relatively immune to the politics of that campus.

As to the charges that Professor Westhues had engaged in "racist" and "unbalanced" comments, the CCLA said, "there is no indication as to precisely *how* Professor Westhues' alleged behaviour fell into such categories".[63] Dr. Mercer's decision contains the following statement: "There is in fact no indication ... of how Professor Westhues' behaviour can allegedly be characterized in these ways."[64] According to the CCLA, "there is nothing in the University's policies which would make the expression of 'racist' or 'unbalanced' views *per se* an offence within the campus community".[65] For his part, Dr. Mercer said, "the expression of 'racist' or 'unbalanced' views *per se* would not constitute an offence however objectionable it might otherwise be".[66] According to the CCLA, "the professor's alleged failure to adequately define 'employment equity' and 'affirmative action' addresses pedagogical techniques not ethical behaviour".[67] According to Dr. Mercer, "the allegedly inadequate definition of 'employment equity' and 'affirmative action' may speak to Professor Westhues' failings as a university teacher but I do not see how they establish a foundation for a formal complaint to the Ethics Committee".[68]

As for the complainant's charge that Professor Westhues had caused her "undue stress, humiliation, and embarrassment", the CCLA said, "professors are not obliged to avoid the expression of opinion that might give offence. . . . the canons of academic freedom have long recognized that legitimate expressions of opinion can sometimes be hurtful".[69] On this issue, Dr. Mercer declared it was not enough that "one of the students felt uncomfortable; discomfort is often the result when any of us is challenged by ideas or opinions that clash with our own".[70] The CCLA went on to qualify this position, pointing out that the only conceivable obligation [professors] would have is "to avoid *gratuitous* offence" [emphasis in original].[71] And, according to the Mercer judgment, a violation of the university policy "would require that Professor Westhues' statements and handling of the topic was gratuitously offensive . . . ".[72]

In view of all this, the recommendation of the ethics committee to impose anything on Professor Westhues must create disquiet about the ethics committee. After all, the faculty members occupying such positions are very likely to be highly intelligent people. It's hard to understand, therefore, why they should be so impervious to the kind of reasons advanced by both Dr. Mercer and the CCLA. This helps to explain the concern that the pressures of political correctness might have overwhelmed the principles of ethical logic.

Needless to say, Professor Westhues was pleased with the decision of the provost to reject the recommendations of the ethics committee. As to the decision of the provost to discipline Professor Westhues in any event, the CCLA argued in its April 2, 1997 letter to the president that since these additional matters had never been the subject of a formal complaint against Professor Westhues, he should not be vulnerable to discipline at such a stage of the proceedings. According to the CCLA: "It is a fundamental prerequisite of procedural fairness that there be a proper opportunity for such accused persons to answer allegations against them *before* they are found culpable"[73] [emphasis in original]. In addition to finding for Westhues on the merits, Dr. Mercer maintained that "procedural fairness precludes [the provost]" from imposing discipline in such circumstances. According to Dr. Mercer, "a necessary prerequisite to the determination of whether to impose . . . a strong disciplinary measure . . . would be to give the opportunity to Professor Westhues to present his side of the story".[74]

This is such a basic and deeply ingrained concept of fair play that, again, it's not hard to understand the agreement between Dr. Mercer and the CCLA. What is hard to appreciate is that an intelligent university official like the provost could fail to see it. And the same goes, of course, for the president. Thus, the disciplinary decision of the provost and the effective abdication of the president strengthen the apprehension that these officials could have become hostages of political correctness.

Yet the most disconcerting aspect of this entire affair is the impact it will likely have on numbers of other professors. In view of what Professor Westhues was forced to endure on the basis of material so obviously devoid of substance, other faculty members can be expected to be exceptionally circumspect about expressing opinions that they believe their students will find controversial. Many faculty members are likely to prefer to be safe than sorry. For many of them, the expression of their views will simply not be worth the risk of becoming enmired in the kind of prolonged proceedings that engulfed Professor Westhues. In short, such professors are likely to wind up muzzling themselves. It's hard to conceive of an outcome so radically at odds with the central mission of a university.

III

A remarkable feature of this new conformity is the role of the students. Historically, students have tended to take the liberal side of social controversies. Thus, you would expect the vast majority of students to denounce—as they have—any manifestations of racism, sexism, and homophobia. But you would also expect students to be liberal about defending free speech—even of those they don't like. On this score, recent student behaviour has been a significant disappointment.

Even before the Rushton case—in the mid-1980s—the student council at the University of Western Ontario adopted a rather disquieting position. It refused to grant recognition to a student organization that was dedicated to promoting a pro-Palestinian solution to the problems of the Middle East.[75] At the time that it made its application for recognition by the university's student council, the group was known as Canadians for Peace in the Middle East. In a memorandum, the council's legal commissioner noted that "the stated purpose of this club has been transformed from a club to promote forums for debate of the Middle East crisis to a club to promote a specific solution for the Middle East crisis".[76] He also pointed out that "membership is predicated upon the prospective member accepting this political solution".[77] The same theme was repeated in an editorial that appeared in the student newspaper:

> ... [the group] has an admitted bias toward the issue ... by precluding other viewpoints in their "intellectual discussion" they have completely negated the possibility of merging minds. Our opposition to this new club rests on these grounds.[78]

The student leaders went to great lengths to demonstrate the partisanship of the group in question. What I can't understand is the relevance of it all. Why should a pro-Palestinian orientation disqualify a campus organization? During the very period when this controversy was flaring, there was a group at the University of Western Ontario known as Christians on Campus. Among its purposes were: "To share the Gospel of Jesus Christ" and "To encourage fellowship among all the Christian students on campus."[79] The Newman Catholic Community also existed, in part, "to be the Catholic presence on campus".[80] There were also political clubs—Conservative, Liberal, and New Democratic. If recognized clubs could pursue activities on the basis of philosophies that were pro-Christian, pro-Catholic, pro-Conservative, pro-Liberal, or pro-New Democrat, it's hard to fathom why there was a problem with a club being pro-Palestinian.

Moreover, it seemed nothing short of bizarre to suggest that it was improper for this club to restrict its membership to those who believe in its pro-Palestinian philosophy. If everybody could join every organization, pluralism on campus would simply not be possible. Indeed, membership restrictions on the basis of an organization's philosophy could be a necessary protection for minority group organizations. How, for example, could a socialist club operate on a campus that had a conservative majority, if the conservatives were permitted, en masse, to join the socialist club and thereby transform it? A Jewish organization could be similarly imperilled on a campus that had a Christian majority.

At some point during the debate, an official of the student council was quoted as saying, "The Canadians for Peace in the Middle East group was denied [recognition] because its name did not accurately reflect the views of its members."[81] This raised the suggestion that somehow the group was committing an act of deception because its name conveyed the idea that it would provide a neutral forum for exploring the Middle East conflict rather than promote a pro-Palestinian solution.

In the real world, many proponents of a point of view try to package it in the most saleable fashion possible. Numbers of groups with competing ideologies have tried, for example, to appropriate the word "peace" for themselves. The student council was undertaking a Herculean task to try and monitor how well groups fulfil the promises of such names. Some have argued, for example, that the Liberal Party is really very conservative and that the Progressive Conservative Party is not really very progressive. The argument has also been made that there is nothing "new" about the New Democratic Party; it is really the old CCF in a new package. It boggles the mind to believe that anyone would have withheld recognition of those clubs on the grounds that they had chosen deceptive names.

Another reason that emerged during the debate was that, by recognizing an organization, "the university student council takes that point of view as well".[82] This, of course, was a simply incredible characterization of the relationship between a student council and a recognized club. Would anyone have suggested, for example, that the opposition of the New Democratic Party Club to cruise missile testing thereby implicated the university student council in that policy? Since the Liberal Club was also recognized, to what extent might its possible support of cruise missile testing be simultaneously imputed to the student council?

The president of the student council was also quoted as saying, "I don't think the way to peace is trying to isolate one part of the issue, or to spark more controversy."[83] While the president of the student council is entitled to have and express such a point of view on the merits of the Middle East conflict, how would that justify refusing to recognize a club with an opposing point of view? Surely, it was not an appropriate function of a student council to evaluate in this way the ideologies or political opinions of groups seeking recognition. That decision was for individual students to make at the point of deciding which, if any, groups they wished to join.

It doesn't require the I.Q. of an Einstein to figure out what was going on. Plainly and simply, the student council was committing political discrimination. Somehow, it considered pro-Palestinian politics unacceptable in a campus setting. Fortunately, a subsequent student council reversed the policy and recognized the group in question. While the change is certainly welcome, it cannot dispel the disquiet over the realization that the principles of intellectual freedom had fallen into such low repute among the students at the University of Western Ontario.

Coincidentally, at around the same time, the student council at the University of Ottawa revoked the recognition that had been accorded to the Jewish Student Union. The basis for this action was the allegedly "racist" character of the State of Israel. The following is an extract from a press release issued by the council:

> Some will accuse us of wishing to deprive the students [in the Jewish Student Union] of their freedom of speech and consequently of acting in an anti-democratic manner. To them we respond: How can those who deny the rights of the Palestinians, the other Arabs, and non-Zionist Jews, claim for themselves the right to propagate their racist ideology which precisely goes against all principles of democracy?[84]

Quite apart from this simplistic description of Israel, it was deeply disturbing to witness a student government behaving in such an authoritarian manner. I would have thought that the role of a university was to encourage—even to sponsor—discussion and debate over the issue of culpability in the Middle East. Instead, this student council arrogated to itself the right to determine for its constituents the opinion they ought to hold. And, to make matters worse, those who held a dissenting view were denied full participation rights in campus life. The one virtue the Ottawa student council can claim over its counterpart at Western was its candour. While the Western student council performed disingenuous handstands in order to rationalize its exclusion of the pro-Palestinian group, the Ottawa student council acknowledged frankly that it regarded Zionism as a taboo position for students to embrace.

Again, the action was reversed at Ottawa and the Jewish Students Union did recover its recognized status, but not without interference by the university administration. In any event, the worrying feature of all this is that repressive measures could have become so acceptable in the supposed heartland of liberalism—the university student community.

On the occasion of the Yaqzan suspension at the University of New Brunswick, the student union took the unusual initiative of running ads in the campus newspaper that sought student testimony to be used in the administration's review of the math professor's history.[85] Understandably, this initiative was labelled a "witch hunt" by the

Association of the University of New Brunswick Teachers.[86] After all, the professor had been suspended for expressing opinions that many found offensive; there had been no suggestion that he had behaved improperly toward any female students. Instead of denouncing the suspension, the student union tried to validate it.

During the fall term of 1993, there was a close call at the University of Toronto. The women's issues officer of the Students' Administrative Council (SAC) proposed a motion to stop Planned Parenthood from distributing pamphlets on birth control and safe sex. The reason? According to the mover of the motion, the founder of Planned Parenthood "thought that certain races should be restricted from having children".[87] Despite the fact that the statement in question was made some seventy years earlier, the SAC came very close to adopting the motion. It was defeated by a narrow vote of thirteen to nine.

In the fall of 1991, the University of Toronto was debating the possible adoption of a speech code.[88] While many professors found the proposed code to be too restrictive, the Graduate Students' Union argued that it was too liberal. In that group's view, the draft policy was too deferential to free speech. Instead of reproducing the terms of the proposed policy, I think it would be more useful to reproduce some of the statements made by the Graduate Students' Union. Here are some extracts from the letter written by that organization:

> ... Rather than tying the limits of debate to a vague notion such as "the reasonable exercise of free speech" (reasonableness as defined by whom, acceptable to whom?) we feel it would be much more productive to limit freedom of expression to ideas and expressions which are free of prejudice.[89]

Incredibly, graduate students are usually the most intellectually sophisticated members of the student community. Imagine trying to outlaw prejudice on a university campus! To paraphrase these students themselves, "prejudice" as defined by whom and monitored by whom? The group failed to indicate how it would go about policing expressions of prejudice. Would the graduate students have banned all speech that provided no evidentiary foundation? Conversely, how would it have treated the work of a Phillipe Rushton that was laced with research and evidence? Would they concede that it's possible to reach some inegalitarian conclusions without being prejudiced? On the other hand, is it possible to reach egalitarian conclusions in a prejudiced manner? Did they propose to be selective about prohibiting prejudice?

I shudder to think that, for many people, their student days are the most liberal they will ever experience. What, then, is likely to happen to the leaders of the Graduate Students' Union as they begin to age?

IV

In making these observations, I do not pretend that freedom of speech, even in a campus setting, is an absolute that can never be fettered. I acknowledge that certain forms of speech could undermine the functions a university is supposed to perform. Speech that amounts to plagiarism or cheating, for example, could not be tolerated. Moreover, speech from persons who exercise power over others could be validly penalized if it attempted to exact sexual favours in exchange for employment or academic advantage. For such purposes, explicit prohibitions would be unassailable.

Defenders of campus speech codes, more restrictive than this, often trot out some story of a professor telling hurtful off-colour jokes about women or homosexuals. The situation is described as one of a professor with power making life intolerable for vulnerable students who lack power. Campus speech codes are needed, their defenders urge, in order to provide some reliable means of redress for such abuses.

To what extent, however, are these speech codes able—and even intended—to muzzle expressions of opinion on political and social issues? When Matin Yaqzan was suspended from the University of New Brunswick for his article on date rape, there was no question of his having made gratuitously crude jokes at anyone's expense. He was merely expressing a non-conforming opinion that happened to offend many of the university's students. Nor was Phillippe Rushton accused of such gratuitous meanness. There are no reports that he targeted minority students in his classes or behaved insensitively towards them as individuals. It was his *scholarship* that people found offensive. Most of the above incidents are similar.

One organization that would be expected to appreciate the distinction between gratuitous harassment and legitimate expression is the professors' pressure group, the Canadian Association of University

Teachers (CAUT). The CAUT drafted a model anti-harassment policy for recommended use in universities. This policy includes a prohibition against "conduct of a sexual nature such as . . . verbal abuse of a sexual nature . . . when . . . such conduct creates an intimidating, hostile or offensive . . . environment".[90] Significantly, the anti-harassment policy at the University of New Brunswick was virtually identical to the model proposed by the CAUT.[91] The hopeless paradox is inescapable. While the CAUT was opposed to the suspension of Matin Yaqzan, its proposed model policy was used to facilitate his suspension.

Nevertheless, it must be acknowledged that certain forms of verbal insult could undermine the operations of an academic community. For these purposes, harassment must be seen as a synonym for taunting, hectoring, or pestering. We can all imagine situations in which verbal expressions of this kind could reach the point of unacceptability. But there is no reason to condition prohibitions in this area on the basis of the categories in the definition. Pestering can become unacceptable even if it has nothing to do with categories such as race, creed, gender, or sexual orientation. By formulating a harassment policy in these terms, a university effectively discourages certain subjects of discussion on campus. Such an outcome clearly violates the university's mission.

Once more, the problem is how to formulate a prohibition precise enough to nail the unacceptable hectoring or pestering without risking the legitimate expressions of opinion that universities are supposed to encourage. Some formulations could certainly reduce the risk more than others. Query, however, whether any prohibition could lower the risk enough to leave a campus in a viable state of intellectual freedom.

In any event, it is appropriate to insist that those who seek to promulgate such restrictions on campus speech have a heavy onus to discharge. They must demonstrate the necessity for the measures they seek. I think it's fair to say that this exercise has never really occurred. I know of no research, for example, that has attempted to indicate how women, racial minorities, and homosexuals would likely suffer without such speech codes on campus. Indeed, even certain officials of Ontario's NDP government, who were earlier involved in promoting the idea, admitted that *they* had never conducted or even examined any such research. It is clear, therefore, that many universities in this country have adopted speech codes, not because the need for them has been demonstrated, but rather because the canons of "political correctness" demanded such action.

In the meantime, I believe that women, racial minorities, and homosexuals would more effectively serve their interests by confirming, rather than rejecting, the liberal values that have contributed so much to the progress they have experienced thus far. As far as the universities are concerned, this means a high tolerance for the free speech of the foes, as well as the friends, of equality. It also means understanding that freedom of speech, like so many other freedoms, has an indivisible quality. You can't curtail the speech of some without seriously imperiling the speech of others. In a university community, this is critical. After all, intellectual freedom is indispensable to what a university is supposed to be about.

Notes

[1] "SAC repudiates SDS action" *The Varsity*, (15 March 1974) 1.
[2] "Blacks support SDS action" National Black Coalition of Canada letter to *The Varsity*,(20 March 1997) 7. For a sampling of professor Banfield's views see *The Unheavenly City*.
[3] "Write on" letters to *The Varsity*, (15 and 20 March 1974).
[4] "Final Report of the Special Committee on Student Societies and Human Rights," University of Toronto, February 15, 1991; "Human rights statement debated" *The Varsity*, (26 Sept 1991) 3.
[5] "Framework Regarding Prevention of Harassment and Discrimination in Ontario Universities," Ontario Ministry of Education and Training, 1993.
[6] "Statistics on Jewish Registration," Minutes of Queen's University Senate, October 29, 1943.
[7] "Engineering students publish newsletter that causes uproar" *Globe and Mail*, (26 March 1990); "Toike controversy heats up" University of Toronto Bulletin, (12 Dec 1988).
[8] Confirmed by Peter Carstors, professor emeritus of anthropology at the University of Toronto.
[9] Richard F. Devlin, "Legal Education as Political Consciousness—Raising, or Paving the Road to Hell" (1989) *Journal of Legal Education* 39:213-229 (hereinafter Devlin).
[10] Devlin, p.227.
[11] "Sexual Harassment and You: What every Student should Know," pamphlet circulated by the York University Sexual Harassment Education and Complaint Centre, 1986, p. 2.
[12] Devlin, p. 226.
[13] "Gay and lesbian day coming to Rye soon" *The Ryersonian*, (30 Nov 1990); "Complaints filed against students" *The Ryersonian*, (7 Dec 1990)1;

"Harassment policy questioned" *The Ryersonian*, (18 Jan 1991) 3; "Right to know" *The Ryersonian*, (23 Jan 1991); "Decision next week" *The Ryersonian*, (25 Jan 1991) 1; "Harassment complaint dismissed" *The Ryersonian*, (6 Feb 1991) 1, 5; "Complaint dismissed" *The Ryersonian*, (13 Feb 1991) 1; "First Annual Report of Harassment Prevention Services, December 1, 1990, to November 30, 1991," Department of Campus Safety and Security, Harassment Prevention Services, Ryerson Polytechnical Instutute, p. 3.

14 "Complaint dismissed" *The Ryersonian*, (13 Feb 1991) 1.
15 "President K.G. Pederson's letter to professor Marjorie Ratcliffe" *UWOFA Review*, (March 1993) 4.
16 University of Western Ontario Race Relations Policy (1990), provision 4.02.
17 University of Western Ontario Human Relations Tribunal case #001 Report, p. 7.
18 *UWOFA Review*, (January 1993) 6.
19 *UWOFA Review*, (January 1993) 17.
20 See, for example, "Faculty vote condemns handling of Ratcliffe case" *Western News*, (17 June 1993); "Faculty condemns president for mishandling of race case" *London Free Press*, (18 June 1993); "Western race policy criticized" *The Varsity*, (5 Nov 1992).
21 *UWOFA Review*, (March 1993) 4.
22 "Phillippe Rushton: honest academic or sinister racist?" *Canadian Press*, (15 Jan 1995).
23 *Canadian Press*, (27 Nov 1993).
24 Ian A Hunter, "Three Johns: Figures of Speech" (1991) 25/2 *Journal of Legal Education* 212; "Informed of hate probe, Rushton cancels speech" *Globe and Mail*, (13 March 1989) A1.
25 "Rushton rating sparks letters of protest" *Globe and Mail*, (31 May 1990) A3; Hunter, *supra*.
26 "Rushton students say learning environment 'poisoned'" *Globe and Mail*, (25 May 1991) A7.
27 "Complaint against professor's racial theories abandoned" *Canadian Press*, (27 Nov 1995); "Complaints against Rushton dropped" *Globe and Mail*, (28 Nov 1995) A5; "Rights body drops racism case against professor" *Toronto Star* (29 November 1995) A13.
28 "Date rape comments cause campus furor" *Globe and Mail*, (9 Nov 1993) A6; *Canadian Press*, (12 Nov 1993).
29 Ibid.
30 Ibid.
31 *Canadian Press*, (4 Jan 1994).
32 Materials on file at the CCLA, including renditions of the actual posters. The outline of the facts, originally conveyed to the CCLA office by some of

the students involved, has been corroborated through a discussion with a Seneca official and an interview with a Seneca teacher.

[33] Ibid.
[34] "Seneca College of Applied Arts and Technology Policy on Discrimination/Harassment" (1992) Articles 6.2.1 and 2.
[35] *supra* note 32.
[36] "Report in Respect of the Political Science Department of the University of British Columbia," Joan I. McEwen, 1995, p. 1 (hereinafter McEwen).
[37] McEwen, p. 22.
[38] Ibid.
[39] McEwen, p. 82, 84.
[40] McEwen, p. 84.
[41] McEwen, p. 96.
[42] McEwen, p. 82.
[43] McEwen, p. 88.
[44] Ibid.
[45] Ibid.
[46] McEwen, p. 70-114, 167-172.
[47] McEwen, p. 71.
[48] McEwen, p. 72.
[49] Ibid.
[50] Ibid.
[51] McEwen, p. 149.
[52] "Reasons for Decision in the matter of an appeal by Professor Kenneth Westhues under University of Waterloo Policy 33 from the decision of the Vice-President Academic and Provost, dated March 11, 1997, arising out of the report of the Ethics Committee, dated August 23, 1996," Dr. Peter P. Mercer, Adjudicator, February 10, 1998 (hereinafter Mercer decision).
[53] University of Waterloo Policy 33: Ethical Behaviour, section II(B)-2.
[54] Mercer decision, p. 1.
[55] CCLA letter to Vice-President Academic and Provost, University of Waterloo, September 3, 1996.
[56] Mercer decision, p. 1.
[57] Mercer decision, p. 2.
[58] Mercer decision, p. 3.
[59] CCLA letter to President, University of Waterloo, April 2, 1997.
[60] Mercer decision, p.3.
[61] Ibid.
[62] Ibid.
[63] CCLA letter to Chair, Ethics Hearing Committee, University of Waterloo, August 27, 1996.
[64] Mercer decision, p. 21.

65. CCLA letter to Chair, Ethics Hearing Committee, University of Waterloo, August 27, 1996.
66. Mercer decision, p. 21.
67. CCLA letter to Chair, Ethics Hearing Committee, University of Waterloo, August 27, 1996.
68. Mercer decision, p. 22.
69. CCLA letter to Chair, Ethics Hearing Committee, University of Waterloo, August 27, 1996.
70. Mercer decision, p. 23.
71. CCLA letter to Chair, Ethics Hearing Committee, University of Waterloo, August 27, 1996.
72. Mercer decision, p. 23.
73. CCLA letter to President, University of Waterloo, April 2, 1997.
74. Mercer decision, p. 10.
75. "UWO Council refuses aid to Mideast group" *London Free Press*, (10 Dec 1982); "CPME loses ratification bid" *The Gazette*, (10 Dec 1982).
76. "Review of the constitution of Canadians for Peace in the Middle East" Memorandum by Nick Davies, November 26, 1982.
77. Ibid.
78. "Taking the blame for opinions" *The Gazette*, (29 Oct 1982).
79. "Christians on Campus Constitution," (1978) Article 2.
80. "Newman Catholic Community Constitution," (1980) Article 11.
81. "Mid-East group denied club ratification by USC" *Western News*, (16 Dec 1982).
82. "New club meets opposition" *The Gazette*, (8 Oct 1982).
83. Ibid.
84. "Press release," Students' Federation of the University of Ottawa, July 7, 1982.
85. "Union to grieve ouster of date-rape professor" *Toronto Star*, (17 Nov 1993) A14.
86. "When free speech and equality don't mix" *Toronto Star*, (6 Oct 1994) A25.
87. "Banned Parenthood" *McLean's*, (30 Aug 1993)12; "Prophylactics draw polemics" *The Varsity*, (10 Aug 1993); "Planned Parenthood back on campus" *The Varsity*, (7 Sept 1993).
88. "Final Report of the Special Committee on Student Societies and Human Rights," University of Toronto, February 15, 1991; "Human rights statement debated" *The Varsity*, (26 Sept 1991) 3.
89. "Letter to Special Committee on Student Societies and Human Rights," University of Toronto Graduate Students' Union, October 31, 1991.
90. "CAUT Policy Statement on Professional Rights, Responsibilities and Relationships," (1992) Appendix II, Article 3.
91. "University of New Brunswick Policy and Procedure on Sexual Harassment," (1990) p. 2.

CHAPTER FOUR

Among Doves

So compelling is the exercise of equality-seeking in some circles that it is also affecting issues of international relations. To many peace activists and doves, equality in the international arena means reducing the role of the superpower United States and commensurately enhancing that of an invigorated United Nations (UN). For such peace activists and doves, it would be hard to imagine anything more unequal than the perpetual domination of the world by a single superpower.

With his customary crispness, Canadian playwright Rick Salutin expressed what for peace activists and doves is probably one of the central issues of international relations:

> ... by what right does the United States assume responsibility for *anything* in the sands of Arabia and the waters of the Persian Gulf? Think about it. What the hell are they doing there? If 500,000 Arab soldiers turned up in, say, Texas, do you think Americans might notice the incongruity? [emphasis in the original][1]

While they attacked in this way the American role in the 1991 Persian Gulf war, many dovish commentators have acknowledged nevertheless the need for *some* semblance of "world order". For them, however, the legitimacy of an intervention would require United Nations, not United States, authorization. Consider, for example, the comments of Douglas Roche, Canada's former Ambassador for Disarmament:

> With a toothless United Nations, the way would be clear for the United States . . . to bestride the world as the lone superpower intervening at will . . . .[2]

Obviously, Douglas Roche very much wanted to avoid giving the United States such freedom of action. There would be no comparable reluctance, however, to empower the United Nations. To many dovish commentators, the alleged emasculation of the United Nations has been the most significant casualty of recent international developments.

Writing in the *Toronto Star*, ethics columnist Tom Harpur made the following remarks about a paper published by the U.S. Defence Department:

> ... for me the worst aspect of the defence department manifesto is its total downplaying of effective, collective action by the United Nations. Obviously we are being prepared for future repetitions of the kind of hijacking of the U.N. by the Americans that was used to justify the 1991 war in the Gulf.[3]

Similarly, Harpur's then fellow columnist Gerald Caplan said of the Persian Gulf war, "the real tragedy in all this is how terribly the credibility of the U.N. has been undermined".[4]

It's clear from the foregoing that these doves are not a group of isolationists seeking to withdraw from the conflicts of the world. What they are seeking, rather, is a moral and legal legitimacy for intervening in such conflicts. In their view, such legitimacy cannot reside in the United States; it must come from the United Nations.

It's not hard to understand these cravings about the United Nations. After all, the U.N. is the only world body that has some legal basis to claim that it represents all of the nations on earth. At the very least, it has embodied many of humanity's historic yearnings for an effective world government. When it was created at the end of the Second World War, it was seen as the vehicle through which we humans could avert yet another world war. This explains why the impact on the United Nations is seen, by some, as the most important consequence of the Gulf war.

In my view, these dovish writers are confusing the realities of the existing United Nations with their fantasies about effective world government. In the result, these commentators have become an influence against a truly *liberal* international order. By this, I mean a world that is relatively safe for the preservation and expansion of democratic self-government.

A substantial majority of voting members in the United Nations are significantly less democratic than are those countries of the traditional

Western bloc. These nations range from what one monitoring agency, Freedom House, calls the "partly free" to the "unfree". Such countries have a majority in the General Assembly, and one of the most repressive—China—has a veto in the Security Council.[5] Thus, they have significantly less or no relationship of accountability to the people on whose behalf they purport to speak. To put the question in Rick Salutin's style: Why the hell should the democracies submit to the political will of such regimes? The American columnist Charles Krauthammer put it even better on a recent television program. He asked why American foreign policy should be vetted by the butchers of Tienanmin Square.

Suppose that the Mafia chose a large number of MPs in our House of Commons. Why should the rest of us who freely elect our MPs submit their decisions to vetting by the representatives of those who don't? A world parliament of democracies would make sense. If we were going to submit our sovereignty to that of others, then those others should also be democracies. This is not to say that the Western nations should necessarily prevail. It is to say that democracy should prevail.

When Messrs. Roche, Harpur, and Caplan get their knickers in such a twist over the status of the United Nations, they could be effectively reducing the influence of the world's democracies. Thus, the world order urged upon us by those commentators would be essentially and increasingly illiberal—all in the name of peace and under the noble banner of world government.

This is not to completely disparage the value of the U.N. The world body performs a number of worthy functions, not the least of which is the peaceful mediation of disputes. My quarrel here is limited to those who seek for this international agency the power to overrule member governments on virtually all international matters.

Unfortunately, these commentators inadequately appreciate the substantial possibilities that the current international power structure creates for their humanitarian aspirations. In all recorded history, it would be hard to remember a time so opportune for enforcing a world order that is relatively safe for democracy. Most of recorded history has been dominated by conflicts between two or more great powers. Invariably, at least one of those powers was an out-and-out dictatorship. Not surprisingly, the enforcement of a liberal order invariably incurred a risk of serious warfare.

In today's world, however, there is only one great power—the United States. No other nation is capable of defeating the United States.

Conversely, the United States is capable of defeating every other nation. At long last, therefore, it might be possible to reasonably ensure an international regime of security and safety for liberal democratic values.

Why should peace-loving, internationalist doves find this situation so unacceptable? Perhaps Tom Harpur expressed the consensus in the course of commenting on that paper published by the U.S. Defence Department:

> ... the defence department, in a policy statement ... now asserts that the U.S. political and military mission in this new, post-Cold War era will be to ensure that no rival superpower is allowed to emerge in Western Europe, Asia, or the territory of the former Soviet Union. ... The idea of a global 'manifest destiny' for the U.S.—a modern version of the ancient dream of madmen for world empire—is an evil, dangerous delusion.[6]

Thus, the United States is seen by some dovish internationalists as the *de facto* reincarnation of Alexander the Great, Julius Caesar, Napoleon, or perhaps worse. That's why, in Tom Harpur's words, "it's the moral duty of all free, peace-loving people to resist and expose [the U.S. plan] before it becomes reality".[7] Such considerations will also explain why former U.S. Attorney General Ramsey Clark, another dovish internationalist, has said, "The U.S. military arsenal ... has grown immensely. There will be little chance for peace on earth until it is dismantled."[8] What a vision for the world! Dismantle American power and give the United Nations—with its majority of less than democratic countries—the effective power on the international scene.

In all of these commentaries and polemics, a critical factor seems to have been overlooked or at least downplayed. It is the factor that distinguishes the United States from those that have previously attempted to foist their will on the international scene. The United States is essentially a democracy. Its government derives its power from the freely given consent of the citizens it governs. Neither Julius Caesar nor Alexander the Great nor Napoleon nor any of the twentieth-century dictators were answerable or accountable to an electorate that enjoyed a large measure of freedom of speech, freedom of assembly, freedom of the press, freedom of association, and secret ballot elections. These freedoms—admittedly imperfect and inadequate—have enabled the citizens of the United States to exert a significant influence over that country's international behaviour.

What else, for example, could possibly explain the dramatic reversal of U.S. policy over the war in Vietnam? Lyndon Johnson, who substantially expanded the war, was forced to abandon his well-known desire to seek another term in the U.S. presidency. Richard Nixon, the tough cold warrior, was forced to retreat from Vietnam under humiliating conditions. The reason is obvious. The American *people* withdrew their political support for the war.

After that experience, it should be clear that those exercising government power in the United States must operate under significant constraints. The American people are not about to risk the blood of their sons and daughters in questionable foreign adventures. Thus, American interventions abroad will invariably require selling the American citizenry on their validity. As we have seen from the U.S. reluctance to get involved in Bosnia and its decision to withdraw from Somalia, this selling exercise is not likely to be an easy one. Even if American military power is virtually certain to prevail, the American people might well regard the costs of those victories as too much for them.

In saying these things, I must, of course, acknowledge the argument frequently made by dovish commentators that the American people are subject to government and media manipulation. According to this argument, those fundamental freedoms to which I earlier referred have often become, in reality, a sham. No one can validly deny the charge that such manipulations have occurred—and are occurring—in the United States. Nor can anyone validly deny the possibility that they could recur. The real world provides no guarantees. What can be said, however, is that, compared to the realistic alternatives, the United States provides the *best hope* for the development of international behaviour that is subject to the influence of a democratic electorate. And this stage of history provides hard, empirical evidence that the American electorate has been largely exercising its freedoms to constrain America's international behaviour.

This is not to suggest for one moment that democracies necessarily behave in a just manner. To be sure, democracies are capable of serious immorality. Indeed, on many occasions, the United States itself has provided an apt illustration of this phenomenon. My point is a less ambitious one: as between democracies and other regimes, there is a significantly better chance that the democracies will resist, avoid, redress, or at least reduce, injustice. The combination of a free press, open debate, and the right of citizens to protest publicly and to replace their governments—in short, the democratic freedoms—are the factors that help to counteract the human propensity to behave unjustly.

In my view, therefore, we should avoid trying to weaken America's ability to act on the international scene. This does not mean supine acceptance of whatever America does. In this regard, it's wise to bear in mind that those of us who live in other democracies are free to write, speak, demonstrate, and organize so as to influence our governments to pressure the United States. While such actions on our part will not as often exert an influence comparable to that of America's citizens, the importance of these actions should not be minimized. The United States usually seeks the support and good will of other nations, particularly those of its democratic allies. Moreover, the American people can be influenced by the behaviour and actions of friendly nations and their peoples.

Again, this is not to downplay the risks of a sole superpower in the world. But it is to recognize that compared to the realistic alternatives—especially those being urged by the dovish critics—America's position in the world today provides a singular opportunity to achieve a workable peace in which democratic societies can enjoy relative security.

Indeed, it may well develop that the United States will be too timid—rather than too eager—about foreign entanglements. Since the humiliation in Vietnam, such timidity has frequently characterized America's responses. Ever since the end of the Cold War, the United States has been a reluctant intervenor. In this regard, the Persian Gulf is more the exception than the rule. Even though the Americans did send a contingent to Somalia, one small bloody skirmish was enough to force the U.S. president to set a time limit on the American presence in that country. There has been little taste for involvement to stop the ethnic slaughters in the former Yugoslavia or the North Korean acquisition of nuclear weapons. And, contrary to the allegations of many dovish commentators, the American Pentagon particularly exhibits little stomach for military interventions.

Significantly, the current U.S. posture is much criticized by Americans who believe that world stability requires a greater American willingness to intervene abroad. Writing in *Commentary* magazine, for example, Edward Luttwak charged that America's emerging doctrine on foreign interventions

> presumes to rule out any U.S. military combat action. . . .
> unless a long list of conditions is met. They include a victory
> fully guaranteed in advance by overwhelming force,
> irrevocable public support for whatever operations are
> undertaken . . . and a precisely defined objective that may
> not, repeat not, be changed in accordance with shifting
> circumstances.[9]

If Luttwak and such other critics are right, the complaints of the dovish commentators begin to look like unwarranted hysteria. Even if Luttwak is exaggerating when he talks about "irrevocable" public support, we should bear in mind that one of the roles of democratic leadership is to create such support. If Franklin Delano Roosevelt had waited for public support, he might never even have supplied Britain with arms at the outset of the Second World War. But Roosevelt believed that part of his job was to persuade his fellow citizens that their long-term interests required such action. In any event, if Luttwak is only partly right, America is more likely to behave—as one writer expressed it—like a "paper tiger than an imperial despot".

Nevertheless, the dovish commentators would impose even further conditions on military interventions. In the course of criticizing the Gulf war, Gerald Caplan, for example, argued that "resort to war should have been unthinkable unless it was conclusively demonstrated that sanctions would not work".[10] Note that Caplan is not requiring proof that sanctions have not worked but rather that they "would" not work. How could a future event ever be demonstrated, let alone "conclusively" demonstrated? In prescribing such conditions on military intervention, Caplan is effectively ruling out military interventions. In his world, we might not have been able to use military power against Hitler. Even then, we would have been unable to "conclusively demonstrate" that economic sanctions would not have worked.

While other dovish commentators may have avoided advocating such blatantly impossible conditions, their prescriptions could also paralyze the military power of the Western democracies. According to former Conservative party chairman, Dalton Camp, for example, "true friends of America, in Canada, should be forgiven for supporting the option of continued sanctions".[11] The Roman Catholic bishops in the United States also complained that sanctions "had not been given time to be effective".[12] Philosophy professor Trudy Govier argued that "the possibility of ending the crisis through sanctions was not exhaustively explored".[13]

My lack of expertise precludes me from pronouncing definitively one way or the other on the question of sanctions. But I am able to question the adequacy of the pro-sanctions arguments employed by these commentators. They all complain that sanctions were not adequately or "exhaustively" explored. But they have little to say about how to determine when such a point would be reached. The very nature of a slow process like sanctions is such that it could be argued at any time that more time is necessary. Unless these commentators would eschew any resort to military means, it is incumbent upon them at least to identify some criteria by which we could decide when sanctions were no longer sufficient.

It must be remembered, of course, that economic sanctions have the capacity to create terrible suffering for the people who live in the targeted countries. We couldn't expect a tyrant like Saddam Hussein to ensure that he and his elites shared the misery of economic privation with the powerless masses who are subject to his rule. *Toronto Star* columnist Michele Landsberg has commented on "the trauma faced by Iraqi women and children coping with the results of U.N. sanctions—the hunger, desperation, primitive conditions and nightmarish 2000% inflation that puts even basic foodstuffs out of reach for the poor".[14]

Thus, if the dovish commentators are right about the eventual success of economic sanctions, they must have been prepared to continue inflicting misery on the ordinary people of Iraq. Indeed, they must have been prepared to increase the misery they inflicted. At the same time, the dovish commentators must have been prepared to tolerate longer periods during which the Kuwaiti people would have had to endure the hardships associated with the Iraqi occupation of their country. Even if some of the horror stories regarding that occupation turned out to be less than true, it was reasonable nevertheless to believe that a regime like Saddam Hussein's would be very likely to behave with unacceptable cruelty.

It is not immediately clear why the expected casualties accompanying military sanctions are significantly worse than the suffering caused by continuing economic sanctions. Granted, war kills and maims irreparably. But sanctions might starve even more people. And that too could be irreparable. Comparative effects would depend upon a host of conditions and circumstances. Again, I am not necessarily asserting the preferability of one solution over the other; I am simply saying that the dovish commentators did not adequately weigh the competing hardships. For them, the desire to avoid a shooting war effectively became the only consideration.

In this regard, one of the more helpful analyses I have seen was that of Professor Govier who did consider the increasing damage that sanctions might cause: ". . . perhaps prolonged sanctions would have led, in the end, to a violent upheaval within Iraq".[15] Having so helpfully acknowledged this problem, Professor Govier made a questionable statement: "Internal violence, however horrible it might have been, would almost certainly have been less harmful overall than war . . .".[16] Not only is there no basis for such a comparison, there is some compelling evidence to the contrary. Numbers of civil wars have been far more devastating than have many international wars. Consider, for example, the civil wars in Bosnia, Angola, Nigeria, and, even during the last century, in the United States. To whatever extent any of the dovish commentators regarded civil war in Iraq as a likely outcome of our economic sanctions, they should at least have harboured some ethical reservations about the course they were advocating.

To be fair, some of the doves did express such qualms during the course of the debates. After detailing the devastation that economic sanctions were causing to the people of Iraq, Michele Landsberg flatly concluded, "We should not be punishing Iraqi civilians for the crimes of their leaders—and ours."[17] But her article failed to address the obvious implication of this argument. If you are unable to immunize the people of a dictatorial regime from the punishment you are attempting to inflict on their leaders, must you, therefore, spare their leaders? Are you prepared to let the Saddam Husseins of this world do what they will and go in peace?

According to the Catholic bishops' statement, a just war requires that "all less violent alternatives . . . must first be exhausted".[18] The bishops complained that "diplomatic initiatives . . . were not vigorously pursued . . .".[19] If these arguments had been made against the justness of Saddam Hussein's invasion of Kuwait, they would have been well taken. Moreover, the bishops argued that "there is little evidence that Iraqi grievances against Kuwait . . . were taken seriously . . .".[20] But once Saddam invades and occupies that country, why should a serious consideration of his grievances be a prerequisite for insisting that he get out? If the pursuit of diplomacy must first be exhausted, surely that must apply, first and foremost, to Saddam Hussein. If he makes a clearly unjust war, why should he be entitled to our diplomatic consideration? I would have thought that we should have made his withdrawal a prerequisite for seriously considering his grievances.

No doubt, the bishops would reply that we have to exhaust diplomatic initiatives before *we* commit violence that will risk so many lives. Again, however, there is a failure on the part of these doves to identify the criteria by which we can determine when our negotiating efforts have been "exhausted". After all, it's not as though negotiations had not been attempted. Prior to the war, there were months of diplomatic activity aimed at peacefully resolving the conflict.

In any event, commentators such as the bishops paid inadequate attention to the likelihood that the Saddam Husseins of this world would perceive unremitting negotiating efforts on our part as a sign of weakness. In saying this, I am not advocating a macho posture for its own sake. But I am suggesting that tyrants like Saddam are likely to be emboldened to commit additional encroachments when they see vacillation in the democracies. This is not necessarily to disagree about the negotiating attempts that had been made then; it is simply to say that it's not good enough to disparage those attempts as insufficient.

In some respects, it could *always* be argued that some additional overture could be made at the diplomatic level. Human ingenuity being what it is, there is always some new compromise that can be suggested. But the problem in a situation such as the Gulf war is that additional proposals for compromise on our part would have risked rewarding Saddam Hussein's blatant invasion of Kuwait. To have continued the negotiating efforts could have signalled to tomorrow's aggressors that the best way to get what they want is to seize it and then the international community will negotiate with them. For all of these reasons, it was not helpful for Professor Govier to ask rhetorically whether standing firm was "virtuous" or "obscene".

In still other ways, dovish internationalists have objectively undermined the prospects for a liberal world order. In a further comment on the justness of the Gulf war, the Catholic bishops made the following remark: "Were it not for the strategic importance of oil resources, it is unlikely that the United States and its allies would have gone to war to protect the national sovereignty of Kuwait".[21]

Here, the validity of the argument becomes confused with the validity of the arguer. Even if America's deepest motive concerned oil, that does not invalidate its argument about protecting the sovereignty of Kuwait. If it were independently justifiable to go to war for Kuwait, it would not matter whether some (or even all) of those who went to war were trying to serve other interests by doing so.

Some Marxists opposed the war against Hitler on the grounds that the primary interest being served for the Allied governments was capitalist markets, not democratic survival. Even if that were so, the rest of us still had to determine whether the war served *our* interest in the survival of democratic institutions. To whatever extent it did, we were justified in going to war—despite the motives of our governments and their supporters.

In the case of the Gulf war, however, the interests of democratic survival were often dismissed in a peremptory fashion. Gerald Caplan, for example, seemed to represent the views of many fellow doves when he made the following statement: "No one accepts that this conflict is about democracy, Kuwait having been a feudal entity run by a few Sheiks and merchants".[22]

Of course, Caplan is right that the issue could not have involved democracy *in Kuwait.* In a very real way, however, the war involved the interests of democracy in other countries. To whatever extent a power-hungry despot like Saddam could have succeeded with this aggression, democratic institutions might well have been threatened elsewhere. If Saddam could have overrun Kuwait with impunity, he might have been tempted to turn his attentions to resource-rich Saudi Arabia. An expanding, richer Iraq in the Middle East could well have created security problems for democratic Israel and even for some of the European democracies in the Mediterranean. Consider also how Iraq's potential acquisition of nuclear, biological, and chemical weapons could have exacerbated this threat.

Once more, my disclaimer. None of this is to definitively justify the war on the basis of preserving democracy. But it is to insist that there was a very good argument for it. In order to oppose the war, the dovish commentators had an obligation at least to *meet* this argument.

When the affected interests are assessed from this perspective, some of the statements made by dovish internationalists are nothing short of remarkable. Remember, for example, the earlier quote from Tom Harpur's attack on the Pentagon paper: "the U.S. political and military mission in this new post-Cold War era will be to ensure that no rival superpower is allowed to emerge in Western Europe, Asia, or the territory of the former Soviet Union".[23] What is hard to fathom about this statement is that it represents, on Harpur's part, a *criticism* of U.S. policy. Is Harpur saying that the world would be safer if another superpower did emerge?

Unless such a superpower were also a democracy—and there is no evidence that the United States would be opposed to *that*—it would likely take the form of a fascist, racist, Islamic fundamentalist, or perhaps even a Communist dictatorship. On the basis of what conceivable analysis could Harpur argue that such a development would be less bad than the status quo in which a democratic America is the only superpower? Indeed, if such other superpowers were to emerge, the survival of both democracy and world peace would undergo significantly increased dangers.

If, on the other hand, Harpur is simply arguing that the dangers of another superpower tomorrow cannot justify American military intervention today, his position still remains assailable. After all the horrors that the twentieth century has visited upon the human race, it is time that we saw the available options in a clearer light. The world rarely affords us the opportunity to choose between pleasantness and unpleasantness. Usually, we are required to choose between or among competing unpleasantnesses. As we learned from the period before the Second World War, it would have been far better to have engaged in a little warfare then in order to stop Hitler, than a great deal more warfare later. There simply was no other choice. Unless Tom Harpur can persuasively demonstrate that human beings—particularly those possessing dictatorial power—are likely to behave differently from here on than they have heretofore, he should endorse America's objective of preventing the emergence of another superpower.

Another alleged American objective that triggers dovish criticism deals with the proliferation of nuclear weapons. In a further comment on the Pentagon paper, Tom Harpur complained that "there is confirmation ... of plans ... for using military force, if necessary, to stop the proliferation of nuclear weapons to nations the U.S. views as threatening".[24] Similarly, *Canadian Forum* editor Duncan Cameron made the following remark:

> Amassing a vast military force in the desert, delivering an ultimatum, and foregoing diplomacy suggest a United States aimed at destroying Saddam Hussein's war machine before he develops a nuclear capacity . . . it also says to the world that only Western nations are entitled to weapons of mass destruction.[25]

What mortal terror these dovish internationalists would have us suffer, if they had their way! Since when and on the basis of what kind of analysis is it improper to try and prevent the proliferation of nuclear weapons? Are Harpur and Cameron suggesting that the world would be safer if countries like, let us say, North Korea, Libya, or Iran acquired nuclear weapons? Or would it simply offend their ethical—and egalitarian—sensibilities if the Western nations enjoyed a virtual monopoly of such destructive power?

In response to this last question (the answer to the penultimate one is obvious), the issue becomes simpler when we go from the abstract to the concrete. At most, any persuasive argument against a Western monopoly would address a world in which nuclear weapons were *first* being developed. Perhaps, it might then have been appropriate for someone to argue that no one should have a nuclear monopoly; all such power should be transferred to a responsible world authority. The problem with this argument, of course, is that there never was a responsible world authority and there is not now. We face a status quo in which the West has a nuclear superiority and the question is: Are humanitarian values better served if the West keeps this superiority or loses it? Put that way, the answer here must also be obvious.

Moreover, these considerations are fuelled by the fact that the Western nations with nuclear weapons are all democracies. Unlike most of the Third World countries that are trying to acquire nuclear weapons, the Western governments remain accountable to their democratic constituencies for any use they may make of these awesome weapons. Compared to all realistic alternatives at this point in history, it is better, therefore, that these Western nations work vigorously to prevent any additional countries from acquiring nuclear weapons. It would be foolish to be persuaded by the kind of abstract ethics urged upon us by writers like Tom Harpur and Duncan Cameron.

Such dubious egalitarianism manifests itself in other ways as well. In their desire to be fair, certain dovish internationalists almost break their backs bending over to avoid double standards. Consider, for example, *Toronto Star* columnist Richard Gwyn denouncing the Israeli kidnapping of Hezbollah leader Sheik Abdul Karem Obeid. Acknowledging that Obeid was likely a terrorist himself, Gwyn concedes that this imparts some political justification to the Israeli act. "But", Gwyn adds, "it invests it with no legal justification whatsoever".[26]

At what point Gwyn abandoned moral for legal argument I'm not sure. Why, however, should he get excited about such legal arguments in the context of the international jungle? In the absence of an international authority capable of enforcing this approach to international law, unilateral observance of it by a democracy would simply put that democracy at an irreparable disadvantage in its dealings with dictators and terrorists. Consider the practical question. What is Israel to do when international organizations like the Hezbollah attack its citizens? Run to the world court? Run to the United Nations? If Israel declines to take tough action, it renders itself a sitting duck. (At this point, I am arguing the ethics, not the prudence, of tough actions.)

As for the comparison between this seizure by Israel and those by the Hezbollah, I would have thought that the material difference is that Israel deliberately targeted a known terrorist. The Hezbollah, on the other hand, has deliberately targeted innocent non-combatants. Thus, Richard Gwyn engages in some dubious moral equivalents when he compares these kidnappings and concludes, "no matter by whom committed or for what motive, terrorism is still terrorism".[27]

Former United Church moderator Bruce McLeod revealed a similar misconception when he said of an aide to Yasser Arafat, leader of the Palestine Liberation Organization (PLO), that "terrorists and resistance fighters are the same, depending on which side of an argument you take".[28] Had it all been left in the abstract, it might not have created a problem. But McLeod went on to embellish this by noting that former Israeli Prime Minister Yitzhak Shamir, when he was a member of the pre-Israel underground, "justified the murder of a British officer who arrested him by saying 'we aimed at achieving a political goal that had to be achieved' ".[29]

In making such comparisons, McLeod completely overlooked the fact that the PLO had deliberately targeted innocent non-combatants, including little children. By what kind of moral somersaults can this be analogized to the killing of a military officer by a person he has imprisoned?

In another example of this phenomenon, Rick Salutin sympathized with actress Margot Kidder, during the Gulf war, for becoming "an instant object of abuse in the United States when she wondered in public why the American government thought it was awful under the Geneva Conventions to parade prisoners of war, but just fine to bomb mothers and infants".[30] I would have thought that the answer was obvious: according to the U.S., America did not deliberately target mothers and infants. The object of the bombing was to destroy military installations, not mothers and infants. But parading prisoners of war had no other object but to humiliate those prisoners of war. They were deliberate targets of extra-military cruelty.

Again, this is not necessarily to absolve the United States for all of its military tactics. To whatever extent there is evidence that the Americans deliberately targeted non-combatant civilians, they would be properly condemned for it. Moreover, they would be properly censured to whatever extent their military activity incurred undue risks of injuring non-combatant civilians. It is not for me, at this point, to determine definitively whether the American military activity fell within either of these categories. It is for me, however, to criticize those who make moral comparisons without even examining these questions.

The regrettable paradox concerning these dovish commentators is how the indiscriminate pursuit of their liberal values is so likely to create an illiberal international order. In their desire to avoid war and create world government, they would make war more probable and the democracies less viable. It's hard to avoid wondering whether these commentators would *ever* find themselves approving an American military intervention.

In this regard, note, for example, the statement made by the Right Reverend Walter Farquharson, then Moderator of the United Church: "But, in light of modern warfare and technological changes in weaponry, we are convinced that ultimately world order is only effectively pursued by non-military means".[31] What is the significance of the word "ultimately"? If Mr. Farquharson is telling us that the objective of our efforts is a de-militarized world in which decisions are made by non-military means, there can be little quarrel. But, if that's all he is saying, he was wasting his breath (or his ink). Who could quarrel with such an ultimate objective? But the practical question is: What do we do between now and the millennium? As a comment on the Persian Gulf war (which is what I think it was), Mr. Farquharson's comment provides little assistance.

It may well be that Tom Harpur expressed some of the inarticulate major premises of certain dovish positions when he said that "it has been the church's greatest betrayal of Christ to have dropped his teachings on violence in favour of the theory of the so-called 'just war'".[32] I cannot tell to what extent Harpur or any of the others subconsciously—or even consciously—prefer a position of absolute pacifism. I am prepared to argue, however, that in order to advance the cause of pacifism in a religiously pluralistic society, it is necessary to consider how such a course of action would be likely to protect the values and the interests that we share. After all, it would not be wise or useful to rely on God's will in a society where there are conflicting beliefs and no empirical evidence as to what that will, in fact, entails.

Thus, Harpur and those who subscribe to his views must focus on why military action against such tyrants is worse, from the standpoint of our shared values and interests, than surrendering to their will. For all of the reasons indicated above, I contend that the dovish position has inadequately addressed this challenge. In the meantime, we should appreciate that the creation, protection, and survival of a liberal world order require a much greater willingness to use the military power of the United States than these doves have hitherto been prepared to acknowledge. In their unwillingness to accept this reality, these doves could well help to bring about the very weakening of democratic institutions that they, more than many, would lament.

Notes

[1] "Thoughts of a Gulf War Watcher," Rick Salutin in *This Magazine* (May 1991) vol. 24, no. 8, p. 35-36.

[2] "Why U.N. must stop Iraqi A-bomb," Douglas Roche in the *Toronto Star*, (12 March 1992) A2.

[3] "Why new global manifesto by U.S. is an evil delusion," Tom Harpur in the *Toronto Star*, (15 March 1992) B7.

[4] "It's still an unjustified war," Gerald Caplan in the *Toronto Star*, (20 January 1991) B3.

[5] According to the 1997-1998 Freedom House "Survey of Freedom", the breakdown of 189 independent countries is 81 "free" and 108 "partly free" or "not free".

[6] "Why new global manifesto by U.S. is an evil delusion," Tom Harpur in the *Toronto Star*, (15 March 1992) B7.
[7] Ibid.
[8] "How Iraqi civilians are suffering," Ramsey Clark in the *Toronto Star*, (18 February 1991) A17.
[9] "If Bosnians were dolphins ...." Edward Luttwak in *Commentary* (October 1993) 29.
[10] "It's still an unjustified war," Gerald Caplan in the *Toronto Star*, (20 January 1991) B3.
[11] "Those advocating war should keep silent," Dalton Camp in the *Toronto Star*, (13 January 1991) B3.
[12] "Statement on the morality of the war in the Persion Gulf," by the American Catholic Theologians and Professors of Religious Studies, p. 4.
[13] "A Just War?" Trudy Govier in *The Canadian Forum*, (March 1992) 13.
[14] "Crimes of Bush and company are killing innocent Iraqis," Michelle Landsberg in the *Toronto Star*, (10 November 1992).
[15] Govier, p. 13.
[16] Ibid.
[17] "Crimes of Bush and company are killing innocent Iraqis," Michelle Landsberg in the *Toronto Star*, (10 November 1992).
[18] "Statement on the morality of the war in the Persion Gulf," by the American Catholic Theologians and Professors of Religious Studies, p. 4.
[19] Ibid.
[20] Ibid.
[21] Ibid.
[22] "This crisis could have been a triumph for non-violence," Gerald Caplan in the *Toronto Star*, (13 January 1991) B3.
[23] "Why new global manifesto by U.S. is an evil delusion," Tom Harpur in the *Toronto Star*, (15 March 1992) B7.
[24] Ibid.
[25] "Editorial: Blood for Oil," Duncan Cameron in *The Canadian Forum*, (March 1991) 2.
[26] "Israeli state terrorism initiated latest spiral in mid-east violence," Richard Gwyn in the *Toronto Star*, (11 August 1989) A19.
[27] Ibid.
[28] "Moderate voices give peace a chance," Bruce McLeod in the *Toronto Star*, (20 December 1988) A17.
[29] Ibid.
[30] "Thoughts of a Gulf War Watcher," Rick Salutin in *This Magazine* (May 1991) vol. 24, no. 8, p. 37.

[31] "Attack on Iraq wasn't necessary Canadian church leaders argue," *Toronto Star*, (18 January 1991) A20.

[32] "The war against Iraq is insane and unjust," Tom Harpur in the *Toronto Star*, (27 January 1991) B7.

CHAPTER FIVE

Among Governments and Their Agencies

Until this point, our discussion has focused primarily on the new anti-liberals who are attempting to influence government. This chapter addresses a number of situations in which new anti-liberals have actually wielded government power. The examples are designed to examine the extent to which certain governments, generally considered progressive, are prepared to adopt anti-liberal measures in order to achieve their progressive, essentially egalitarian, objectives—in these cases, the objectives of protecting French, securing abortion rights, and combatting discrimination.

PROTECTING FRENCH

No one with a grain of empathy could fail to grasp the significance of the rallying cry that emanated so often from Quebec's former separatist premier, the late Rene Lévesque. Time and again, Mr. Lévesque declared that, for the French-Canadians, the dominant issue was dignity.

Small wonder. For generations, the economic life of the French majority in Quebec was largely dominated by the English minority there. Despite their relative smallness numerically (less than 25%), the Anglo-Saxons held the greatest number of the decision-making positions in the economy. From manufacturing to finance, the Anglo-Saxons called the shots. And, what in some respects was even worse, the language of commerce was English. Despite the promises of Confederation and their overwhelming majority status, French-Canadians could not adequately function in their own language in their own province.

It is no surprise that the indignities caused by this subordination triggered, in turn, the growth of nationalism among French-Canadians.

"Le Québec au Québecois" and "maître chez nous" reverberated through the streets and meeting halls of la belle province. Marches, rallies, and demonstrations proliferated as the French-Canadian masses expressed their determination to assert their dignity. By the late 1960s, this nationalism found expression in respectable politics. An avowedly separatist party with a mainstream leadership entered the political arena. Inevitably, this development pushed even the non-separatist parties in an ever more nationalist direction.

It's one thing, of course, for nationalism to protect the legitimate interests of those who have suffered unjust discrimination. But it's another thing entirely when that nationalism begins to intrude unjustly on the interests of others. In certain important respects, such a development has characterized the French-Canadian nationalism of the late twentieth century.

In the wake of the turbulent 1960s, the non-separatist Liberal Party was elected as the government of Quebec. By the early 1970s, the new government introduced the controversial Bill 22, which was designed to ensure the predominance of the French language in the educational, industrial, and commercial life of the province. The bill substantially reduced eligibility for free public education in English as the language of instruction. There was also a requirement for programs of francization to be implemented throughout the business sector.

Whatever quarrels some may have with certain features of the bill from a Confederation standpoint, it's hard to portray them as infringements of human rights or civil liberties. From the standpoint of fundamental rights, Quebec is no more obliged to ensure free English instruction than Manitoba is obliged to provide free Ukranian instruction. And the promotion of French in commercial transactions derives its justification from the need to ensure that the francophone majority can function in its own language.

But, like many other forms of nationalism, this one went overboard. It wasn't enough for Bill 22 to promote the use of the French *language*, it also sought to enhance the position of French *persons*. Among other things, Section 29 of the bill required francization programs to encourage a "francophone presence in management".[1] What a message this must have sent to the non-francophone minority. No matter how hard non-francophones worked at mastering French, they would have to face certain official disabilities.

This was, in effect, an affirmative action program in favour of the majority. Apart from its moral dubiousness, there were even questions as to its necessity. In a situation where there is a French-speaking majority, a provision to use French would be very likely to assist that French-speaking majority. The operation of francization and the market could be expected to enhance francophone employment. That being the case, why should the law explicitly push francophone employment at the expense of everyone else?

In 1976, the separatist Parti Québécois (PQ) was first elected as government of Quebec. The new government at first favoured and then removed this contentious provision.[2] But the PQ introduced Bill 101, which contained some other inequities. One of the most notable was a section requiring that, in general, public commercial signs and posters be published in the French language *only*.[3] Again, there is an argument for the stipulation that such public communications be conveyed in French so that the French-speaking majority would be able to understand them. But why was it necessary to *restrict* such communications to French?

At the very least, therefore, this provision must be seen as an unwarranted encroachment on freedom of expression. But that's not all. It is also a form of cultural discrimination. It tells the Greeks, Italians, Jews, Portuguese, as well as the English that they cannot use their respective languages on commercial signs. The PQ government tried to redress the indignity that the French-Canadians had been suffering by inflicting a comparable indignity on everyone else. And what is most significant—this indignity contributed nothing to the legitimate protection of the French-Canadian majority.

There is some indication that this provision had a ludicrous, as well as a repressive, dimension. In the course of explaining Bill 101 to a special meeting of affected entrepreneurs, a government official pointed out that advertisements by way of door-to-door flyers must be in French only unless the occupant of the home specifically signs a card requesting another language. But, in such event, the card must be kept by the distributor to be shown on request to government inspectors.[4] Thus, those having the effrontery to distribute bilingual materials had better be careful to cover themselves.

For some business operations, the difficulties were compounded by the fact that their names do not readily translate into French. Since they cannot use both English and French, this could produce a substantial change of name. Consider, for example, the difficulty confronted by George's Steak House. The French language has no apostrophes. Among the suggestions that emerged at the above meeting were Grilladerie George or La Steak à George.[5] One of the business representatives asked how to handle the word "pizza". The response was, "if pizza has a French translation we'll find it".[6] Imagine what would become of the restaurant currently known as "Pizza Pizza"!

A sign maker asked the government officials whether the new law meant that he would no longer be able to sell English signs in Quebec. He was told that it would be permissible for him to sell such signs to clients outside Quebec. But, as for signs inside Quebec, as of a certain date, they would have to be in French only.[7] The sign maker replied, "then I'd better sell off all my English signs right away before I go bankrupt".[8]

To be fair, there were numbers of French-Canadian Québecois who urged a policy of solicitude regarding minority groups. Unfortunately, however, there were others who argued that the government had not gone far enough. The Conseil des Hommes d'Affaires Québecois, for example, proposed a ban on English subtitles in French movies and the suspension of operating permits for any firms that failed to comply with the requirements of the bill.[9] The vice-president of Les Isolants du Québec Inc. urged the government not to give in "one centimetre or even one millemetre. The biggest error you can make is not to hit hard enough."[10]

Certain sociologists who gathered data for the Quebec government's Office du Langue Française raised an even more alarming possibility. Perhaps, they suggested, the only way to achieve economic equality is to "appropriate" the better paying jobs for francophones.[11] As far as the Montreal chapter of the 145,000 member St. Jean Baptiste Society was concerned, anglophones who disagreed with the new language charter could always leave the province. In the words of that organization's brief, "an unhappy anglophone can always find asylum several kilometres to the west, and south of the border of Quebec".[12]

In situations such as this, political rhetoric can sometimes be as damaging as statutory enactments especially when the rhetoric comes from the cabinet minister in charge. In the case of Bill 101, the PQ government's chief spokesperson was its minister for cultural development, Dr. Camille Laurin. While Dr. Laurin frequently insisted that he and his colleagues were sensitive to the plight of minorities, his rhetoric often revealed a disquieting insensitivity.

On the rights of anglophones, for example, Laurin declared, "we are not trying to remove their right... we're simply reducing their privileges a little, much like a diet which leaves a person with the basics without endangering his health".[13] And then speaking more directly to the insecurity of the anglophone business community, Laurin noted how he would have liked to spare them. But he went on to remind his audience that the francophone community had known such insecurity "for a long time". He maintained that the kind of problems they were suffering can be healthy "it can bring about a healthy reaction like the one our own insecurity has provoked in us".[14]

This statement sounded more like vengeance for the francophones than solace for the anglophones. Don't worry, Laurin effectively said to the anglophones, if you suffer somewhat the way we have, you, like us, will be the better for it. It's not without significance to remember that these words of ostensible consolation were spoken by a psychiatrist.

Some people, of course, will find it hard to generate sympathy for the Anglo Saxon business interests which dominated Quebec life for so long. But the principles of human rights and civil liberties have to be applied to all, even the formerly powerful, without discrimination. To whatever extent the legitimate interests of the French-Canadian majority could be achieved without encroaching on the interests of the English minority, a democratic government would be duty-bound to follow such a course.

In any event, Dr. Laurin's insensitivity was directed also against smaller ethnic groups that had never exercised such power in Quebec. He reacted testily, for example, to a proposal made by the Fédération des Groupes Ethniques du Québec Inc. that there should be a right of appeal to the courts against the administrative decisions of the bureaucracy under the language bill.

> I find a trace of this distrust, this apprehension, in the certitude which the Fédération des Groupes Ethniques has that the civil servants will necessarily resort to unjust measures or to excesses in the application of the law under study.[15]

In response, a spokesperson for the federation accused the minister of double standards.

> We say the same thing as the representatives of the Stock Exchange said. We say the same thing as the [Quebec] Bar

said. When the Bar asked for [appeal to] the courts, it was taken as a proposal to be considered. When we ask for the same thing we are told: the ethnic groups don't trust the future civil servants. . . .[16]

Again, to be fair, it must be acknowledged that not all PQ representatives were guilty of comparable insensitivity. To be sure, the then Premier Lévesque frequently went out of his way to promote rapprochement with the various ethnic minorities. Nevertheless, Lévesque and his more sensitive colleagues must bear not only a political but also an ethical responsibility for the behaviour of Dr. Laurin. They gave him the job of selling the language legislation and they declined to rebuke or remove him when his rhetoric escalated. What is most disquieting is the idea that Laurin may have been reflecting the views of a significant sector of both the Parti Québécois and the Quebec community.

Unfortunately, there was a subsequent development in which key representatives of the Parti Québécois made even more contentious statements. Consider, for example, the comments of (now Premier) Lucien Bouchard, the party's spokesperson for the "Yes" side in the 1995 referendum campaign, and those of then PQ Premier Jacques Parizeau at the end of the campaign. Bouchard openly lamented the low birth rate of "white" francophones[17] and Parizeau blamed monied interests and the "ethnic" vote for the defeat of the "Yes" side.[18] Chilling manifestations of xenophobia.

I have already made the point that one of the most disconcerting aspects of the civil liberties infringements in bills 22 and 101 was their gratuitous character. Both government bills exceeded the legitimate goal of enabling the francophone population to function effectively in its own language. This conclusion can be reached on the basis of a strictly logical examination of what the bills contained. But it is strengthened immeasurably by an inquiry into the actual experience of the 1970s, an experience whose main features have continued.

In 1971, 46% of those questioned by the SORECOM opinion research firm reported they had encountered difficulties with using French at work. In 1979, the number of people reporting such difficulties had shrunk to 1%. In 1971, 70% of those questioned said that in restaurants and stores they had experienced trouble being served in French. By 1979, such complaints had dropped to below 5%.[19]

Sociological research conducted for the Quebec government's Office de la Langue Française revealed that, between 1971 and 1978, the number of francophones in the Quebec workforce rose by more than 450,000 while the number of non-francophones declined by more than 28,000. And, despite mythology about the state of French in the city of Montreal, a similar pattern occurred there. The number of francophones in the Montreal workforce increased by more than 84,000 and the number of non-francophones declined by more than 16,000.[20]

During this period, the aggregate income of francophones increased by 64.5% while the aggregate income of non-francophones rose by only 9.8%. Francophones acquired an additional 20,000 of the prestigious management and administrative jobs while non-francophones lost nearly 8000 such positions.[21]

On the basis of these dramatic and apparently irreversible trends, Quebec governments are hard put to demonstrate the need for a law that prohibits the use of any language but French on commercial signs, flyers, and catalogues. Indeed, in 1988, the Supreme Court of Canada ruled that the law unconstitutionally infringed freedom of expression.[22] Subsequently, however, the then Liberal government of Quebec invoked the "notwithstanding" clause of the Charter to protect this legislation against further judicial interference.[23] Despite the seemingly permanent changes in the status of the French language and the increased mobility of the francophone people, a non-separatist government said it was necessary to adopt the exceptional measure of excluding the operation of the Charter of Rights and Freedoms.

Remarkably, after five years, the invocation of the notwithstanding clause was allowed to expire, and successive Quebec governments have opted not to re-invoke it.[24] Unless it is re-invoked, however, it no longer applies. Thus, Quebec's language law could be constitutionally challenged once again. In the meantime, there has been a further refinement in this law. At last, a provision was adopted permitting languages other than French to accompany French on public signs and posters. Even so, however, French must be "markedly predominant," that is, at least twice as large as any other language.[25] And the government has been empowered, on its own, to create exceptions.[26] Hence, in addition to the vast number of circumstances in which French must prevail over other permissible languages, there are rare situations in which there may be exclusive use of other languages, some situations in which other languages might enjoy equal billing, and yet further situations in which French, once again, must be exclusive.[27]

While this development represents some liberalization, the issue remains: apart from the arguable need to require French as a way of ensuring that people can effectively function in French, what justification is there for this panoply of state intrusions on people's communications? Again, the experience fuels the argument.

In December of 1997, a gravestone-maker who serves the Jewish community received a letter from Quebec's language inspectors instructing him to change his sign or face prosecution. Although he used Hebrew and French letters on his sign, the Hebrew letters were slightly taller. Despite the Jewish character of his clientele, he was told that the French language must predominate.[28] The French population must be heartened to realize that the deference to French is extending even to Jewish cemeteries.

SECURING ABORTION RIGHTS

One issue that has long united feminists and civil libertarians is the right to perform and receive abortions. Both constituencies have generally been solid supporters of the "pro-choice" position. Conflicts have developed, however, over the appropriateness of using certain state powers to protect abortion rights.

In the first few years of the 1990s, both Ontario and British Columbia had New Democratic Party (NDP) governments that were committed to a progressive social democratic philosophy. Not surprisingly, both those governments were strongly pro-choice on the abortion question. An issue that tested them concerned the rights of their opponents from the "pro-life" movement. Anti-abortion activists had set up picket lines around abortion clinics and the homes of certain doctors who performed abortions. On many occasions, the picket line activity was marred by violence, obstruction, and a number of ugly incidents. Both NDP governments responded by invoking state power.

In Ontario, the government applied to the courts for an injunction to restrain what it saw as unacceptable picket line behaviour.[29] To the extent that the application focused on clearly unlawful acts such as assaults and obstructions, there might not have been a substantial controversy. But this injunction application went much further. It sought also to prohibit "insulting", "abusive", and "defamatory" language and indeed all picketing within 500 feet of the targeted premises.[30] The premises at issue included both the private residences of the doctors and the clinics where the operations were performed.

The significant factor in this strategy was the use of an anti-liberal mechanism by a social democratic government. After all, the social democratic and labour movements had fought for years against the use of injunctions to restrain labour picketing. In this situation, those same constituencies were attempting to use such a weapon against *their* adversaries. Indeed, there are real questions concerning the appropriateness of a government seeking an injunction in a dispute among private citizens. Normally, injunctions are considered civil remedies available to those who feel aggrieved to invoke against those who are injuring them.

Thus, if the government was going to act, why didn't it prosecute? After all, its injunction application accused the pickets of having "persistently counselled or committed acts of assault, mischief, intimidation, vandalism, or unlawful interference with persons or property".[31] These constitute allegations of criminal behaviour. To whatever extent such behaviour provokes a response from government, such response usually takes the form of a prosecution. But there was no indication that the government even attempted to prosecute for these picket line excesses. Indeed, if the government had adopted such a policy, much of the objectionable behaviour might have been brought under effective control. Prosecution can be a tough remedy.

But prosecution also has civil libertarian virtues. Among them is the panoply of safeguards available to those who are accused, including any available statutory defences. Unfortunately, such safeguards are not as available in injunction proceedings. Affidavits generally displace oral testimony. The injunction also tends to cast too wide a net. It operates not simply against people who have committed wrongs in the past but also against those who might do so in the future; not simply against those who are named in the injunction application who can come to court and defend themselves but also against those who may act merely with knowledge of the injunction's existence. Defendants are not simply subject to discernible penalties, as in criminal cases, or a calculable amount of damages, as in most civil cases. Rather, they are subject to the vastly enhanced contempt powers of the courts to fine and jail them.

This enormous potential for abuse materialized on many occasions during the century that the labour injunction was so readily used.[32] As a consequence of that experience, Ontario law was amended to provide that, before an injunction may be obtained in a labour dispute, there must be convincing evidence that, without it, the police would not be able to protect the public peace and the rights of the parties.[33] Yet, here we had the labour-supported New Democratic Party choosing this anti-liberal device without first exhausting—or even attempting—the normal processes of law enforcement.

To make matters worse, the government's application went well beyond what was necessary to achieve its legitimate objectives. For the purpose of this discussion, I will leave aside the issue of picketing private residences. Admittedly, that is a more contentious issue raising as it does possible infringements of personal privacy.

But what about the picketing of clinics where the actual operations were occurring? The terms of the government's proposed injunction were so broad that they could arguably have prohibited even silent, peaceful, information picketing within easy view of the abortion clinics. A restriction against physical obstruction is one thing; a ban on informational picketing is another thing entirely.

Of course, government representatives did point out that, if their injunction were granted, such informational picketing could occur beyond 500 feet from the targeted premises. But, to keep pickets that far away, is effectively to require telescopes to see them and mega-microphones to hear them. This situation proved to be a classic illustration of a comment I once made in a different context: "In Canada, we don't ban demonstrations; we re-route them".

And what are we to make of the government's attempt to prohibit language or gestures that are "insulting" or "abusive"? So long as such language falls short of threatening physical violence, it is not necessarily unlawful. Moreover, a restriction of this kind would also suffer from vagueness and incomprehensibility. At what point do unkind words become "insulting" or "abusive"? Imagine the impact of such a precedent on the picket lines of trade unionists, environmentalists, consumer boycotters, and aboriginal activists! And, as we imagine this impact, we must be aware of the irony that all those picketers would owe any such new restrictions to a pro-labour social democratic government.

The proposed prohibition against "defamatory" language was also defective. By and large, defamatory words are unlawful only in a civil sense. The problem with enjoining such language by injunction is the chilling effect that could be created for the kind of polemics that the abortion conflict inevitably produces. To what extent, for example, would epithets such as "sinner" or "baby-killer" be considered defamatory? Such a measure might have posed less difficulty if the government had attempted to curb a repetition of some particular expression that the pickets had already used. But to invoke the contempt power of the courts against allegedly defamatory language that has not yet been used is to threaten people with jail for what they *may* say in the heat of controversy—a situation hardly compatible with a viable free speech.

In saying all this, I acknowledge the possibility that, where health facilities are concerned, there is a case for picketing restrictions that would not be justified in other situations. As regards those seeking health care, it might be acceptable to protect them from some of the upsetting encounters that picket lines often produce. Even so, however, there remains no excuse for the *breadth* of the prohibitions that were being sought in this situation.

Fortunately, the Ontario Court of Justice proved to be more liberal about the rights of pickets than was the NDP government. The injunction that finally issued was much narrower than the one the government had sought. In short, a member of the judicial "establishment" turned out to be more liberal regarding the rights of protesters than was the party of the proletariat.[34]

While the Ontario New Democrats responded to the excesses of anti-abortion picketing with an injunction, their British Columbia counterparts also enacted legislation. The B.C. legislation effectively prohibits "any act of disapproval ... with respect to ... abortion services, by any means, including, ... graphic, verbal or written ..." within fifty metres of certain abortion clinics.[35] In short, anti-abortionists may not express their disapproval of abortion within half a football field of such abortion clinics.

Again, it's one thing to protect doctors and patients from physical obstruction; its another thing entirely to immunize them from social disapproval. Nor is it any answer to say, as some have, that the anti-abortion protesters can always express their views somewhere else. That's like telling labour strikers and consumer activists that they can picket anywhere but at the premises of the dispute. To re-route picket lines in this way is to transform freedom of communication into freedom of soliloquy. The pickets must have *some* access to those whose behaviour they are trying to influence. Of course, the protesters must not be so close as to create physical intimidation, but they should be close enough to convey ethical disapprobation. Without such an opportunity, their right of protest becomes quite impotent.

As an example of how excessive these restrictions might be, certain clinic staff members demanded that the police arrest some protesters for merely praying within a prohibited zone.[36] Under the terms of the B.C. law it appears that such praying may well be illegal. In this regard, consider a comment made by the then president of the British Columbia Civil Liberties Association:

> We also recommend that the police continue to use the admirable discretion they have shown in ignoring such symbolically political, but literally private actions as silent prayer in the restricted zones.[37]

This statement is tantamount to an acknowledgement that the B.C. law does, in fact, prohibit praying in the restricted zones. It is disappointing to see as stalwart a defender of civil liberties as the B.C. Civil Liberties Association (BCCLA) reduce its role to recommending wise police discretion. I would have thought, on the basis of its admirable record, that the BCCLA would vigorously criticize a law that was *capable* of suppressing the right to pray in such a situation.

Again, this is not necessarily to rule out some additional restrictions on picket line activity, in the case of a health facility, beyond what might be permissible elsewhere. Be that as it may, there can be no excuse for prohibiting such prayers within fifty metres of abortion clinics.

Consider the consequent paradox. With the support of a civil liberties organization, a left-wing, progressive government unduly curtails a freedom it usually defends—picketing. While the NDP government of British Columbia validly sought to protect the free choice of patients and doctors, it failed to adequately protect the free speech of protesters and pickets. An unfortunate development.

COMBATTING DISCRIMINATION

While it is not appropriate for government power to curb the discrimination that people practise in their private personal interactions, such power is properly invoked against the more serious forms of discrimination in public market transactions. Thus, those attempting to sell their goods and services on the public market are appropriate targets for legislation if they practise discrimination against potential and actual employees, customers, and tenants on grounds such as race, creed, ethnicity, sexual orientation, and gender. In this connection, every jurisdiction in Canada has enacted human rights laws that deal with such forms of discrimination. And every such jurisdiction has created a human rights commission to administer and enforce those laws. With minimal encroachments on liberty, these laws have achieved substantial increases in equity.

Not surprisingly, these governmental efforts have long enjoyed support from many sectors of the liberal constituency. Indeed, my previous organization of liberals and social democrats—the Labour Committee for Human Rights—made the attainment of such laws and the creation of such commissions a high priority in its race relations program. We conducted vigorous and spirited campaigns because we believed that well-administered human rights legislation would significantly promote equality and dignity throughout the country.

During the past few years, however, some new developments in the human rights field have begun to undermine the liberal foundations on which these laws and practices have been based. Certain human rights commissions have begun to take aim at discriminatory *speech*. There would have been little problem if such measures had been content to target speech that was part and parcel of discriminatory *acts*. Thus, it has long been regarded as unlawful for businesses to advertise that "no blacks need apply".

Unfortunately, however, these new measures have gone much further. They have attempted to restrict certain expressions of opinion. As we noted in the chapter on minorities, a section of the federal Human Rights Act purports to prohibit telecommunications that are "likely to expose" people to "hatred or contempt" on the grounds of race, creed, ethnicity, and so on.[38] With the aid of this provision, the Canadian Human Rights Commission took action against the hotline operated by the white supremacist Heritage Front[39] and the Internet website operated by Holocaust-denier Ernst Zundel.[40] We have also seen how the British Columbia Human Rights Commission used a comparable provision in that province's Human Rights Code against the anti-Jewish columns written by journalist Doug Collins.[41] Moreover, in the mid 1990s, hate speech was the theme of a conference organized by the Canadian Association of Statutory Human Rights Agencies (CASHRA).

To be sure, much of the impugned speech was pretty repugnant stuff. But it was also repugnant to use state censorship against such material. After all, one of the most fundamental or our society's values is freedom of speech. Moreover, as indicated in the minorities chapter, the particularly broad test in these statutes could readily be used against important political, historical, and social commentary.

One of the earliest assaults on free speech committed by a human rights commission in Canada occurred during 1980 in the province of Saskatchewan. That province's human rights legislation included a provision making it unlawful to ridicule people because of their "race, creed, religion, colour, sex, marital status, physical disability, age, nationality, ancestry or place of origin".[42] The Saskatchewan Human Rights Commission established a board of inquiry into a complaint involving a Saskatoon businessman who had posted a display in the window of his business premises. The display contained the reproduction of an angry letter he had written to the premier of the province in which he inveighed against the alleged incompetence of a government department. His last two sentences became the subject of the human rights complaint.

> I would highly recommend the government of this province hire the handicapped; the situation could only improve if they hired the mentally retarded too. Or is this being done already?[43]

A woman suffering from an epileptic condition became angered by the above sentences and filed a complaint under the Human Rights Code. In her opinion, the letter equated physical disability with incompetence.

While the board of inquiry acknowledged that the respondent "did not intend his statements to be interpreted as disparaging comments about the physically disabled", it found nevertheless that the display in the window had such an effect.[44] In the result, the board ordered the respondent to delete the two sentences in question from any copy of the letter which was displayed or published on his premises.[45]

Although I have no particular interest in defending the merits of this businessman's exhibit, I have a considerable interest in questioning the propriety of invoking state power to remove it from the window of his business premises. As the board of inquiry acknowledged, his display was not an attack on the disabled; it was an attack on the government. Moreover, it's hard to believe that his exhibit would have discouraged job applications or potential patronage from disabled people. The references to disability, however tasteless, were beside the main point he had to make.

Would the human rights commission have taken such action if the businessman's impugned statements had appeared on picket signs outside government offices rather than on a display in his window? After all, the relevant section of the Saskatchewan Human Rights Code applied to "any printed matter" which a person "controls". If the commission had taken such action, it would have become a general censor of certain material in bad taste.

In the case of the Ontario Human Rights Commission, the handling of some feminist initiated complaints creates further concern about freedom of expression. In 1993, a board of inquiry was established to hear the complaints of two women who alleged that certain convenience stores in Toronto were discriminating on the grounds of gender because they were offering for sale some allegedly pornographic magazines including *Playboy* and *Penthouse*. According to the complaint, the sale of these magazines created a "hostile environment for women".[46] It is important to note that no case of this kind could reach a board of inquiry without the approval of the Ontario Human Rights Commission. In order for the commission to recommend a board, it must believe that "the evidence warrants an inquiry".[47]

Consider the implications of the commission's action. According to the logic of this complaint, bookstores could run afoul of the Human Rights Code for selling *Oliver Twist* by Charles Dickens or *Satanic Verses* by Salman Rushdie. After all, Jewish customers might regard Dickens' characterization of Fagan as creating "a hostile environment" for Jews, and many Muslims have already complained about how Rushdie's "blasphemy" offends them.

Thus, the distribution of any material that someone in a protected group finds offensive could be banned in virtually any public place, including even libraries. The mere appearance of such material in such places could arguably make those settings "hostile" for someone. Apparently, the Ontario Human Rights Commission was prepared to have the Ontario Human Rights Code become the authority for pervasive censorship. (It should be pointed out that the issue here was not the public display of pornography; a Metro Toronto by-law already required such material to be concealed discreetly from general public view.)[48]

As an indication of the mentality that apparently influenced the Ontario Human Rights Commission at that time, I remember encountering one of its upper echelon officials at a banquet. When I told him that the commission's position in this case could logically support the forced removal of Salman Rushdie's *Satanic Verses* from libraries, his reply was nothing short of incredible. "How would you like it," he asked, "if libraries carried *Mein Kampf*?" Perish the thought that any libraries should make available a book of such historic importance!

I would have thought that the issue of discrimination concerns not *what* materials may be offered for distribution but *how* such transactions are facilitated. In short, the commission has no business vetting the contents of what the public may read, but it should address the behaviour of those who are disseminating the material to the public. On this basis, the commission should confine its scrutiny to how prospective patrons are treated. If a prospective patron receives rudeness, neglect, or outright refusal because of gender (or race, creed, ethnicity, etc.), that could involve discrimination and therefore be the business of the commission and the code. By going as far as it did in this case, the Ontario Human Rights Commission embarked on a very dangerous course. In doing so, it placed itself in opposition to some of our society's most fundamental liberal values.

Through their involvement in such cases, human rights commissions are not only threatening liberal values, they are also weakening the important parts of their own mandates. The case involving the convenience stores was launched in 1988 and the board of inquiry did not convene until 1993. Moreover, the commission indicated that it expected almost fifty days of hearings.[49] In view of the fact that agencies like human rights commissions have limited resources, we can only wonder what impact all of this is having on the commission's ability to deal with complaints of discrimination in jobs and housing—if I may say so, the important areas involving discrimination. And we can only wonder how these cases are exacerbating the well-publicized backlog of unaddressed discrimination complaints. As one who organized campaigns during the early 1960s for the creation of the Ontario Human Rights Commission, I lament this change in the commission's direction.

Yet, at around the same time as the Ontario Human Rights Commission was processing this case and the CASHRA conference was devoting itself to hate speech, there were reports that complaints of job discrimination were comprising more than 70% of certain commission caseloads. Moreover, we had learned from the previous census (mentioned earlier) of the disproportionately high unemployment experienced by the black community. At around this time also, the Canadian Civil Liberties Association disclosed its survey (also mentioned earlier) showing how few aboriginal people were employed by retail establishments in communities with large aboriginal populations.

Of course, little of this material had the sensational quality associated with hate mongers. Yet the covert inequities connected with these employment practices were likely causing much more harm to minorities than the overt invective used by hate mongers. In my view, therefore, human rights commissions should be less concerned about radicals who hate than about moderates who don't hire.

Government efforts at combatting discrimination have been at odds with still other liberal principles. Consider again the case of employment equity. In an earlier chapter, I acknowledged the positive features of this concept and registered against some of its negative features. For now, it will suffice to identify certain governmental pronouncements and then to consider how such pronouncements may have affected public opinion.

Again, I draw my examples from the record of Ontario's NDP government. In an attempt to sell a program of employment equity for Ontario's police forces, one of the NDP's solicitors general said that the "ultimate objective" is for every police department to have an equal number of men and women.[50]

Once more, we are dealing here with a progressive government sincerely attempting to counteract discrimination. Nevertheless, we have to ask why it was necessary or even desirable to push the principle as far as the above statement implies. Is there any reason to believe that, in today's society, such a large number of women would actually want to be police officers? If not, why must we change their minds? We should, of course, try to broaden their perspective: help them appreciate that policing could be a viable option and then ensure that they do not face discrimination. But why anything beyond that?

The Ontario New Democrats were dedicated, nonetheless, to the idea that workplaces should, as soon as possible, reflect the mix in the population outside. Such an objective could logically propel you to use numerical goals as a way of playing "catch-up". It was, therefore, seen as permissible—and, in some respects, even as desirable—to actually prefer some of the disadvantaged groups such as women and racial minorities at the expense of white males. Workplaces that preferred such groups could more quickly achieve a mix that reflects the population outside.

Thus, the Ontario government itself published an employment advertisement that seemed to discourage applications from white males. When asked about this apparent discrimination against white males, NDP Management Board Chairperson Brian Charleton reportedly said, "their time will come ... there is only a problem until the workforce is in balance".[51] While Charleton argued that such job restrictions are only temporary, he also acknowledged that temporary could mean fifteen years—in many situations, much of a person's working life.

What a message this must have conveyed to the public at large and to white males in particular! According to this official representative of the Ontario government, it had become acceptable to sacrifice fairness for white males in order to achieve the government's concept of employment equity. Small wonder that there was a backlash against this governmental attempt to redress discrimination. And small wonder that the Conservatives who replaced the New Democrats in government acted so swiftly against the entire employment equity law. Moreover, it was so unnecessary. As indicated earlier, substantial progress for women and racial minorities never required such extreme government measures.

The casualty of the NDP rejection of liberal principles was the whole idea of a vigorous government effort against discrimination. This was a classic case of left-wing confusion fuelling right-wing reaction.

Notes

[1] Bill 22, *Official Language Act,* S.Q. 1974, c. 6, section 29(b).
[2] Mark Rosenstein, "'Bill 101' and Affirmative Action: Francization vs. Francophonization" in *Meredith Memorial Lectures, 1976-77, Language Regulation of Business,* (McGill University, Faculty of Law, 1978), p. 151-159.
[3] Bill 101, *The Charter of the French Language,* R.S.Q., c. C-11, sections 1 and 58.
[4] "Quebec sign painters get the message: French-only is the new rule" *Globe and Mail,* (16 May 1978) 1, 2.
[5] Ibid.

6   Ibid.
7   Ibid.
8   Ibid.
9   "PQ's language bill not harsh enough, business group says" *Globe and Mail*, (23 June 23 1977).
10 "Dr. Laurin prescribes 'diet' for anglophones" *Globe and Mail*, (3 August 1977).
11 "William Johnson in Quebec: A tour de force of shoddy thinking" *Globe and Mail*, (23 August 1979).
12 "Baptiste society wants English curbs tougher" *Toronto Star*, (17 June 1977).
13 "Laurin wins few converts to his 'diet' for English" *Toronto Star*, (3 May 1977).
14 "Dr. Laurin prescribes 'diet' for anglophones." *Globe and Mail*, (3 August 1977).
15 "The Laurin way: Treat anglophone witnesses as if their views are to be refuted." *Globe and Mail*, July 8, 1977, p. 9.
16 Ibid.
17 "Bouchard remarks spark outcry" *Globe and Mail*, (16 October 1995) A1.
18 "Parizeau promises to 'exact revenge' for sovereigntist loss" *Globe and Mail*, (31 October 1995) A1.
19 "William Johnson in Quebec: Quebec stereotype dies hards" *Globe and Mail*, (6 September 1979).
20 "William Johnson in Quebec: A tour de force of shoddy thinking" *Globe and Mail*, (23 August 1979).
21 Ibid.
22 *Ford v. A.G. Quebec*, [1988] 2 S.C.R. 712, 54 D.L.R. (4th) 577.
23 *Canadian Press*, (20 December 1988).
24 "PQ Government suffers embarassing setback" by Jack Branswell, *Canadian Press*, (23 November 1996).
25 *Canadian Press*, (22 April 1996).
26 "The Charter of the French Language" R.S.Q. c.C-11 S.58, cited in "The Language of Business and Commerce in Quebec". Office de la langue française publication, May 1995.
27 Ibid., s.58.
28 "Language Police crackdown on Hebrew sign maker" *Canadian Press*, (16 December 1997).
29 Attorney General of Ontario, "Notice of motion" in *A.G. Ontario v. Dieleman* 20 O.R. (3d) [1994] 229; "Why completely ban in-the-street protests against abortion" *Globe and Mail*, (21 April 1993) A7; "Ontario seeks court order" *Globe and Mail*, (20 April 1993); "New abortion battle pits individual vs. free speech" *Toronto Star*, (21 April 1993) A19.
30 Ibid.

[31] Ibid.
[32] For a history see A. Carrothers, *Report of a Study on the Labour Injunction in Ontario,* vol. 1 (Toronto: Ontario Department of Labour, 1966).
[33] *Ontario Judicature Act,* R.S.O. 1980, c. 223, s. 20(3).
[34] *A.G. Ontario v. Dieleman.* 20 O.R. (3d) [1994] 229.
[35] Bill 48, *Access to Abortion Services Act,* S.B.C. 1995, section 2(1)(b).
[36] *R. v. Lewis* (8 October 1996), Vancouver Registry No. CC960120 (B.C.S.C.); "Prayer and the police" *The Province (Vancouver),* (20 September 1995) A30; "Score one for the pro-lifers: a provincial judge punctures the NDP's 'bubble-zone' law" *British Columbia Report,* v. 7(23), (5 February 1996) 16-28.
[37] "On Bubble Zones: A Reconsideration by Kay Stockholder" *The Democratic Commitment,* (October 1995) 14.
[38] *Canadian Human Rights Act,* R.S.C. 1985, c. H-6, s.13(1).
[39] *Canada (Canadian Human Rights Commission) v. French* [1996] F.C.J.
[40] "Genocide viewed as fable: Witness" *Canadian Press,* (16 October 1997).
[41] "Freedom's just another word . . . " *Saturday Night,* (November 1997) 59.
[42] Saskatchewan Human Rights Code, 1979, section 14.
[43] *McKinlay v. Dial Agencies* (1980) 1 C.H.R.r. D/48 (Saskatchewan Human Rights Commission, Board of Inquiry), paragraph 2132 [hereinafter *McKinlay*].
[44] *McKinlay,* para. 2136, 2140.
[45] *McKinlay,* para. 2141.
[46] Ontario Human Rights Commission Complaints Nos. 60-023, 60-024, 60-025, (the "Findlay" complaints), 60-026, 60-028 (the "McKay" complaints); "The centrefold war: Do skin magazines violate human rights?" *MacLean's,* (10 May 1993) 14,16; "Human rights commission drops suit against store" *Hamilton Spectator,* (13 May 1996) A5; "Adult magazine complaint killed" *Toronto Sun,* (11 May 1996) 22.
[47] *Ontario Human Rights Code,* R.S.O. 1990, section 36(1).
[48] The municipality of Metropolitan Toronto, By-Law No. 51-86, To regulate the display of adult books and videotapes in the Metropolitan Toronto, Schedule 1, section 2.
[49] The centrefold war: Do skin magazines violate human rights? *MacLean's,* (10 May 1993) 14,16.
[50] "Hire more women, police told" *Toronto Star,* (11 April 1991)A1; "Ontario boosts hiring quotas" *Montreal Gazette,* (11 April 1991) A15.
[51] "Job policy bars whites for years, NDP admits" *Toronto Star,* (10 November 1993) A9.

CHAPTER SIX

Among Theoreticians

No discussion of the new anti-liberals would be adequate without an examination of the contributions that are being made by at least some of their theoreticians. What makes these theoreticians particularly noteworthy is the way they combine a strong sense of egalitarianism with an open hostility to liberalism.

While the ensuing comments do not attempt to address all of the theoreticians in this category, they do deal with some of the more influential ones. For convenience, I have divided my treatment of this subject by issues rather than by individuals.

ON PREFERENTIAL TREATMENT

One of the most controversial issues in North America today concerns a subject that has arisen a few times in this book—the extent to which employers and educational institutions may be required, or even allowed, to make decisions on the basis of categories such as race and gender. Programs known as "affirmative action" in the United States and "employment equity" in Canada have been increasingly adopted and criticized. Such programs have been praised for enhancing the state of equality and scorned for promoting quotas and "reverse discrimination". While affirmative action and employment equity contain a number of differences, one of the common features is an attempt to produce numerical results: the hiring, promotion, and admission of specified numbers of people who have traditionally suffered discrimination, for example, blacks, aboriginals, and women.

Stanley Fish, an English professor and critic from Duke University in the United States, has mounted an ambitious counter-attack on those who criticize the idea of preferential treatment. Quoting from George Bush's 1991 address to the United Nations on the Zionism equals racism resolution, Fish castigates those who have equated the Jewish priorities of Zionist Israel with the Aryan priorities of Nazi Germany. What such equivalence ignores, according to Fish, "is the *historical* difference between them, the difference between a program of genocide and the determination of those who escaped it to establish a community in which they would be the makers, not the victims, of the laws" [emphasis in original].[1]

Fish applies this logic to a defence of preferential treatment. In his view, it is downright "bizarre" to equate the black-centred preferential treatment of today's affirmative action with the white-centred preferential treatment that preceded it. After all, according to Fish, the hostility of the whites stems not from any wrong done to them "but from the wrongs [they have been] able 'to *inflict*'" [emphasis in original].[2] Fish admonishes his readers to observe the distinction "between the ideological hostility of the oppressor and the experience-based hostility of those who have been oppressed".[3] In Fish's view, "reverse racism is a cogent description of affirmative action only if one considers the virus of racism to be morally and medically indistinguishable from the therapy we apply to it".[4]

I have no trouble agreeing that Fish is quite right to repudiate such equivalence mongering among the critics of affirmative action. But the question remains: So what? Why is it necessary to equate these forms of preferential treatment in order to criticize them? Why can't we acknowledge that one form is worse than the other but insist nevertheless that they are *both* wrong? The answer, of course, is obvious. Professor Fish has devoted his considerable intellectual energy to the demolition of a straw man that he himself has created.

In my view, racial and gender discrimination in the employment and educational market is presumptively unacceptable, even if it enures to the benefit of women and ethnic minorities instead of white males. People should not generally be made to suffer such a disability simply because of their colour or gender.

Indeed, Fish himself acknowledges the inadequacy of the equivalence argument. He attempts to rebut the notion that "if it was wrong to treat blacks unfairly, it is wrong to give blacks preference and thereby treat whites unfairly".[5] At this point, he tries to demonstrate why it will not suffice simply to prohibit traditional discrimination.

> When the deck is stacked against you in more ways than you can even count, it is small consolation to hear that you are now free to enter the game and take your chances.[6]

On this score, Fish's analysis is valid. Generations of discrimination have created a most unlevel playing field. The mechanisms for assessing candidates are often racially and culturally biased. To leave blacks, for example, at the mercy of such mechanisms is to load the dice against them. To be sure, it is not enough simply to outlaw discrimination. Special measures are required in order to redress the imbalance of the tilted playing field.

But Fish's conclusions don't necessarily follow from his analysis. The recognition that some additional measures are called for does not make the impugned preferential treatment one of those measures. Such preferential treatment and the status quo do not exhaust the range of options. Consider, for example, devising ever more effective "head start" programs as a way of providing disadvantaged people with some of the skills that they will need in order to compete more equitably. Why not also consider improving upon the various testing mechanisms that are used to assess people's ability? If we are able to recognize cultural bias, we should be able to reduce its influence. Even if we are not able to render such instruments completely bias-free, we should be able at least to make significant improvements in that direction.

Moreover, there are substantial numbers of non-whites and women who are well qualified to compete on the job market and in our educational institutions. There is no reason to doubt the ability of such people to pass many of the merit tests that are now in use. If significant numbers of them don't get available jobs and aren't admitted to centres of higher learning, there will be strong grounds to suspect inadequate recruitment efforts, intentional discrimination, and/or systemic impediments.

Such barriers can be reduced without preferential treatment. There is no reason why employers and educational institutions could not be encouraged (through the lure of incentives) or required (through the threat of sanctions) to engage in vigorous outreach efforts so that the target groups will learn of available opportunities and be induced to apply for them. With a little effort—on the part of voluntary organizations and government agencies—systemic barriers can be increasingly detected and corrected.

Moreover, it might even be appropriate, in certain situations, to set numerical goals that employers and educational institutions would have to achieve unless they provided a reasonable explanation for their failure to do so. As long as the numerical goal is chosen fairly (a reasonable assessment of how many would be selected if vigorous recruitment efforts were made, fair eligibility requirements were adopted, and there was no discrimination in the ultimate selections), such a system could well be acceptable. As indicated in the chapter on the feminists, sensible numerical goals would look more to the pool of qualified people than to the community at large. They would also avoid playing "catch-up". It should be clear that numerical goals of this kind would not amount to preferential treatment. They would be a device to enforce a policy of no discrimination.

On the basis of all these factors, there is good reason to believe that women and racial minorities can make significant progress without preferential treatment.

To his credit, Fish squarely faces the impact of preferential treatment on the innocent white male. "Why me?" is the question that invariably greets those programs that would discriminate against white males in favour of women and racial minorities. Why, it is asked, should innocent white males who have never participated in discrimination against women and racial minorities find themselves the victims of such discrimination?

Recalling a situation in which he was bypassed because he is a white male, Fish contends, "it was obvious that the policy was not directed at me... nor was it directed even at persons of my race and gender".[7] Since the policy was driven by other considerations, Fish concluded that the situation was not "unfair". But why should it matter whether the policy was directed at Fish himself or white males in general?

Years ago, it was discovered that the city of Toronto had only two non-white firefighters out of more than 1100. When the situation was investigated, it was learned that fire-fighting jobs were never publicly posted. The personnel officials would interview from only one source: a file of applicants that had been accumulating over the years. Since the choices were made according to how long the applications had been on file, the system effectively precluded hiring recently arrived immigrants, despite their qualifications. Since the policy was not directed at any one immigrant in particular or at immigrants in general, would Fish therefore have excused it? Not bloody likely. Indeed, this is exactly what is considered a "systemic impediment": a policy, otherwise unreasonable, that has the effect, if not necessarily the intent, of discriminating against certain categories of people.

If white males are bypassed, despite superior qualifications, in favour of women and racial minorities, that too would represent discrimination. The fact that you are shut out with a smile, instead of a growl, would hardly compensate for the loss of an important economic opportunity. In both cases, the system deliberately subordinates considerations of ability to those of ethnicity, gender, or date of application. Again, these two types of systemic discrimination are not equal, but, presumptively at least, they are both wrong.

In saying these things, I must acknowledge that the evaluation of ability is a complex subject. Conceivably, for example, an aboriginal graduate with B+ grades who endured the poverty of a reserve or the alienation of a city might be considered more qualified than certain graduates with A grades who studied in more advantageous surroundings. The aboriginal could well claim something special for fortitude and character. In short, I can agree with Fish that traditional assessment methods are not the only—or the best—way to evaluate applicants. But I disagree with the notion that considerations of merit—if validly assessed—should be so readily trumped by considerations of race and gender.

None of this is necessarily to discount the acceptability of some forms of preferential treatment in certain exceptional circumstances. It is, however, to rule out preferential treatment as a standard operating policy.

ON FREEDOM OF SPEECH

Since the late 1970s, Professor Kathleen Mahoney, of the law faculty at the University of Calgary, has been a prominent champion of feminist causes in Canada. She has argued in court, written scholarly articles, and addressed many public conferences. One of her favourite targets is the liberal conception of free speech. At the core of her convictions on the subject are the following propositions:

> ... an egalitarian society may be impossible to achieve when the dissemination of racist ideas is permitted.[8]

> ... if true equality is to be achieved between male and female persons, society must guard against misogynist materials....⁹

Thus, Professor Mahoney would have our democratic society impose restrictions on free speech in order to hasten the day when equality will be enjoyed. On the basis of such a rationale, I cannot avoid wondering how extensively Mahoney would support the use of censorship. In this regard, she assures us that "the law is not intended to prohibit anything but extreme forms of speech".[10] She points out that "mere contentious, irritating, and annoying speech" would not be caught by the current prohibitions.[11]

It appears that, despite her ideology, Professor Mahoney may have retained some of the liberalism she tries so hard to eschew. If the purpose of censorship is to remove potential obstacles on the road to equality, I would have thought that she should have set her sights on some of the veiled, less extreme forms of racist and sexist expression. After all, Zundel, Keegstra, the Heritage Front, and the Aryan Nations have a combined appeal that hovers near zero.

In today's society, the veiled code word has much more impact than does naked invective. Thus, on racial and ethnic matters, the more effective anti-egalitarians talk not about the inferiority of racial minorities but rather about the potential disharmony caused by Third World immigration. On gender matters, mainstream commercials depicting women as nitwits are likely to produce more misogyny than will peripheral pornography. If nothing else, the commercials will be seen by substantially more people. Thus, if Mahoney were consistent, the allegedly narrow range of our restrictions on speech should be a cause for lamentation not commendation.

Along with many others, Professor Mahoney cites the example of Hitler's Third Reich as evidence of how hate propaganda can "drive reason from the field".[12] In view of such experiences, she endorses the opinion of those who have declared that "absolute faith in a rational, free marketplace of ideas [is] not only wrong-headed, but irresponsible"[13]. But not all critics of our anti-hate laws have faith in a "rational, free marketplace of ideas", let alone absolute faith in such a phenomenon. In my case, for example, I don't have such great faith in the marketplace; I simply have much *less* faith in the law enforcement authorities. In the Canada of today and the foreseeable future, I think the government will likely cause more damage to legitimate dissenters than Canadian neo-Nazis will cause to ethnic minorities.

As indicated in an earlier chapter, our unavoidably vague anti-hate laws invariably wind up being invoked against legitimate dissenters. This has already happened to anti-American protesters, French-Canadian nationalists, anti-apartheid activists, a pro-Zionist book, and a Jewish leader, among others. At the same time, the neo-Nazi movement in this country is minuscule and universally condemned. Even though the marketplace of ideas and pressures is far from completely rational, it has nevertheless been relatively immune to extremist invective. That is why, in pragmatic fashion, I balance the competing risks against the anti-hate law. Even if Professor Mahoney might prefer to debate with absolutists or those with naïve beliefs about the human condition, it would be useful for her to devote more energy to the arguments of her more pragmatic opponents.

One of the leading ideologists of the pro-censorship movement among feminists in North America is Michigan law professor Catharine MacKinnon. Together with writer Andrea Dworkin, MacKinnon has campaigned vigorously for legislation against pornography and hate speech. At one point, this dynamic duo actually drafted a municipal ordinance creating a right of civil lawsuit for "victims" of pornographic material.[14]

For purposes of assessing MacKinnon's theory, I use her aptly entitled book, *Only Words*. At the heart of the book's analysis is the following declaration:

> Speech acts .... In the context of social inequality, so-called speech can be an exercise of power ....[15]

And, in explaining the above ordinance, she says, "Pornography is not restricted here because of what it says. It is restricted through what it does."[16] According to Professor MacKinnon, the very production of pornography is abusive to women. In order to make sex pictures, she alleges that "women are hurt and penetrated, tied and gagged, undressed and genitally spread and sprayed with lacquer ...."[17] In order to further drive home her point that pornography consists of action, not just expression, MacKinnon asks an intriguing question: If blacks were lynched in order to make photographs of lynchings, would such material thereby become protected speech?[18]

Like Mahoney, MacKinnon might prefer to debate with her more doctrinaire opponents. But I, for one, am a congenital non-absolutist. As such, I am not prepared to defend genuine snuff films. I quote from my 1988 book, *When Freedoms Collide*:

> To the extent that certain particularly repugnant crimes are committed for the purpose of titillating a potential audience or readership, there is an arguable case for a legal prohibition of the resulting film or literature.[19]

It is important to note that this exception on my free speech position requires the commission of certain actual crimes. To whatever extent adult actors *consent* to play scenes in which they are bound, gagged, penetrated etc, it is likely that no such actual crime would have been committed. To whatever extent Professor MacKinnon denies the possibility of such consent, her position is based on ideological fiat rather than empirical evidence. It is not appropriate to patronize those adult women who participate in pornographic productions. That's why, in my view, the test should involve legal criminality. On this issue, MacKinnon's comments are quite remarkable.

> Paying the woman to appear to resist and then surrender does not make the sex consensual: it makes pornography an arm of prostitution.[20]

But stigmatizing a transaction as prostitution does not necessarily deprive it of voluntariness. If, on the other hand, MacKinnon insists that all prostitution is coerced, she must equally insist that she knows better than do the prostitutes themselves. The same goes for those who play in porn films. While it appears that some of them have been forced into these roles, others have adamantly argued that such is not the case.[21] This creates a dilemma for Professor MacKinnon. How can she simultaneously demand that society respect these women and then deny them the most elementary components of her own respect—acceptance of the proposition that they are more expert than she about how they should live?

In addition to her bitterness about what she says happens to women during the production of pornography, MacKinnon is upset about what supposedly happens to everyone from the consumption of pornography. As she says, "it is what it takes to make [pornography] and what happens through its use that are the problem".[22] In response to the argument that pornography is speech entitled to the free speech protection of the First Amendment to the U.S. Constitution,[23] MacKinnon argues that "it is not the ideas in pornography that assault women: men do, men who are made, changed, and impelled by it".[24]

In this regard, she draws considerable sustenance from the decision of the Supreme Court of Canada, mentioned in an earlier chapter, that upheld the constitutional validity of the Criminal Code section on obscenity. As noted, the Court in that case said, "if true equality between male and female persons is to be achieved, we cannot ignore the threat to equality resulting from exposure to audiences of certain types of violent and degrading material".[25]

Thus, according to MacKinnon, pornography is not simply speech. It is also a form of action that discriminates against women. Men exposed to it are considered more likely to assault women and, under its influence, people in general are believed to be attitudinally more disposed to devalue women. Professor MacKinnon goes to considerable lengths to demonstrate that some forms of speech are not simply speech. The words "you don't belong here" in furtherance of racial segregation are indeed more than speech.[26] They effectuate the act of racial exclusion. Similarly, MacKinnon argues, pornography acts as well as speaks. In her words, "It is used as sex. It therefore is sex." And, in even more colourful language, she says, "It is not ideas [men] are ejaculating over. Try arguing with an orgasm sometime".[27]

Whoever said that freedom of expression is concerned only with ideas? What about emotions? Much expression is designed, for example, simply to make people laugh. Is it fair, therefore, to say that since such comedy is used to produce laughter, it *is* laughter? And might we then deny such comedy the protection of free speech with the explanation, "try arguing with laughter sometime"? Moreover, upon seeing a magnificent painting or hearing a beautiful symphony, many people respond, as the artist and composer intended, with awe and even tears. If ideas were not involved, would these aesthetic expressions be deprived of constitutional protection under a MacKinnon regime? Would she say, "try arguing with awe or tears sometime"?

Professor MacKinnon's analysis addresses the traditional American distinction between speech and acts. According to one theory of the First Amendment, free speech is a virtual absolute, but acts can more readily be restricted. Thus, those Americans who favour restrictions will often go out of their way to demonstrate that what they seek to restrict is not speech at all but acts.

Of course, MacKinnon is right that speech "acts" as well as it "says". If it didn't, it would not be the potent instrument that the theory of democracy intends it to be. As far as political matters are concerned, speech is the method for redressing people's grievances; it is the democratic system's substitute for violence as the way to resolve disputes. As for aesthetic matters, "speech" or "expression" is the vehicle of self-fulfilment for both producers and consumers. It serves, therefore, as a source of potential enrichment. MacKinnon is also right, however, that the acts performed by speech can be negative as well as positive and harmful as well as helpful.

But, even if we were to accept this part of Professor MacKinnon's analysis, where would it get her? She would still find it necessary to formulate a prohibition for a legal enactment. At this point, her intellectual edifice would be likely to crumble. As I have indicated in the earlier "feminists" chapter and elsewhere,[28] there seems to be no way to define pornography, for legal purposes, so as to avoid a significant risk of nailing a considerable amount of material apart from what is targeted. Human language is not sufficiently precise to make such distinctions.

MacKinnon's ordinance, for example, refers to the "graphic sexually explicit subordination of women through pictures and/or words that also includes . . . women [being] presented in postures or positions of sexual submission . . .".[29] The court judgment nullifying her ordinance as unconstitutional contains several examples of mainstream films that could be caught by this definition.[30] The brief of the American Civil Liberties Union in that case expands on these examples with numerous works of classical art and literature.[31] The problem, in a nutshell, is that legitimate material must be able to portray evil as well as virtue. Thus, legitimate speech itself is likely to be imperilled by MacKinnon-influenced attempts to catch pornographic "discrimination".

In discussing the comparable issue raised by the censorship of hate propaganda, MacKinnon pays homage to the Supreme Court of Canada. In her view, "because the Canadian law of equality . . . knows the difference between disadvantaged groups and advantaged ones, it is less worried about the misfiring of restrictions against the powerless and more concerned about having nothing to fire against abuses of power by the powerful".[32] Presumably, by the "Canadian law of equality", MacKinnon means the Canadian courts. In view of our courts' traditional and current conservatism on so many matters, MacKinnon's faith emerges as uncharacteristically naïve.

In any event, even if the "law" knows the difference between advantaged and disadvantaged groups, do the *police*? In the real world, their judgment about what constitutes "hatred" or "obscenity" is critical. Since they usually decide which persons to investigate and frequently which ones to prosecute, they are in a position to intimidate. The ultimate acquittal of a person, improperly targeted, will rarely redress the damage that such police activity may have caused. Moreover, the absence of censorship does not mean that there is "nothing to fire against abuses by the powerful".[33] As indicated in both the feminist and minorities chapters, there are all sorts of other weapons available.

Thus, the question that must be faced is whether the magnitude of harm caused by pornography is sufficiently great to warrant the inevitable risks to legitimate material. In this regard, MacKinnon repeatedly discusses the dangers to women when men are exposed to pornography. Yet the most eminent of the relevant social psychologists, such as Edward Donnerstein, have warned that such conclusions are not valid.[34] Even the Supreme Court of Canada, whose obscenity decision she seems to admire, has acknowledged the virtual impossibility of demonstrating a causal relationship between anti-social deeds and exposure to pornographic material.[35]

Professor Donnerstein has suggested, however, a possible connection between porn and anti-social *attitudes*. But, in the absence of imminent peril to life or limb, censorship is a dangerous course for a democracy. Attitudes stand to be influenced by expression on many subjects. On this basis—as indicated in the chapter on the feminists—the Communist Manifesto, the Bible, and the television news would all be potential candidates for suppression. Moreover, attitude formation is a slow process, allowing time for longer term measures—also mentioned in the feminist chapter—to counteract the possible messages in pornography.

In commenting on the "equal rights" section of the Fourteenth Amendment to the U.S. Constitution, Professor MacKinnon says that "Fourteenth Amendment equality . . . has grown as if equality could be achieved while the First Amendment protected the speech of inequality . . . and without considering equal access to speech as central . . .".[36] Thus, according to her, ". . . there is a relation . . . between the use of the word 'nigger' and the fact that a disproportionate number of children who go to bed hungry every night are African-American . . .".[37]

Acknowledging as she must that American society is a long distance from the equality she seeks, MacKinnon seems to believe that legal restrictions on the speech of inequality will help significantly to pave the road to equality. But, as noted, experience reveals that a law of this kind—unless it protected only ethnic minorities and other disadvantaged people as such—will be used, at some point, against those it was designed to benefit. Remember, for example, how Canada's anti-hate law was used against a film supporting South Africa's Nelson Mandela.

Thus, Professor MacKinnon's problem is whether, on balance, the cause of greater equality is advanced or set back by such restrictions on free speech. Since her proposed restrictions will likely inflict some burdens on the very groups she wants to protect, she will be commensurately driven to depend on the good faith of the existing power structure. As indicated earlier, equality seekers are better off relying more on their own ability to agitate and less on the power structure's willingness to deliver.

Perhaps, then, Professor MacKinnon would favour more selective restrictions on speech. There is a suggestion of this in her discussion of the proposed Nazi march in Skokie, Illinois. MacKinnon objects to how "the position of those with less power is equated with the position of those with more power".[38] But, as between the handful of Nazis who were universally reviled and the large Jewish community that was quite well-respected, it is palpably inaccurate to say that the Jews of Skokie had less power than did the Nazi interlopers.

If it doesn't help to resolve these conflicts on the basis of redressing advantages in power, is there some other way MacKinnon can get the outcome she wants? In this regard, she points out that if one party is promoting inequality and another is resisting it, the constitutional preference for equality should be taken into consideration.[39] Perhaps this might work in some situations, but, in so many others, it would likely exacerbate, rather than illuminate, the issues in contention.

Between the free speech of "pro-life" and that of "pro-choice" advocates, which is pro-equality? The women's movement has long argued that reproductive choice is an important way to advance the equality of women in our society. But their "pro-life" opponents can make a comparable claim for their position. After all, numbers of them believe that fetuses should enjoy a level of equality with other members of the human species. How, then, is the principle of equality supposed to determine which speech ought to enjoy priority?

As for the rights of aboriginal people, there are many conflicts between native communities who seek self-governing powers and others who believe that aboriginals should be fully integrated into Canadian society. The former group would argue that self-government is the most effective way to redress the accumulated inequalities indigenous people have suffered for generations; the latter group denounces such an approach as special treatment—the very antithesis of equality.

All of these positions make egalitarian claims. According to liberal theory, they should all fight it out in the political marketplace and ultimately the public will choose. It is not clear to me how far Catharine MacKinnon would be prepared to muzzle some of these views in order to reduce impediments on the road to equality. If she is not prepared to do so, I am not sure—on the basis of her arguments—why not. If she is prepared to do so, she would wind up denying the public access to important policy debates.

Perhaps Professor MacKinnon would reserve these censorship powers for the most extreme forms of inequality expression? She did cite, for example, the Ku Klux Klan and the proposed Nazi march in Skokie. To be sure, both of those groups advocate an extreme and even monstrous form of inequality. But, as indicated, a law that does not name such groups in particular would likely wind up—despite its intent—muzzling other expression as well. General terminology is not uncommonly stretched to apply beyond what its drafters intend. That's what explains our earlier example of how the Canadian anti-hate law was used against the film supporting Nelson Mandela.

In fairness, MacKinnon has commented somewhat on this problem. I am not sure, however, that her comments contribute significant clarity.

> This does not mean that ideas to the contrary [of equality] cannot be debated or expressed. It should mean, however, that social inferiority cannot be imposed through any means including expressive ones.[40]

By and large, I don't think any ideas as such should be imposed. But what constitutes impermissible imposition? If psychology Professor Phillipe Rushton conducts research and reaches the conclusion that some racial groups have more or less intellectual capacity than do others, should he be free to teach these things in his classes? Does that constitute "imposing" social inferiority? And, if Catharine MacKinnon reaches the opposite conclusion, with or without doing the research, to what extent should she be free to say so in her classes?

Should the academic proponents of equality be entitled to special privileges not accorded to their adversaries? In this regard, MacKinnon has explicitly criticized the notion that, for First Amendment purposes, there is no such thing as a false idea.[41] She sees no reason why the advocacy of inferiority should be accorded the same free speech rights as the advocacy of equality. Since the ideal of equality is entrenched in both American and Canadian constitutions, she sees no reason to deny equality advocates a free speech advantage.

I have already spelled out why a sensible free speech regime should not confer such advantages. In so many situations, it will be no easy task to determine just who the equality advocates are—pro-life or pro-choice advocates, those in favour of more autonomy for aboriginal communities or those against it? Moreover, the attempt to prohibit the speech of inequality can wind up harassing those it was designed to protect, as our anti-hate and obscenity laws have done.

Despite the theoretical appeal of MacKinnon's position, it remains beset with all kinds of practical difficulties. When some such speech is to be restricted or even denigrated, someone must be empowered to do the restricting or denigrating. Who is worthy of such trust? In general, the liberal prefers to let members of the public make these decisions for themselves. We liberals are uneasy about trusting the authorities to screen out what people may see and hear. As indicated, it's not that we necessarily have boundless faith in the people; it's that we have much less faith in the authorities. Thus, for all her professed commitment to equality, there is an unavoidable elitism in Catharine MacKinnon's position. She is prepared to repose a great amount of trust in the authorities to vet what is available to the people. Thus, the very logic of her analysis propels her to a profoundly anti-egalitarian outcome.

ON "POLITICAL CORRECTNESS"

At the Queen's law faculty in Kingston, Ontario, Professor Sheila McIntyre has distinguished herself as an outspoken feminist scholar. In a lengthy journal article, she took on the critics of "political correctness" (PC).[42] A wide-ranging essay, it contains some telling problems.

In the course of launching into her vigorous counter-attack, Professor McIntyre makes the following statement:

> The anti-PC movement—and it is a movement—is clearly an organized campaign arising out of the coalition of right-wing interests that currently dominate American political and economic institutions.[43]

While acknowledging that the charges of the anti-PC movement are not *"per se* suspect because of their right-wing origins",[44] Professor McIntyre insists that "for all its defence of timeless, universal truths and disinterested scholarship", anti-PC literature "is *political* in origin and aspiration . . ." [emphasis in original].[45]

Let us concede, for a moment, the validity of Professor McIntyre's two main points: the anti-PC movement is essentially a right-wing phenomenon and it is essentially political in character. What follows? Absolutely nothing. The fact that the origin of a position may be right-wing does not necessarily make it wrong. Conversely, the fact that the Communist Party campaigned to prevent the execution of atom spies Julius and Ethel Rosenberg did not make it right to electrocute them. A position must be accepted or rejected on its own merits, not on the basis of its proponents or opponents.

Similarly, nothing follows from labelling the anti-PC movement as "political". Even if the label were warranted, it could then be argued that support for more campus free speech is politically preferable to support for less of it. Again, the position would have to rise or fall on its merits rather than on the justification for the label.

In any event, the growing opposition to "political correctness" cannot be so readily pigeon-holed as essentially a front for society's right-wing powerholders. The opposition to "political correctness" also contains a number of liberal and left-wing voices. In the United States, for example, among PC's fiercest critics is the American Civil Liberties Union, hardly a right-wing mouthpiece.[46] In Canada, the opponents of PC include Pierre Berton, June Callwood, and the Canadian Civil Liberties Association—all long-time battlers against various right-wing orthodoxies.[47]

Near the inception of her analysis, Professor McIntyre makes a strategically astute concession: "My stance, then, is no more neutral than that of the anti-PC lobby."[48] After rebuking her adversaries for hiding their interests behind a veil of presumed objectivity, she wisely confesses her own partisanship. The concern, however, is not with the neutrality of her critique, but with its validity. At key points, the validity of her analysis is undermined by some questionable arguments.

In the course of admonishing those university professors and administrators for what she believes is their inauthentic support for equality, Professor McIntyre makes the following statement:

> If one genuinely supports equality, one does not react with outraged denial, resentment or a bruised ego when advised one's conduct has been experienced as oppressive by members of a class one recognizes as oppressed; one changes.[49]

To whatever extent professors or administrators are *civilly* advised that their behaviour is inappropraite, of course they should react with commensurate civility. But suppose the "advice" is communicated in abusive tones? If that were to happen, I see no reason why the belief in equality should inhibit an indignant response. Moreover, there is no reason for professors or administrators to change their behaviour unless such behaviour, in the circumstances, was really inappropriate. (In saying this I acknowledge two possibilities: (1) in the context of the frank exchange of views that universities should encourage, hurt is sometimes unavoidable; and (2) where hurt can be avoided, a considerate person, consistent with the requirements of integrity, might well make changes to avoid *needlessly* hurting someone else—whether or not that "someone else" belongs to an oppressed class).

Professor McIntyre's comment appears to be based upon an assumption that support for equality means agreeing with the members of oppressed classes whenever they collide with the members of other classes. If that is the case, her statement would become a mandate for patronizing the members of oppressed classes. In my view, such a posture would represent the very negation of what equality requires.

One of McIntyre's recurring charges is that the anti-PC literature creates a "false symmetry between powerholders and those they disempower".[50] Such observations would appear to provide the rationale for a denial of support to those academics who are accused of racism, sexism, and homophobia.

> By insisting that calling someone a racist is as intimidating, chilling of speech, and harmful to education as being racist, racism becomes an idea whose articulation becomes dissent.[51]

Here, Professor McIntyre is essentially saying that by equating the accusation of racism with its practice, the anti-PC people are conferring upon racism the status of legitimate dissent. Significantly, this hierarchy of evils fails to include the *false* accusations of racism. I have no reason to believe that Professor McIntyre would deny that false accusations are, in fact, made. But I see no point in attempting to rank such evils. The requirements of fundamental justice, as well as the interests of education, require condemnation of both racism and false accusations of racism.

And what are we to make of McIntyre's warning that, from this allegedly wrongful symmetry, racism becomes effectively legitimated? Is she implying here that *no* expression of racism warrants the protections of academic freedom? For all of the reasons spelled out in the chapter on professors and students, such a position has the ability to undermine university life.

At a number of points, Professor McIntyre rightly challenges a key criticism made by what she calls the "anti-PC camp". The following rather crisply expresses her objection:

> In the discourse on political correctness . . . describing remarks or policies as racist or sexist amounts to censorship, critique amounts to propaganda and dissent and protest amount to intimidation or totalitarianism. . . .[52]

It is true, as McIntyre alleges here, that a number of PC critics accuse PCers of "censorship" simply because of the latter's vehement polemics. Yet, no principle of intellectual freedom protects members of the campus community from criticism, even from harsh and biting criticism. On the contrary, intellectual freedom encourages all campus members to speak their minds. This includes students from historically oppressed classes as well as professors from historically privileged classes. To whatever extent such professors reject criticism of themselves as censorship, they are engaging in the self-serving exercise that McIntyre describes. More to the point, they are trying to discourage the very intellectual freedom they claim to be defending.

But if that were all the anti-PC camp was complaining about, Professor McIntyre's analysis would be virtually incontestable. But that's not all there is to it. The charges of censorship go beyond name-calling. They include threats of discipline and discharge. Such threats do amount to a form of censorship. And that does infringe the requirements of intellectual freedom. Moreover, as indicated in the chapter on professors and students, these job-related threats have not been confined to behaviour that is gratuitously abusive. These threats have been applied to expressions of opinion on important subjects. Even if some students are offended by such expressions of opinion, that is not sufficient reason for anyone to face explusion from the campus community.

In this regard, McIntyre draws consolation from her claim that "even in their own accounts, none of the men named as casualties of the PC menace has been disciplined, let alone discharged".[53] Moreover, according to her, "only one tenure denial is even cited and it dates from the 1970s ...".[54]

Even apart from the fact that Professor McIntyre's piece was published before cases such as those of UNB Professor Yaqzan, the paramount problem with her argument here is the measure it uses: discipline, discharge, denial of tenure. At this point, she neglects even to mention how the mere threat of such sanctions can muzzle legitimate expression. Freedom of speech suffers not only when sanctions are actually imposed but also when they are seriously threatened. You cannot enjoy a viable free speech when the fear of legal or employment reprisals makes you look over your shoulder. McIntyre's discourse is remarkably insensitive to this phenomenon. Elsewhere in her piece, she consoles herself further with the concessions made by her opponents.

> All the complaints about 'silencing', 'thought control', and 'censorship' ... concede that the marketplace of ideas cannot ensure that the truth will prevail if words are backed by social or political power. But this is what the [pro-political correctness side] has been saying all along, for instance, in

supporting the criminalization of hate propaganda and in tracking how rights are unequally established, distributed, exercised, and enforced.[55]

Even if the marketplace of ideas cannot ensure the triumph of truth, it does not follow that hate propaganda should be criminalized. Moreover, why assume that such criminalization will contribute significantly to the triumph of truth even in the area of its jurisdiction? As already indicated, the anti-hate law has been used against a wide variety of constituencies that don't bear the slightest resemblance to racist hate mongers. Indeed, it has been invoked even against the very minorities it was supposed to protect.

Thus, the issue is: In a world without guarantees, where shall we repose our trust? In the law enforcement authorities or in the marketplace of pressures and ideas? For all of the reasons I have advanced in both this chapter and the one on minorities, I believe it is wiser, at this point in Canadian history, to trust the marketplace rather than the government—or at least, to mistrust the marketplace less than the government. In any event, the question is not answered by merely assuming—without substantiation—that the government is the more reliable guarantor of truth.

Toward the end of her essay, Professor McIntyre attacks the idea that "historically subordinated groups ... are expected to pay a price—their own equality, dignity, expression—for the [freedom of expression] of that larger society whose history is marked by securing privilege at their expense".[56] This statement seriously misconceives the free speech argument. To opt for the priority of free speech in such circumstances does not involve any neglect of the "subordinated groups". On the contrary, it is to insist that such groups are beneficiaries of a vigorous free speech. They have enjoyed the greatest amount of progress at those times when both the universities and society in general protected a wide right to dissent. Moreover, as indicated earlier, the subordinated groups have too frequently been the victims of the very restrictions on speech that had been originally conceived for their protection. Unfortunately, Professor McIntyre's article fails to address this point.

ON "SMALL—L" LIBERALISM

Among theoreticians, some particularly provocative opposition to liberalism is expressed by certain writers who are ardent champions of Israel and the Jews. In these circles, the departure from liberal values is not just a matter of growing proclivity, it's a matter of conscious philosophy. Consider, for example, the influential American Jewish magazine *Commentary*. The editors openly proclaim that their position is neo-conservative—they have even dropped the neo—and they are highly critical of political liberalism.

In Canada, one of the most noteworthy representatives of this conservative development in Jewish intellectual life is Ruth R. Wisse, professor of Yiddish and English literature at McGill and Harvard universities. Professor Wisse has written frequently for *Commentary* and has also appeared in *The New Republic*. Fortified by a compelling writing style, she is a highly respected scholar and commentator on Jewish and Israeli issues. In her recent book, *If I Am Not For Myself... The Liberal Betrayal of the Jews*, Professor Wisse alleges that devotion to liberal ideals is responsible for undermining vital Jewish interests.[57] Among other things, she sees modern liberalism as eroding the kind of political will that is needed to combat anti-semitism and to ensure the survival of Israel.

The heart of her position is philosophical. Professor Wisse argues that the defeat of anti-semitism "requires . . . a temporary sacrifice of the liberal optimism upon which the whole of democracy is founded".[58] As anti-semitism grows, she sees it forcing "a choice between defense of Jews on the one hand and faith in the essential moderating reasonableness of human nature on the other".[59]

As intriguing as this argument may be, it's grounded largely in intellectual quicksand. Since when has democracy been based on such an optimistic view of human nature? Every democracy contains checks and balances among competing centres of power. In the United States, for example, a constitutional bill of rights endows the courts with the power to strike down laws enacted by majority-elected legislatures. This will happen when such laws are seen as infringing fundamental freedoms. But, even in the United Kingdom, which believes in parliamentary sovereignty, the judicial power to interpret and apply the law acts as a check against parliamentary power. I would have thought that these separations of power reflect anything but optimism. In fact, they reflect a deep-seated distrust of human nature. The admonitions of Ruth Wisse to the contrary notwithstanding, one of the most pervasive assumptions of the democratic system is that *no* one can be trusted with a large concentration of power.

Thus, what is very much at issue in Professor Wisse's analysis are fundamental misconceptions of the liberal philosophy. She says, "liberals believe in progress and in the progressive improvement of human society".[60] If there are any people—liberal or otherwise—who, after living through the horrors of the twentieth century, still believe in the inevitability of progress, they would indeed be the mush-heads that Professor Wisse implies they are. In fact, however, liberalism never believed that progress would necessarily happen; liberalism believed simply that progress could happen. The difference, of course, is considerable.

Admittedly, she acknowledges the phenomenon she calls "the conditional or skeptical liberal" who responds with tough-mindedness to uncomfortable realities.[61] But this concession is contained in essentially one sentence. She focuses her attention on what she calls "the liberal fundamentalist" who prefers to deny the existence of the uncomfortable realities.[62] In this regard, she talks about how certain kinds of misconduct in the world require "liberal optimism" to suspend its belief "that the world *is* liberal" [emphasis in original].[63] Again, I cannot deny that there are some liberals who suffer from such delusions about the world. But large numbers—I believe even most—of them do not believe that the world *is* so liberal; indeed, their efforts are especially designed to *make* it so.

The proof of the philosophical pudding is in the historical eating. The battles that liberals have so vigorously waged against all forms of social injustice testify to their acknowledgement of evil in the human condition. When liberals "sat in" at lunch counters in the southern United States, they were confronting what they regarded as the evil of racial segregation. When liberals such as auto workers' leader Walter Reuther "sat down" in auto plants at Flint, Michigan, they were confronting the evil of exploitative capitalism. And when liberals such as Emile Zola went to bat for the Jewish Alfred Dreyfus, they were confronting the evil of anti-semitism.

Moreover, by engaging in confrontation tactics like "sit-ins" and "sit-downs", these earlier generations of liberals showed their unwillingness to "trust in rationality" (Professor Wisse's words) to win their victories.[64] Since they didn't harbour naïve notions about human nature, they knew that rational argument would not suffice; they needed to use unpleasant pressure as a key instrument of persuasion. Perhaps some liberals have been paralyzed by their fantasies about the human condition, but large numbers of them have been quite invulnerable to the charge.

Professor Wisse goes on to repeat a familiar theme: liberals have been too soft on Communism. Here are some of her words on the subject:

> Why, in particular, did the liberal community in North America continue to waltz to what the American writer Vivian Gornick called "the romance of Communism" long after the music had choked on the blood of 60,000,000 of its own subjects?[65]

Again, an eloquently expressed statement. Again, however, a flawed statement of the facts. Admittedly, there were many liberals who were once genuinely guilty of these allegations, but that group has significantly dwindled over the years. In any event, how can Professor Wisse ignore or belittle the scores of liberals who have long been in the vanguard of the struggle against Soviet Communism? Her book fails to mention the fact that, in the years immediately following the Second World War, large numbers of American liberals went on the offensive against the international Communist movement. Indeed, such liberals have supported the policy of "containment" against Communist expansion since that anti-Communist policy was conceived in the 1940s.[66] Her book fails to mention such liberal U.S. senators as Hubert Humphrey, Henry Jackson, and Paul Douglas, to name just a few, who were both champions of civil rights and the welfare state on the one hand and tough-minded cold warriors on the other hand. She also neglects to mention the leading twentieth-century American liberal intellectual John Dewey who went to the political barricades as long ago as the 1930s to protest the atrocities of Stalinism. In doing so, Dewey was supported by such eminent anti-Communist liberals as Horace Kallen and socialist leader Norman Thomas.[67]

Moreover, Professor Wisse makes no mention of the leftish liberal leaders of the American labour movement who, in the 1940s, purged the Communist-dominated unions from the American Federation of Labour

(AFL) and the Congress of Industrial Organizations (CIO). An account of the role played by some of their Canadian counterparts is described in Cameron Smith's book on the Lewis family, which provides details of how the socialist David Lewis and his allies in the socialist and labour movements fought to wrest control of the Canadian labour unions from the Communist Party.[68] All of these events preceded the collapse of Soviet and east European Communism by decades.

The same is no less true of America's long-standing commitment to Israel. In general, the liberal community has been associated with the bipartisan, pro-Israeli posture of the United States for the last fifty years. And, for the most part, the liberals have continued this support. Among the few names that Wisse mentions as anti-Israel Jews is the linguist, Professor Noam Chomsky.[69] But few of those who are generally regarded as liberals would consider Chomsky to be one of their number. Moreover, I suspect that he too would disavow the label.

Finally, Professor Wisse goes so far as to disparage the attempt to defend Jewish interests on the basis of universalist principles. Noting how certain Jewish human rights activists "wish to transcend parochialism by defending the rights of all people everywhere", she contends that their argument "overlooks just one detail—the opportunity the Jew-hater will find in each new general principle to exclude from it his designated enemy".[70] To illustrate her case, she describes how a lecture series on human rights at the McGill Faculty of Law was distorted by a proposal that it include a lecture on "Israel's abuse of the rights of Palestinian Arabs".[71] The following is the lesson that Wisse extracts from this experience:

> Thus can a general principle like "human rights" serve the double purpose of furthering anti-Jewish propaganda while depriving Jews of one of their moral props.... the only way to overcome it is to resist the seductive temptations of the universalist illusion and to engage in the defense of that very particularity against which the ideology of anti-semitism has always been at war.[72]

At this point, Professor Wisse's position becomes incomprehensible. In view of the fact that, in North America and the world, Jews are a small minority, they will usually need allies in order to effectively counteract anti-semitism. Indeed, Wisse acknowledges this earlier when she says that anti-semitism "cannot be cured without the intervention of Gentiles...".[73] Unless Jews appeal to general human rights principles, why should non-Jews assist them? If anti-semitism is simply a particularity involving anti-semites and Jews, there is no reason for non-Jews to become involved in it. In the final analysis, Professor Wisse prescribes a recipe for defeat.

The surest way to win allies is to persuade them that the values and interests they share with Jews are also threatened by anti-semitism. Inevitably, this means appealing to the very liberal values that Professor Wisse impugns. But, to invoke them in the defence of Jews requires a recognition that they can also be invoked against Jews. For a minority as small as the Jews, the values of liberalism provide the best hope for creating the kind of coalitions that are needed to defang the anti-semites. But the exercise means that the Jews as well must submit their behaviour to the single standard scrutiny of liberal values.

There is no principle of liberalism that denies to any constituency the ethical right to fight like hell for its own interests. But liberalism does require that this fight be conducted on the basis of universal principles applicable to everyone. In this regard, Ruth Wisse and those who share her philosophy would effectively undermine the best interests of all, including those of the Jews.

Stanley Fish carries his critique of liberalism far beyond the particularist interests that engage Ruth Wisse here. But, like Ruth Wisse, he focuses his attack squarely on the liberal philosophy. Indeed, Stanley Fish makes no bones about it. He openly declares that "the structure of liberal thought ... is my target...".[74] Fish sees his role as one of debunking the liberal claims to objectivity. According to him, "the liberal strategy is to devise (or attempt to devise) procedural mechanisms that are neutral with respect to point of view and therefore can serve to frame partisan debates in a nonpartisan manner".[75] Fish argues, however, that such nonpartisanship is impossible. For Fish, there is no disinterested objective truth that stands above the battle; all positions are political and very much part of the battle. In commenting on some of the current campus controversies, Fish has said, "debates between opposing parties can never be characterized as debates between political correctness and something else, but between competing versions of political correctness."[76]

Fish's attack goes to the very roots of liberalism. "Reason is a political entity, and never more so than when its claim is to have transcended politics."[77] Then, he moves in for the kill, "liberalism cannot finally claim to be different from its competitors", he argues, because, no less than others, liberalism depends upon faith.[78] In the case of liberalism, the faith at issue is placed in reason. Thus, as far as Fish is concerned, the clash between liberalism and fundamentalism, for example, is a clash between two faiths with incompatible first principles, in their case, "empirical verification and biblical inerrancy."[79] He argues that not only do fundamentalists not subscribe to argument and evidence as the best way to resolve differences, "they stigmatize [argument and evidence] as the diabolical tools of godless humanism."[80]

The moment that the methods of reason are denuded of their special claims to objectivity, they can no longer be invoked as authority to resolve disputes. Indeed, according to Fish, conflicts could no longer be thought of as being waged "between fairness and bias but between the sense of fairness that follows from one form of bias . . . and the sense of fairness that follows from another".[81]

Thus, it would seem to follow that since complete objectivity is impossible, complete subjectivity is permissible. But Professor Fish balks at the notion that his position must amount to relativism. At this point, I find his argument incoherent. I quote him again:

> It is true that there is nowhere to go, no locus of judgment to which disputants can appeal for an authoritative announcement. But this doesn't mean that they must throw up their hands or toss the dice; it means that they must argue, thrash it out, present bodies of evidence to one another and to relevant audiences, try to change one another's mind. To be sure, the process is not guided by an unchallengeable authority, but authority, not unchallengeable but temporarily regnant, is what is fashioned in the course of it. That is to say, authority does not *preside* over the debate from a position outside it, but is the prize for which the debaters vie. [emphasis in original][82]

How in the world can a sensible debate be conducted unless there is some criterion (or criteria) against which the contending positions can be measured? Moreover, I cannot, for the life of me, understand Fish's point that this authority is the "prize for which the debaters vie" rather than the standard by which they measure their respective positions. Without such a standard—no matter how non-absolute and temporary it may be—debate is nothing but meaningless noise. Elsewhere, Fish seems to acknowledge this when he says: "If you propose to examine and assess assumptions, what will you examine and assess them *with*? And the answer is that you will examine and assess them with forms of thought that themselves rest on underlying assumptions" [emphasis in original].[83] The implication is clear: at some point, everything we believe in is dependent upon some assumption or value judgment that cannot be rationally sustained. Must we, then, give up the quest for objectivity and neutrality? Is liberalism simply a different—albeit more subtle—form of fundamentalism?

Despite his considerable sophistication, I think that Professor Fish is wrong—profoundly wrong. Granted, there is no perfect objectivity. But there are degrees of imperfect objectivity. In short, some positions are more objective than others. In saying this, I acknowledge the non-rational component of all our value judgments. In this, Fish is right. To whatever extent any of us are pushed to spell out our assumptions, we will inevitably articulate some that we cannot justify in rational terms. The claim to greater objectivity grows out of the extent to which those affected by a particular problem or situation harbour *shared* interests or values. Since problems are solved one at a time rather than all at once, there is no need for an infinite regression to first principles. We live in the middle of history and not at the beginning. Thus, we already have a very substantial number of shared values.

As soon as we can identify a shared interest or value, we can employ reason to help us discover a solution that, *more than others*, serves this interest or value. That is what a liberal means by objective validity—a proposed solution that is more inter-subjectively valid than the alternatives.

There is no need to attribute absoluteness or even transcendence to the shared interest or value against which we measure our proposed solutions. To use Fish's words, that barometer value is "temporarily regnant". It derives its exalted status from the fact that it is the common ingredient to those who will be affected by the problem at hand. As soon as the problem changes, that common value becomes, like other values, subject to challenge and modification. But, even if that common value might be challengeable in another situation, it is not challengeable in *this* one. Again, our values are subject to challenge one at a time, not all at once. On this basis, liberals are enabled, without recourse to absolutes, to make respectable claims that some positions are more objectively valid than are others.

Thus, even if all positions may be tainted with politics, they are not all equally so in every situation. Some criterion of measurement would be able to stand above the fray by virtue of the shared reverence for it in that situation. And, while it may be forced to relinquish its throne in another situation, it is quite entitled to enjoy this superiority in the meantime. None of this means that numerical might is the equivalent of ethical right. Invariably there will be situations in which minority positions will more validly fulfill shared interests than will majority positions. Thus, it is possible to lose politically and still be right morally.

As far as reason is concerned, Fish rightly remarks that it always serves some other end or interest. But, so long as the interest it serves is shared by all who are affected by the problem, reason can help to illuminate the most workable—or, in this sense, most objective—of possible solutions.

What, then, shall we make of Fish's claim that liberalism is really no different from its competitors? Just as fundamentalism might require faith in God, liberalism requires faith in reason. Are these faiths, as Fish implies, equally irrational?

In order to obey God's will, we must first know what it is. This necessitates reliance upon a revelation from God to one or more humans. But humans are, as they say, only human. How can we be satisfied that the human recipient of a claimed revelation could discern that the communicant at the other end was God? How can a mere human being recognize God? Moreover, how can we be so sure that the purported recipient got the message straight? Could there not have been a "not" that the recipient may have missed?

All this requires that we repose a hefty chunk of faith not in God, but in some human or humans who claim to have encountered Him. But what justifies reposing so much faith in mere humans? After all, God, the Bible, and science all agree that human beings are finite, limited, and imperfect. Thus, even if God is always right, humans could nevertheless be wrong. This means, therefore, that they could also be wrong with respect to having been at the other end of a "revelation". Some have responded to this argument by insisting that God would ensure the integrity of the encounter. To say this, however, is to claim some knowledge of God. But, in the absence of a revelation, how could we finite mortals presume to attribute any characteristics to God?

This raises the problem of multiple and competing claims to revelation. After all, Abraham, Moses, and Jesus are not the only figures in history who have made such claims. Numbers of mass murderers and torturers have also explained their activity on the basis of Divine revelation. How do we separate the authentic claims from those of the charlatans and lunatics?

The one thing we cannot do is base our judgments on any knowledge of God's character. How can we finite mortals presume to tie God to our notions of right and wrong? Thus, we cannot dismiss a revelation claim simply because it produced a command to do what we regard as evil. It is profoundly self-contradictory to judge the ultimate by a more ultimate standard. In short, our knowledge of right and wrong comes from God and not the other way around. This means that the only way we can distinguish the genuine from the phony revelation claims is through faith. Unavoidably, however, that faith must be reposed in one or more finite humans.

There is another problem connected to the phenomenon of Divine-human communication. God's commands (or commandments) should, by virtue of their source, be regarded as absolute. That means they should not be subject to human criticism, challenge, or correction. But humans, by virtue of their finiteness, must avoid attributing absoluteness to their beliefs. As indicated, even if God must be right, they may still be wrong. Thus, they must ever be willing to subject their beliefs to question, challenge, and correction. How is it possible to regard the very same command (or commandment) as being both immune and subject to challenge at one and the same time?

Some people have answered this dilemma by insisting that faith is not rational and, therefore, cannot be judged by rational standards. This reply is more cute than right. Religious believers are no more exempt than is anyone else from certain requirements of reason. At the very least, believers must avoid contradiction. To the extent that they contradict themselves, they are talking gibberish. This does not mean that their faith is wrong, but it does mean that their explication of it must be wrong. Even religious people are not entitled to say it is and it isn't about the same thing, in the same way, at the same time. To the extent that they purport to do so, it is clear that they are making a mistake.

In short, I contend that religious believers are entitled to be extra-rational, that is, they may operate outside of reason. But they are not entitled to be contra-rational, that is, they may not contravene the requirements of reason. In my view, the doctrine of revelation propels the religious believer into the position of contravenor. This does not disprove the existence of God; it simply disentitles humans from asserting any knowledge of God. Without such knowledge, God, as the embodiment of perfection, becomes operationally irrelevant to human moral judgment.

Even if it is not possible to justify faith in reason on a rational basis, such faith, at worst, is extra-rational; it does not contravene rationality. Unlike the situation with revelation, faith in reason does not lead to hopeless contradictions.

There is another reason for adherence to reason. It is the one faculty that both fundamentalists and liberals can—and do—share. Indeed, it is the faculty that makes it possible for people of different philosophies to co-exist. In this respect, Fish is wrong in his characterization of fundamentalists as people who stigmatize argument and evidence "as the diabolical tools of godless humanism". That description of fundamentalist thinking is derived from Fish's imagination, not from the circumstances of everyday life.

Fundamentalists might ultimately revere revelation as the central truth, but in the meantime, they, like everyone else, use reason in order to cope with the vicissitudes of everyday life. Like liberals, they want to raise healthy children in a safe environment. Like liberals, they believe in kindness, consideration, charity, and good sportsmanship. Even if they would attribute those beliefs ultimately to God, they nevertheless share such beliefs with liberals and most other members of our society. These are the common values that enable reason to do its work of pointing the way to those policies, laws, and measures that are most likely to make such values operational. To the extent that both fundamentalists and liberals prefer to live rather than to die, to co-exist rather than to not exist, and indeed, to the extent that fundamentalists and liberals share a plethora of interests and values—reason is the most reliable instrument for everyone.

Suppose, however, that some might prefer, for example, destruction to existence. How, Fish might ask, can liberals claim that the desire to go on living is more objectively valid than the alternative? The answer is: they can't. But that doesn't mean that the liberals lose. For liberals, there is no *a priori* preference for life over death under any and all circumstances. Indeed, there may be some extreme circumstances in which the risk of death might be preferable to certain kinds of life. But this is a conclusion that, to a liberal, would only be justified if it best accorded with the shared interests and values of those who would be affected.

If fundamentalists opt for death over life and base it on anything other than the best way to fulfil the shared interests and values of those affected, they would likely be invoking—or making deductions from—a claimed revelation. And, at that stage, their position is likely to become enmired in the contradictions referred to above.

For all of these reasons, I believe that Stanley Fish—despite his sophistication—has wrongly attacked the fundamental principles of liberalism. In doing so, he has strengthened the hand of the traditional conservative and reactionary forces in society that have been seeking, for more than two centuries, to discredit the legacy of the Enlightenment.

Notes

[1] Fish, Stanley, *There's No Such Thing As Free Speech*, (New York: Oxford University Press, 1944), 60 (hereinafter Fish).
[2] Fish, p.61.
[3] Ibid.
[4] Ibid.
[5] Fish, p. 62.
[6] Ibid.
[7] Fish, p. 67.
[8] Kathleen Mahoney, "Language as Violence v. Freedom of Expression: Canadian and American Perspectives on Group Defamation" (1988/89) 37/2 *Buffalo Law Review* 337 at p. 345 (hereinafter Mahoney).
[9] Mahoney, p. 348.
[10] Mahoney, p. 350.
[11] Ibid.
[12] Ibid.
[13] Ibid.
[14] Catharine A. MacKinnon, *Only Words*, (Cambridge, MA: Harvard University Press, 1996), 121 note 32 (hereinafter MacKinnon).

15 MacKinnon, pp. 30-31.
16 MacKinnon, p. 23.
17 MacKinnon, p. 15.
18 MacKniion, p. 34.
19 A. Alan Borovoy, *When Freedoms Collide*, (Toronto: Lester & Orpen Dennys, 1988) 64.
20 MacKinnon, p. 28.
21 Wendy McElroy. *A Woman's Right to Pornography*, (New York: St. Martin's Press, 1995), 104-109.
22 MacKinnon, p. 15.
23 U.S. Constitution, First Amendment:

> Congress shall make no law respecting an establishment of religion, or prohibiting the free exercise thereof; or abridging the freedom of speech or of the press; or the right of the people peaceably to assemble, and to petition the government for a redress of grievances.

24 MacKinnon, p. 15.
25 MacKinnon, p. 101 quoting from the case of *R* v. *Butler* [1992] 89 D.L.R. (4th) 449 at 479.
26 MacKinnon, p. 13.
27 MacKinnon, p. 17.
28 Borovoy, pp. 53-66.
29 MacKinnon, p.121-2, note 32.
30 *American Booksellers Association Inc.* v. *Hudnut*, 771 F.2d 323 (1985) at 330.
31 Brief of the American Civil Liberties Union and the Indiana Civil Liberties Union, *Amici Curiae*, submitted to the United States District Court, Southern District of Indiana, Indianapolis Division, June 22, 1984.
32 MacKinnon, p.103.
33 Ibid.
34 Donnerstein, Edward, "Aggressive Erotica and Violence against Women," *Journal of Personality and Social Psychology*, Vol. 39 (1980), pp. 269-77.
35 *R.* v. *Butler*, [1992] 1 S.C.R. 452 at 501.
36 MacKinnon, p. 72.

U.S. Constitution, Fourteenth Amendment, section 1:

> All persons born or naturalized in the United States, and subject to the jurisdiction thereof, are citizens of the United States and of the State wherein they reside. No State shall make or enforce any law which shall abridge the privileges

or immunities of citizens of the United States; nor shall any State deprive any person of life, liberty or property, without due process of law; nor deny to any person within its jurisdiction the equal protection of the laws.

37 MacKinnon, p. 74.
38 MacKinnon, p. 105.
39 MacKinnon, pp. 106-110.
40 MacKinnon, p. 106.
41 Ibid.
42 McIntyre, Sheila, "Backlash Against Equality: The 'Tyranny' of the Politically Correct" (1993) 38/1 *McGill Law Journal* 1 (hereinafter McIntyre).
43 McIntyre, p. 7.
44 Ibid.
45 Ibid.
46 See the ACLU Policy on Free Speech and Bias on College Campuses, summarized on the ACLU webpage at http://www.aclu.org.
47 "Why muzzle tenured profs and campus rags" Pierre Berton in the *Toronto Star*, (4 December 1993); "Tangled dealings at Dalhousie" June Callwood in the *Toronto Star*, (24 January 1985) M8; "Reeking herring in swimming pool distracts from real abuse cases" June Callwood in the *Toronto Star*, (12 April 1989) A2; see, for example, the following letters from the Canadian Civil Liberties Association: March 28, 1991 to Terry Grier, President, Ryerson Polytechnical Institute re: anti-harassment policy; November 12, 1991 to Dr. J. Dimond, Secretary of Governing Council, University of Toronto re: anti-harassment policy.
48 McIntyre, p.25.
49 McIntyre, p.21.
50 McIntyre, p. 54.
51 McIntyre, p. 55.
52 McIntyre, p. 58.
53 McIntyre, p. 53.
54 Ibid.
55 McIntyre, p. 35.
56 McIntyre, p. 57.
57 Ruth R. Wisse, *If I Am Not For Myself . . . The Liberal Betrayal of the Jews*, (New York: The Free Press, 1992) (hereinafter Wisse).
58 Wisse, p. 46.
59 Wisse, pp. 46-7.
60 Wisse, p. 21.
61 Wisse, p. 135.
62 Wisse, p. 135.

⁶³ Wisse, p. 135.
⁶⁴ Wisse, p. 25.
⁶⁵ Wisse, p. 184.
⁶⁶ See Athan Theoharis's "The Politics of Scholarship: Liberals, Anti-Communism, and McCarthysim," reproduced on the internet for the University of Pennsylvania at http://www.english.upenn.edu/~afilreis/50s/theoharis.html. Also see Arthur M. Schlesinger, Jr., *The Vital Center: The Politics of Freedom*, (Boston: Houghton Mifflin Company, 1949).
⁶⁷ Sidney Hook, *Out of Step: An Unquiet Life in the 20th Century*, (New York: Harper & Row, 1987), 225.
⁶⁸ Cameron Smith, *Unfinished Journey: The Lewis Family*, (Toronto: Summerhill Press, 1989).
⁶⁹ Wisse, p. 65.
⁷⁰ Wisse, p. 66.
⁷¹ Wisse, pp. 66-7.
⁷² Wisse, pp. 67-9.
⁷³ Wisse, p. 46.
⁷⁴ Fish, p. 16.
⁷⁵ Fish, p. 16.
⁷⁶ Fish, p. 9.
⁷⁷ Fish, p. 18.
⁷⁸ Fish, p. 138.
⁷⁹ Fish, p. 136.
⁸⁰ Fish, p. 137.
⁸¹ Fish, p. 9.
⁸² Fish, pp. 10-11.
⁸³ Fish, p. 18.

A Perspective

Undoubtedly, many conservative elements in our society will salivate over the spectacle of rifts among the equality seekers. In this regard, the best I can do is to urge small "l" liberals to be neither deterred nor seduced by any bursts of applause from the right-wing.

As for the risk of seduction, it would be wise for liberals to re-dedicate themselves to their libertarian *and* egalitarian agenda. This means doing double duty: resisting the excesses of equality seekers and also promoting equality. For an idea of how such a balanced approach might work, I offer, for consideration, the experience with which I am most familiar, that of my organization, the Canadian Civil Liberties Association.

During the same period that we were polemicizing against the excesses among many employment equity advocates, we were conducting surveys designed to demonstrate the need for new equity initiatives. Such surveys documented the willingness of employment agencies to screen out visible minority job applicants and the shortage of native people holding retail positions in communities with large native populations. Thus, we were enabled to argue that, while some forms of employment equity went too far, the Human Rights Code did not go far enough. Moreover, we had no difficulty rebuking the black newspaper *Share* for its anti-Jewish polemics during the *Showboat* flare-up and then defending the leadership of the black community when it was subjected to police intelligence gathering.

The CCLA also demonstrated that, on one day, it could challenge the rape-shield and privacy-shield legislation advocated by many feminists and, on the next day, it could join these feminists in a challenge of the Ontario government's revival of the notorious and sexist "spouse in the house" rule for welfare recipients. Logically, of course, there is no inconsistency between opposing many of the equality seekers on one issue and siding with them on another issue. Politically, it is becoming increasingly important to do just that.

As for the risk of deterrence, I recognize the discomfort that right-wing approval is likely to create for dedicated liberals. It might help, however, for these liberals to review the evidence in this book of how counter-productive the excesses of the new anti-liberals have been. This, of course, is one of the central themes of what I have written here. A number of equality-seeking organizations have taken anti-liberal positions that have produced unintended consequences that include injury to the very goal of equality itself.

As indicated, the attempts of feminist organizations to censor pornography have wound up hurting an important sector of the feminist constituency—a publication for lesbians. Similarly, another egalitarian goal of the feminists—employment equity—has suffered major setbacks that appear to have been influenced by the kind of pressures feminists and other equality seekers have generated. We have seen how the Mike Harris Tory government completely repealed Ontario's employment equity law after the predecessor NDP government burdened it with some foolish excesses. Indeed, feminist-inspired equity plans such as the one at the Ontario College of Art—where women get a ten-year priority on certain jobs—must have increased public hostility to the whole concept.

Early in its term, the Harris government also cut some $700,000. from the budget of the Ontario Human Rights Commission. Not long before, the commission had undertaken hearings into those ill-conceived complaints against the Toronto convenience stores for selling allegedly pornographic magazines. A commission that invokes state coercion in such questionable ways will likely find itself devoid of support when the right-wing wields the budget-cutting axe.

We have also seen how the anti-hate law promoted by the Canadian Jewish Congress and other ethnic minority organizations has backfired in a number of ways. This law has already been invoked against anti-American protesters, French-Canadian nationalists, anti-apartheid activists, a pro-Zionist book, and a Jewish community leader. Not surprisingly, a number of these targets have been from minority groups, themselves the frequent victims of discrimination. Although these cases did not result in enduring convictions, it's bad enough to suffer property detentions, arrests, charges, prosecutions, and police investigations.

As for the universities, we have already seen how the attempts to muzzle the enemies of equality have produced restrictive measures against a pro-Palestinian organization (at the University of Western Ontario) and a pro-Zionist organization (at the University of Ottawa). As for the excesses of the French-Canadian nationalists, there can be little doubt that they contributed to phenomena such as the rise of the Reform Party with its accompanying opposition to Canada's policies on bilingualism. Indeed, the apparent decrease in national support for bilingualism probably also owes something to Québecois excesses. In a political climate where excesses are committed on one side, those on the other side feel legitimated in doing likewise.

This is what comes of the breakdown in support for liberal values. The excesses of equality seekers beget counter-excesses on the part of *inequality* defenders. One casualty of the exercise, therefore, is the quest for equality itself. I fear that we have only begun to see how these developments have hurt the egalitarian cause.

One way to redress these losses is to restore support for liberal values. These values hold out the best hope there is for restraining excess on all sides. They encourage a commitment to principles that transcend our various self-interests. In that way, they challenge all of us to reach beyond ourselves. The measure of validity, then, becomes not what serves this or that sectarian interest, but what best serves the principles we share. Within such a framework, we can all pursue our various conceptions of the good life. But, if the framework itself becomes weakened, we undermine both social cohesion and the more worthy of our separate pursuits.

A promising hope for reversing this anti-liberal tide lies within the affected groups themselves. Fortunately, none of them are monolithic. Significant numbers within these groups disagree on many issues with each other as seriously as any outsiders could. Indeed, I have long believed that, in most groups, there are at least three conflicting tendencies. The first is an appeasement tendency that seeks, through a series of obsequious gestures, to placate the powers that be. The second is a nationalist tendency that seeks the well-being of the group at the expense of virtually everything else. The third is a universalist tendency—the liberal approach—that seeks the betterment of the group through the vindication of universal principles applicable to everyone. Of course, no one person or faction falls completely into one of these categories and outside of the others. That's why I have found it more realistic to describe the phenomenon as one of competing tendencies.

One can find evidence of all three tendencies among virtually all of the groups at issue. Fortunately, the appeasement tendency is in considerable disrepute everywhere. Unfortunately, as indicated in the foregoing chapters, the nationalist tendency has acquired considerable hegemony at the expense of the universalist tendency.

It is important, however, to acknowledge and build on whatever signs of the universalist tendency that we can find. In this connection, I am encouraged by the creation, in the United States, of an organization known as Feminists for Free Expression. Including among its leaders such outstanding feminists as Betty Friedan (the author of the *Feminine Mystique*), Erica Jong (the author of *Fear of Flying*) and Nadine Strossen (president of the American Civil Liberties Union), this organization has become one of the most vigorous critics of the pro-censorship feminists.

Another encouraging development in the United States is the 1998 election of former Georgia state senator Julian Bond as Chairman of the National Association for the Advancement of Colored People (NAACP). Bond distinguished himself as a civil rights activist when he marched with Martin Luther King in the 1960s. More recently, he distinguished himself further by his denunciation of Louis Farrakhan and the anti-semitism associated with Farrakhan's organization. Shortly after being elected as NAACP chairman, Julian Bond reached out to the Jewish community. In a speech to the Anti-Defamation League of B'nai Brith, he talked about the importance of "the coalition between blacks and Jews" and he said, "I want to return to that day when we work hand in hand."

In Canada, committed feminists such as Varda Burstyn, June Callwood, and (now Judge) Lynn King collaborated to publish the book *Women Against Censorship*. In the universities, academic feminists such as Jamie Cameron and (now Judge) Katherine Swinton have written scholarly articles on feminist subjects in which they have advanced the cause of liberal values. Margaret Wente's column in *The Globe and Mail* was a model of sensible feminism. A young feminist, Donna Laframboise, wrote a regular column for the *Toronto Star* in which she courageously attacked the dogmas of anti-liberal feminists, as did her book *The Princess at the Window*. Another noteworthy example of the universalist tendency is retired Manitoba educator Sybil Shack, a lifelong feminist who, for years, was the national president of the Canadian Civil Liberties Association.

While there are a number of Jews who have been vigorously defending liberal values, there have been increasingly few who have done so while maintaining an active involvement in Jewish life. Among the more noteworthy examples of the latter category are the late Toronto lawyer, J.S. Midanik who, for years, served as chairman of the Canadian Jewish Congress Community Relations Committee and was simultaneously a leader in the Canadian Civil Liberties Association. Midanik fought long and hard, both inside and outside the Jewish community, against the anti-hate law and government funding of Jewish day schools. Professor Michael Marrus, a University of Toronto historian, has distinguished himself as the author of scholarly books on the Holocaust and as a courageous opponent of the censorship proclivities within the Jewish community. McMaster philosophy professor Louis Greenspan has been a lifelong promoter of Zionist causes but nevertheless a critic of the Jewish drift from liberalism. It is also encouraging to see York University professor Irving Abella, in his role as representative of the Canadian Jewish Congress, speak out on issues such as redress for the wartime internment of the Japanese Canadians and the general treatment of refugees seeking asylum in Canada. Such involvement is in the best traditions of Jewish liberalism.

One of the last public speeches made by the late Wilson Head, a long-time leader in the Canadian black community, was a plea for blacks to "move from a preoccupation with blacks" to become more involved in the broader issues facing all Canadians. Another significant example of eminent blacks who have been resisting the anti-liberal tendencies is Dr. Daniel G. Hill, former Ontario Ombudsman and the first director of a human rights commission (Ontario) in Canada. At the time of the *Showboat* controversy, Dan Hill co-authored an article in the *Toronto Star* that criticized the extent to which certain black commentators had made an issue of the Jewishness of those associated with the *Showboat* production. On many occasions, Hill has also told audiences of his fellow blacks that the most victimized people in the country are aboriginals.

Another notable example of such liberalism among minorities is the decision made a number of years ago by Dr. Joseph Wong and his colleagues on the Chinese Canadian National Council. After the group's successful campaign of community protest, CTV apologized for having aired a program insulting to the Chinese community. As part of the settlement, the network undertook to produce another program emphasizing the important contributions made by people of Chinese origin. But Dr. Wong and his associates decided on a broader theme. They opted for a program that would alert Canadians to the general evils of racism. The Chinese Canadian organization chose to be universalist rather than nationalist.

As for the universities, the book *Moral Panic* by Trent English professor John Fekete has torn several strips off the "political correctness" crowd. Yet Fekete remains on the social democratic left of the political spectrum. At the time of this writing, McMaster University sociologists Cyril Levitt, Scott Davies, and Neil McLaughlin are organizing a book that attacks "political correctness" from an essentially left-wing perspective.

There are, of course, numbers of others in the affected constituencies who have been attempting to re-assert the primacy of liberal values. As important as it is to encourage every development of this kind among the groups in question, it is no less important for liberals everywhere to challenge the new anti-liberals. If we make the mistake of letting these people off the hook simply because of certain shared objectives, we will wind up immeasurably strengthening those opponents of liberal *and* egalitarian values who inhabit the conservative right-wing. And, as an added corollary, we will help to make a liberal comeback increasingly unlikely.

For liberals, it never required much courage to take on the police, the security establishment, or the right-wing politicians. In liberal circles, to challenge them was always a badge of honour. On the other hand, it was always difficult for liberals to take on the equality seekers and the left. In liberal circles, that was always an unpopular thing to do.

It has become, nevertheless, an important thing to do. If our erstwhile allies continue to assault liberal values without being challenged by the liberal community, they will succeed in polarizing our society. Increasingly, this will give people essentially only two choices: the anti-liberals of the conservative right and the anti-liberals of the equality-seeking left. It has never been more important for the supporters of liberal values to speak up.